The Illustrated ROBERT LOUIS STEVENSON

A Selection of the Stories, Travel Writings, Essays, and Poems
Edited and with an Introduction
BY
Roy Gasson

London
Jupiter Books (London), Ltd.
1977

This edition first published in 1977 by
JUPITER BOOKS (LONDON) LIMITED
167 Hermitage Road, London N4.

ISBN 0 904041 81 6

Typography by Anthony Frewin.
Composed in 12-point Monotype Garamond, Series 156,
and printed and bound in Great Britain by
R. J. Acford Limited, Chichester, Sussex.
115gsm Antique Laid paper supplied by
A. H. James and Company Limited, London.

Sing me a song of a lad that is gone,
Say, could that lad be I?

Contents

List of Illustrations

Introduction

MY FATHER gave me Stevenson's *Treasure Island* as a present for the Christmas before my eighth birthday, and so I first read it at the ideal age and, for that matter, under ideal conditions – by the light of a bicycle lamp under the bedclothes. At the time, I thought it a splendid book, with all the ingredients that anyone could ask for. Above all, it got on with the story, so that even a small, impatient boy read every word without skipping. I remember my delight at two particularly encouraging passages. One is when Dr. Livesey and Squire Trelawney have finished examining the map of Treasure Island:

> "Livesey," said the squire, "you will give up this wretched practice at once. Tomorrow I start for Bristol. In three weeks' time – three weeks! – two weeks – ten days – we'll have the best ship, sir, and the choicest crew in England."

The key, thrilling, word was "tomorrow." There were to be no delays, no interminable discussions, no philosophizing, no doubts, no hesitations. "Tomorrow I start for Bristol."

The other passage is when Jim Hawkins goes to Bristol to join the *Hispaniola* as a cabin boy. Straightaway, he runs into Squire Trelawney.

> "Here you are," he cried, "and the doctor came last night from London. Bravo! the ship's company complete!"
>
> "Oh, sir," cried I, "when do we sail?"
>
> "Sail!" says he. "We sail tomorrow."

If there is a more satisfying chapter ending in any adventure story in English, I have still to read it. Again, that magic word "tomorrow" promised an immediate continuance of the action with the turning of the page.

Unhappily, I can never recover the excitement of that first discovery, but I still reread *Treasure Island.* It remains for me one of that select band of books known since childhood that can combat adult depression and even act as antidotes to letters from my bank manager.

I see now that it is not the perfect story, faultlessly told, that I once thought it. The sense of half-understood terror and foreboding that permeates the opening chapters set in the Admiral Benbow inn gives way, the moment Jim Hawkins and his mother make their escape, to an atmosphere of more overt and open adventure that is exciting in a quite different, less chilling way. The story is not precisely broken-backed, but it is divided by a slipped disc. The two sections are hallmarked by the differing threats characterized by blind Pew and by Long John Silver. The flow is interrupted again by the change of narrator, from Jim Hawkins to the doctor. Making the doctor the narrator for just three chapters in the middle of the book is a too facile device, a clumsy mechanism set in motion to overcome the problem of describing events that happened in the original narrator's absence. And Long John Silver's ambiguities of character are provided with insufficient motivation. *Treasure Island* was intended as a boy's adventure story, not as fodder from which Stevenson's commentators could create theories about his preoccupation with the duality of evil.

My second meeting with Stevenson was less happy in its beginnings but equally fortunate in the event. I had to study *Travels with a Donkey in the Cévennes* as a set book at the age of fifteen, which is too young to appreciate the mannered choreography of contrived, self-conscious prose. But I was lucky. I was guided through *Travels with a Donkey* by an English teacher who combined a disciplined approach with enthusiasm and who managed to transmit something of her appreciation to her unwilling and unreceptive pupil.

I had read *Treasure Island* at an age when it did not occur to me that books had actually to be written by someone. Or, rather, I knew that names were attached to them and that these were the names of their authors; but I had no concept that a real, live person had first to pen or type the words that appeared on the printed page. A book was something of an act of God, a complete and perfect apparition, like a tree or, for that matter, a wireless set. So Robert Louis Stevenson remained only a name on a title page and I had to make the laborious connection between the Stevenson who wrote *Treasure Island* and the man of the same name who wrote *Travels with a Donkey*. I had enjoyed both books – the first with simple and the second with skilfully tutored pleasure – but they seemed miles apart in style, in manner, and in theme. Had I by then come across *The Strange Case of Dr. Jekyll and Mr. Hyde* I would have been even more puzzled.

In so far as that puzzle is a real one, its solution is reasonably simple. Stevenson was a truly professional writer, by which I mean not only that, like every other writer, he wrote for money, but that places, people, and happenings were all grist to his mill. Quite trivial events, memories, and dreams, and particularly scenes and places, were enough to spark off his imagination. *Treasure Island*, for example, had its genesis in a map drawn in fun for Stevenson's stepson, Lloyd Osbourne. The map, Stevenson later wrote, "was elaborately and (I thought) beautifully coloured: the shape of it took my fancy beyond expression; it contained harbours that pleased me like sonnets; and with the unconsciousness of the predestined, I ticketed my performance *Treasure Island*. . . . as I pored over my map of Treasure Island, the future characters of the book began to appear there visibly among imaginary woods; and their brown faces and bright weapons peeped out upon me from unexpected quarters, as they passed to and fro, fighting, and hunting treasure. The next thing I knew I had some paper before me and was writing out a list of chapters. . . . it was to be a story for boys, no need of psychology or fine writing. . . ." *Dr. Jekyll and Mr. Hyde* had its origin in a dream. One night Stevenson had a nightmare so intense that he screamed aloud in terror and his wife, Fanny, in pity woke him up. ("I was dreaming a fine bogey tale," he complained.) He had dreamed the transformation of the good Dr. Jekyll into the evil Mr. Hyde. He began writing the story next morning and in three days had completed the first draft of nearly 40,000 words.

It sounds almost too easy, and of course it is. Neither story welled up from Stevenson's subconscious, whole and complete, in this effortless way. A variety of components went to make the finished product. Into *Dr. Jekyll and Mr. Hyde* went some childhood recurrent nightmares in which Stevenson had dreamed that he was leading a double life, working by day in a doctor's surgery and living at night in the old slums of Edinburgh. To these were added the changes brought about by alcoholism in Stevenson's old friend Walter Ferrier, whose "fine, kind, open dignity of manner" was demolished by drink, which turned him into "a temporal wreck" and finally killed him. The liquid that Dr. Jekyll drinks – which for some readers seems too mechanistic and unconvincing a way of achieving a basic character change – comes from Stevenson's own lifelong acquaintanceship with the effects of doctors' potions. *Treasure Island* incorporates memories of the scenery of the Californian coast and some sea-lore, as well as the famous set-piece scene in the apple barrel, from Stevenson's father. The name John Silver came from the tiny island of Earraid off Mull, where Stevenson as a young man had gone with his father to see a new lighthouse being built; it was the name of one of the stonemasons working there. Long John Silver's character, however, was based upon another old friend, the poet and critic William Ernest Henley, who had had a foot amputated as a result of tuberculosis. "It was the sight of your maimed strength and masterfulness," Stevenson told Henley, "that begot John Silver."

In other words, Stevenson hoarded experiences, which he brought out from store and used when a theme presented itself to him.

Many of these experiences were grounded in Stevenson's childhood in Scotland. He was born in Edinburgh on 13 November 1850. His father was a lighthouse engineer. His mother was an invalid throughout most of his childhood. As a result, Stevenson was looked after by a succession of nurses, the last of whom, and the one who stayed longest, was Alison Cunningham, the daughter of a Fife fisherman. "Cummy," as Stevenson called her, became an influence from which he never escaped. Because he did not learn to read until he was seven, Cummy would read to him – improving books like *The Pilgrim's Progress* and grim tales of the Covenanters, the Scottish Presbyterians who were savagely persecuted after the Restoration. Her stories gave him either nightmares or sleepless nights and, in both cases, Cummy was his comforter. She turned her small charge into a conscience-stricken Puritan with a terror of hellfire.

Stevenson's gratitude to such a woman, which lasted until his death, seems inexplicable. But he never forgot Cummy. When he was thirty-five he dedicated to her his book of poems for children, *A Child's Garden of Verses*:

For the long nights you lay awake
And watched for my unworthy sake:
For your most comfortable hand
That led me through the uneven land:
For all the story-books you read:
For all the pains you comforted:
For all you pitied, all you bore,
In sad and happy days of yore:
My second Mother, my first Wife,
The angel of my infant life –
From the sick child, now well and old,
Take, nurse, the little book you hold!

Cummy, and his sickly, circumscribed childhood, made it hard for Stevenson to achieve any relaxed relationship with women. Any man who can, in early middle age, describe his nurse as "my first Wife" can be regarded only with the deepest suspicion, poetic licence notwithstanding. Throughout Stevenson's life, women were difficult for him to cope with.

As an undergraduate at Edinburgh – a city then notorious for the number of its brothels and prostitutes – he sought out women of the streets. Probably he was no more dissolute than most of his fellow undergraduates, but his strict Calvinistic upbringing, combined with the fact that he was at the time making a tortured rejection of Christianity, meant that he suffered from sick feelings of guilt mixed with an adolescent sense of bravado. He could write, no doubt over-self-consciously, about "the swinging gait of harlots," of girls

. . . at play in a corner of waste-land.
Tumbling and showing their legs and crying out to me loosely,

and even exclaim rebelliously, "Give me the publican and the harlot." But he could also confess:

I have left all upon the shameful field,
  Honour and Hope, my God, and all but life. . . .

Then, at twenty-three, Stevenson fell in love with a woman twelve years his senior. This was Frances Sitwell. She was living apart from her clergyman husband and, unable to get a divorce, was waiting for her husband to die so that she could marry the critic and scholar

Sidney Colvin, who in 1873, the year in which Stevenson first met Frances, had just been elected Slade Professor of Fine Art at Cambridge. Stevenson became her lover in all but the act, and she became his support and confidante. He called her "Madonna" and was apparently content – apart from a single lapse into lust that Frances instantly repelled and reproved – to accept her as his unattainable chaste love, a figure out of chivalric romance. He kept this up for a considerable period, all the time in the knowledge that Frances's first devotion was to Colvin. Frances was, by general consent, an attractive and intelligent woman, well liked by all who knew her. She was constricted by Victorian morality and its marriage laws and her first love was Sidney Colvin (whom she eventually married in 1901). But, when all that is allowed, the mildest term it is possible to apply to her behaviour to Stevenson is coquettish, and franker adjectives are more appropriate.

After three years of this unenviable experience in sex education Stevenson met, in 1876, the woman he was to marry and to remain with for the rest of his life. Coincidentally, her name, too, was Frances, although she was always known as Fanny. Like Mrs. Sitwell, Fanny Osbourne was older than Stevenson – more than ten years older. Like Mrs. Sitwell, she was a married woman separated from her husband, and a mother. Unlike Mrs. Sitwell, she quite soon became Stevenson's lover. Unlike Mrs. Sitwell, she was American and she could get a divorce. But she was unpredictable and mentally unstable, and there were constricting influences bearing down upon her – her parents were Indianapolis Presbyterians. She went back to America, leaving a lonely and bemused Stevenson uncertain whether she had decided to divorce her husband or not. Then, at the end of July 1879, he received from her a cable whose contents are unknown to us, but which made him drop everything and make a dramatic dash to America to rejoin her. She was divorced in December 1879 and they were married five months later, on 19 May 1880, in California.

Although there is no reason to doubt that the Stevensons remained devoted to each other until the end, Fanny's role was an unorthodox one. Cantankerous, sometimes harshly critical of Louis' work and of his friends, subject to nervous breakdowns which, when they lived in Samoa, were once or twice so extreme that she had to be held down on her bed, and a hypochondriac, she was no easy, comfortable partner.

But she lavished upon Stevenson a devoted care. To a large extent, if Cummy was Stevenson's "first Wife", Fanny was his second nurse.

Stevenson publicly attested his devotion and gratitude to Fanny several times. To her he dedicated his last, unfinished novel *Weir of Hermiston,* in terms that make it clear that it was no merely formal dedication:

> Take thou the writing: thine it is. For who
> Burnished the sword, blew on the drowsy coal,
> Held still the target higher, chary of praise
> And prodigal of censure – who but thou?
> So now, in the end, if this the least be good,
> If any deed be done, if any fire
> Burn in the imperfect page, the praise be thine.

(After his death, Fanny added the touching vignette: "He pinned it to my bed curtains when I was asleep. . . .")

His most famous poem about Fanny – much admired by the Victorians, much anthologized, and much raided for dictionaries of quotations – is, however, one that reads today as three over-artificial, purple-passage stanzas:

> Trusty, dusky, vivid, true,
> With eyes of gold and bramble-dew,
> Steel-true and blade-straight,
> The great artificer
> Made my mate.
>
> Honour, anger, valour, fire;
> A love that life could never tire,
> Death quench or evil stir,
> The mighty master
> Gave to her.
>
> Teacher, tender comrade, wife,
> A fellow-farer true through life,
> Heart-whole and soul-free
> The august father
> Gave to me.

It is hard to detect a real, live woman behind these lines, and indeed even in his fiction Stevenson never coped very well with depicting his women characters. As much as possible he avoided them, and women are conspicuously absent, or play minor roles, in most of his stories; his only convincing heroine is the dark-haired Kirsty in *Weir of Hermiston*. *Treasure Island* gives him away. He wrote of that – and it was clearly with relief – "Women were excluded." His friend and near-contemporary, the novelist Henry James, once pointed to *Dr. Jekyll and Mr. Hyde* as an example of what he called Stevenson's "heartless independence" of the need to introduce women into his fiction.

He was equally unhappy with children, in spite of writing one of the best-known books of poems for children and one of the best-known adventure stories for boys. Fanny said of him that "he had little understanding of children in general." A Stevenson enthusiast, and fellow-Scot, Compton Mackenzie, has written:

> . . . in re-reading *A Child's Garden of Verses* it is easy to understand Mrs. Stevenson's comment. The grown-up reader, remembering vividly his own childhood, plucks with delighted recognition the first flower in that garden.
>
> In winter I get up at night
And dress by yellow candle-light.
In summer, quite the other way,
I have to go to bed by day.
>
> But when that same reader plucks the next flower:
>
> It is very nice to think
The world is full of meat and drink,
With little children saying grace
In every Christian kind of place.
>
> the smell of it will be unrecognizable as a flower of his own childhood.

As to *Treasure Island*, it is an exception. One of the lasting pleasures of that book is the by no means simple characterization of Jim Hawkins – a mixture of daring and doubt, of adult acceptance of responsibility and a childish dependence, all combined in his ambivalent relationship with Long John Silver, who at times seems to be

1. Robert Louis Stevenson, 1850–1894; woodcut from *The Bookman,* 1913.

2. This and the following two plates, showing the Edinburgh that Stevenson knew (and whose weather, in particular, he always remembered – "one of the vilest climates under heaven"), are from the 6th edition of his *Edinburgh: Picturesque Notes* (London, 1896). They are engravings made from drawings by S. Bough and W. E. Lockhart for the first edition of the book, a folio volume published in 1879. This plate is of Advocates' Close: "You go under dark arches, and down dark stairs and alleys. The way is so narrow that you can lay a hand on either wall; so steep that, in greasy winter weather, the pavement is almost as treacherous as ice."

3. John Knox's house in Edinburgh High Street: "the man who made Scotland over again in his own image, the indefatigable, undissuadable John Knox."

4. Greyfriars, Edinburgh: "The open shows many slabs and table tombstones; and all round the margin, the place is girt by an array of aristocratic mausoleums appallingly adorned . . . we Scotch stand, to my fancy, highest among nations in the matter of grimly illustrating death."

5. A pencil drawing from the sketchbook Stevenson carried on the walking tour of the Cévennes he described in *Travels with a Donkey*, at a time when he liked to see himself as "a literary man who drew landscapes." This sketch, of *Chateau Neuf, from the Gazeille*, was made when he was staying in the town of La Monastier. His description of his stay was to have formed the opening chapter of *Travels with a Donkey*, but either he or his publisher decided to omit it and to plunge straight into the story of Modestine. The missing chapter was eventually, in 1896, published in the United States as a pamphlet, under the title *A Mountain Town in France: a Fragment*.

6. The frontispiece by Walter Crane for the first edition of Stevenson's first published book, *An Inland Voyage* (London, 1878). *Arethusa* was the cedar canoe used by Stevenson. *Cigarette* was the canoe paddled by his companion, Walter Simpson; it was made of oak, "as we knew so keenly on portage."

7. The frontispiece, again by Walter Crane, for the first edition of *Travels with a Donkey in the Cévennes* (London, 1879).

8. The frontispiece by Edward Ardizzone for *Travels with a Donkey in the Cévennes* (London, 1967).

replacing the boy's lost father. Perhaps this is the clue to the successful delineation of the boy's character. When he wrote *Treasure Island* Stevenson had a stepson, with whom he had achieved a relationship of almost fraternal affection. That stepson, Lloyd Osbourne, was thirteen when Stevenson read *Treasure Island* to him, chapter by chapter as it was written.

Stevenson never became a father – although a young man claiming, falsely, to be his bastard son paraded himself briefly around Edinburgh in the 1920s. Fanny had three children by her first marriage, a girl and two sons. The younger son died at the age of four, just before Fanny met Stevenson. There were good practical reasons for Stevenson's childlessness. Fanny was forty at the time of her marriage, Stevenson was a sick man, and money was a problem. But this was not the whole explanation. Stevenson did not want to have children. Partly, perhaps, he was deterred by memories of his own stifled, nightmare-spattered childhood. Partly, too, he remembered the unhappiness he had caused his own father when, as a young man, he had rejected practically all his father stood for. He had abandoned the three generations old family tradition of a career in engineering, become what he later described as a "red-hot Socialist," and questioned the Christian beliefs cherished by his father. All this brought about a rift between father and son that made them both desperately unhappy. Although the rift was later healed, the scars remained.

Stevenson was also more conscious than most that children can be "hostages to fortune" in another, more tragic, way. In America, waiting for Fanny's divorce, he had lodged in San Francisco with an Irish family whose four-year-old son developed pneumonia; Stevenson sat by the boy's bedside for hours, and was appalled by his suffering. Afterwards he wrote to Sidney Colvin, "O never, never any family for me! I am cured of that." Then Frances Sitwell's eighteen-year-old son died in 1881 at Davos, where Stevenson and his wife were also staying. For the lad's mother Stevenson wrote his "In Memoriam F.A.S.":

Yet, O stricken heart, remember, O remember
  How of human days he lived the better part.
April came to bloom and never dim December
  Breathed its killing chills upon the head or heart.

Doomed to know not Winter, only Spring, a being
Trod the flowery April blithely for a while,
Took his fill of music, joy of thought and seeing,
Came and stayed and went, nor ever ceased to smile.

Came and stayed and went, and now when all is finished,
You alone have crossed the melancholy stream,
Yours the pang, but his, O his, the undiminished
Undecaying gladness, undeparted dream.

All that life contains of torture, toil, and treason,
Shame, dishonour, death, to him were but a name.
Here, a boy, he dwelt through all the singing season
And ere the day of sorrow departed as he came.

These perhaps rather sentimental words of comfort to a bereaved mother conceal rather than reveal Stevenson's grief at Bertie Sitwell's death, which seems to have finally confirmed his pre-marital decision "never any family for me!" After all, death had taken a son from both the women he loved.

He appreciated the precariousness of life more than most. He wrote to Sidney Colvin about the dying Bertie Sitwell: ". . . I feel a great deal, that I either cannot or will not say, as you well know. It has helped to make me more conscious of the wolverine on my own shoulders." The wolverine was death, which throughout Stevenson's life was a menacing shadow, never far away. As a boy he was always sickly. "My ill health," he recalled much later, "principally chronicles itself by the terrible long nights that I lay awake, troubled continuously by a hacking, exhausting cough, and praying for sleep or morning from the bottom of my shaken little body." Adulthood brought no cure. All his life he suffered from recurrent bouts of haemorrhaging from the lungs; even an everyday cold was a threat to him. He survived several dramatic crises. In America, waiting for news of Fanny's divorce, he went camping in the Santa Lucia mountains. He collapsed and was found by a bear-hunter under a tree where he had lain for two days and nights in the open "in a sort of stupor." Six months later he was ill again, "on the verge of a galloping consumption, cold sweats, prostrating attacks of cough, sinking fits in which I lost the power of speech, fever, and all the ugliest circumstances of the disease." In 1884 he was so critically ill in Nice that his doctors told Fanny there was no hope of his recovery. He spent the last five years of his life in Samoa, whose climate gave him relief from the symptoms of his disease; when, once, he set out on a return visit to Britain he got only as far as Australia before collapsing again.

It has been argued recently that Stevenson suffered not from tuberculosis, as has generally been assumed, but from bronchiectasis, a disease with similar symptoms, equally distressing but less of a killer. Certainly it was not tuberculosis that caused his death. He died, suddenly and quickly, on 3 December 1894, of a cerebral haemorrhage; he was forty-four. But the name of the disease scarcely matters; what does matter is that death was always peering over his shoulder.

It may have been the debility of ill-health that caused him often to have trouble finishing work that he had started with some gusto. On every one of his novels he ran out of steam before the end. *Prince Otto* he put aside for a year when he was within two chapters of the end. He dropped *Kidnapped* after a couple of months' work, did not touch it for another two months, and then completed it in three months – "one of these months entirely over the last chapters, which had to be put together without interest or inspiration, almost word by word." Even *Treasure Island* did not go smoothly: after having written fifteen chapters he, in his own words, "ignominiously lost hold"; he forced himself to complete it because he had to – it was already being serialized. Nevertheless, the point at which he picked up the work was the first chapter to be narrated by Doctor Livesey instead of Jim Hawkins; a change which may mark a certain exhaustion of the imagination.

The truth is that Stevenson was happier with shorter pieces than with the novel. None of his novels sustain to the end their opening promise; only care and craftsmanship keep them going. His "natural" length in fiction was the long short story. The way in which *Dr. Jekyll and Mr. Hyde* was written makes the point. As we have seen, Stevenson wrote the first draft in three days. Then he read it to his wife and stepson. Fanny was critical; she said that it was a mere horror story, a waste of a theme that should have been used as an allegory. Lloyd Osbourne remembered later that "Stevenson was beside himself with anger." But he went away and thought it over, and concluded that Fanny was right. "Then ensued," Lloyd relates, "another three days of feverish industry . . . of awed glimpses of him, sitting up in bed, writing, writing, writing, with the counterpane littered with his sheets. The culmination was the *Jekyll and Hyde* that everyone knows; that, translated into every European tongue and many Oriental, has given a new phrase to the world."

Dr. Jekyll and Mr. Hyde was the first of Stevenson's books to find a wide, adult popularity; 40,000 copies were sold within six months of publication. It is a story in which Stevenson's control never relaxes, he builds up unerringly from the first, quiet walk of the lawyer and his friend through the Sunday streets to that high moment when Jekyll's servant tells the lawyer, before they break into the doctor's laboratory, "Once I heard it weeping," and sustains interest through the dénouement. His cool, descriptive prose is perfectly suited to the horror – imagine the exclamation marks, the cumulative adjectives, the hysterical repetition with which Edgar Allan Poe would have clothed the same story.

But this craftsmanship is apparent in everything that Stevenson wrote, not only when his imagination was flowing but when he was flogging himself on to finish a long novel. He was always, I repeat, professional. It is typical of his approach to writing that when he was young he deliberately undertook an apprenticeship in writing. He began to write as a young boy, and never doubted that he wanted to make it his career. Later, as an undergraduate and law student, he set himself a course of writing practice. "Whenever I read a book or a passage that particularly pleased me, in which a thing was said or an effect rendered with propriety, in which there was either some conspicuous force or some happy distinction in the style, I must sit down at once and set myself to ape that quality. I was unsuccessful and I knew it . . . , but at least in these vain bouts, I got some practice in rhythm, in harmony, in construction and the co-ordination of parts. I have thus played the sedulous ape to Hazlitt, to Lamb, to Wordsworth, to Sir Thomas Browne, to Defoe, to Hawthorne, to Montaigne, to Baudelaire, and to Obermann. . . . That, like it or not, is the way to learn to write. . . ." Well, possibly. But it has disadvantages, one of which is that the trainee may find a style of his own, as Stevenson did, but never find a métier.

Stevenson's work is bound together by a number of themes – a sense of place, of history, of occasion. But it is hard to see in his collected works the coherence that exists, for example, in that of his near-contemporary Thomas Hardy. This is because of what we have noted earlier, that he wrote as a subject presented itself to him and, perhaps, never thought his themes through as, in an ideal world, he might have done. It is also because of his large and varied output. He tried everything – short stories, essays, travelogues, historical novels, adventure novels. He wrote in prose and in verse.

No one, I think, would now claim Stevenson as a major poet. I am one of those many who find the poems in *A Child's Garden of Verses* coy and mushy. They have always appealed more to nostalgic adults than to children. Much of the rest of his poetry gives a feeling of contrived cleverness, rather as though Stevenson were still at his practice, testing how neatly and satisfyingly he could versify or render an effect "with propriety." Sometimes, however, he is capable of expressing rather obvious sentiments in a way that we all immediately and gratefully recognize. He does this, for example, in "Consolation" (p. 247) – a poem that is easy to mock but which expresses a hope that few bereaved people have not clung to. "Requiem" (p. 250), the most famous of his poems, is another of the same type. It has had its detractors, who have found a false, smug note of heroism in its lines

> Glad did I live and gladly die,
> And I laid me down with a will

but its strong lilt expresses a simple, fundamentally optimistic sentiment that appeals to the romantic in us all. It has become, because of this, a small scrap of the British literary heritage.

Stevenson himself was modest to the point of detraction about his poetry. He described himself at various times as "a kind of prose Herrick, divested of the gift of verse," "a weak brother in verse," and "a person with a poetic character and no poetic talent." He was, as always, too harsh with himself. Janet Adam Smith, who edited, impeccably, the standard edition of Stevenson's poems, has summed him up with her usual precision: "If we are looking for poetry that has mature passion and mystery, that explores sensibility, that drills down into the subconscious, we shall not come to Stevenson. But if we care for the dance of sounds and meanings, for the verse that, elegantly or humorously, can always rise to the required occasion, for the great commonplace made memorable by style – then Stevenson has a great deal to offer." To put it rather more clumsily, Stevenson would have made a first-class poet laureate. He would never have produced anything disturbingly original and he could have been relied upon to express generally acceptable sentiments with skill and dexterity.

In any case, it is hard to carp at a poet who disarmingly prefixed a book of poems with the modest appeal:

> Of all my verse, like not a single line;
> But like my title, for it is not mine.
> That title from a better man I stole:
> Ah, how much better, had I stol'n the whole!

(The title was *Underwoods*, and the "better man" Ben Jonson.) I have to confess also to being an Englishman, which means that I have to take on trust the opinion of many sound judges that Stevenson's Scots poems should be rated higher than the English.

In prose – and I am not now considering the novels – Stevenson maintained an impressively high standard. Rereading the works with which I was familiar and reading for the first time works new to me to make the selection for this anthology, I found it hard to put much in the reject pile. So this volume has ended up as a Stevenson taster rather than a Stevenson distillation. I have tried to show Stevenson as an essayist (for want of a more relaxed word) and to demonstrate something of the range of his storytelling, from the horror of "Thrawn Janet" and "The Merry Men" to the sustained mocking humour of "The Treasure of Franchard."

It is unfashionable today to appreciate *An Inland Voyage*, which was, the reader should be reminded, Stevenson's first published work, written when he was twenty-five. There seems to us something faintly artificial about undertaking a journey simply to be able to write about it. We have lost the habit of savouring the mannered introversion and carefully formulated prose that Stevenson gives us here. For these reasons *An Inland Voyage* is in danger of being underrated. Stevenson himself was the first to undervalue it. He wrote of it to his mother: "what rubbish these reviewers did talk. It is not badly written, thin, mildly cheery, and strained." But then, as we have seen in connection with his poetry, one of Stevenson's many attractive traits was his cheerful devaluation of his own work. In our own time, even so normally an appreciative critic as James Pope Hennessy wrote, dismissively, that *An Inland Voyage* "is an agreeable, lively book, full of observation. . . ." The trouble is that the book demands a certain cooperation of the reader, an almost deliberate act of immersion, a leisurely appreciation that in our rushed, neurotic lives we find hard to extend to it.

Travels with a Donkey, because it has more humour and is less self-conscious, has remained more popular than *An Inland Voyage*. The journeys described in the two books were very different. The canoe trip of *An Inland Voyage* was undertaken with a companion – Walter Simpson, son of the surgeon Sir James Simpson, the discoverer of chloroform. On his walking tour in the Cévennes Stevenson was alone – for no more significant a reason than that Walter Simpson was not a good walker. But at the time Fanny, still undivorced, had gone back to America, and for Stevenson the solitude of the trip turned into loneliness. This accounts for the later book's less artificial tone; the whimsy has turned to wryness. Although Stevenson wrote to a friend while on his trip, "For the first time in a year I feel something like peace," underlying his whole account is a pensive longing. In a sense *Travels with a Donkey* is a diary addressed to Fanny: "For there is a fellowship more quiet even than solitude, and which, rightly understood, is solitude made perfect. And to live out of doors with a woman a man loves is of all lives the most complete and free." But it is still, because of the obstinate mouse-coloured donkey Modestine, a funnier book than *An Inland Voyage*. Perhaps the most surprising thing about it is that it is so full of descriptions of quietly eventful days and quietly pensive nights, of meetings with travellers and innkeepers, that it is hard to realize that the journey it describes took just ten days. Its pace is the leisured pace of Modestine.

"Walking Tours," a later essay, is a more formal composition, written in tranquillity. It is included here, although it belongs to an unfashionable genre, simply because it puts Stevenson firmly in the same rank as the great English essayists like Lamb and Hazlitt to whom, in his apprentice years, he "played the sedulous ape."

To choose the stories for this volume involved much heart-searching. Almost every one of Stevenson's stories has its pleasures that seemed to demand its inclusion. Moreover, almost every one seems to have its committed supporters among the commentators. Some of this support seems, admittedly, to be misjudged or over-enthusiastic. I find it hard to follow the critic who called "Markheim"

– the story of a murderer who rejects the temptations of a supernatural visitor and confesses his crime – "one of the greatest short stories ever written." Nonetheless, "Markheim" had to be a candidate for admission, and I am sure that many readers will resent its omission. "The Body Snatcher" also seems to me to be often over-rated. I find it a piece of not very frightening sensationalism, a Hammer-film horror story. On the other hand, only its length disqualified the melodrama "The Pavilion on the Links."

So this is a personal choice of stories, and one that better minds than mine can easily fault. "Thrawn Janet" is here. It is the best of all Stevenson's stories of the supernatural. Henry James called it "a masterpiece in thirteen pages." Although it is written in Lallan Scots, even an Englishman can read it with a very small initial effort. "The Merry Men" is a longer story, approaching the length at which Stevenson was always most at home. In it his descriptions of the isolated island and his knowledge of the ways of currents and tides combine with an overall atmosphere of evil to produce the strongest sustained tale he ever wrote. "The Treasure of Franchard" shows Stevenson at his most relaxed, telling a light-hearted story with gently mocking humour. In the "Story of the Young Man with the Cream Tarts," one of a set of highly artificial stories produced for a magazine, we see a more sophisticated exercise in grey humour.

This anthology includes, as a matter of principle, no extracts from the novels. But Stevenson did his best work outside the novels, with the one notable exception of *Treasure Island* – and no extract can do justice to that. Had he lived longer it might have been different. David Daiches, the most sensitive and perceptive of Stevenson's modern critics, and one who distributes his superlatives with careful judgement, has called *Weir of Hermiston*, the novel on which Stevenson was working on the day he died, an "unfinished masterpiece," adding that in it Stevenson put "his topographical sense most memorably at the service of his sense of human character and destiny." Whether Stevenson could have sustained this power is a question that the wolverine on his shoulder tragically prevented him from answering.

Bibliographical Note

The Strange Case of Dr. Jekyll and Mr. Hyde was published in London in January 1886.
"Thrawn Janet" was first published in *The Cornhill Magazine,* London, October 1881.
"The Merry Men" also first appeared in *The Cornhill Magazine,* in the June and July issues, 1882.
"The Treasure of Franchard" was first published in *Longman's Magazine*, April-May, 1883.
"Story of the Young Man with the Cream Tarts" is one of a series of tales called "The Suicide Club" which first appeared in *London: The Conservative Weekly Journal of Politics, Finance, Society and the Arts* between February 1878 and April 1879.
"The Donkey, the Pack, and the Pack-saddle"; "The Green Donkey-driver"; and "A Night among the Pines" are from *Travels with a Donkey in the Cévennes,* London, 1879.
"The Oise in Flood"; "Noyon Cathedral"; and "Changed Times" are from *An Inland Voyage,* London, 1878.
"Walking Tours" is taken from the June 1876 issue of *The Cornhill Magazine.*
The poem "Consolation," although written in 1872, was first published only in 1899, in R.L.S. *Teuila*; *being fugitive verses and lines by Robert Louis Stevenson now first collected* by Isobel Strong (Stevenson's stepdaughter). This was privately printed.
"*Nous n'irons plus aux bois*," written in 1895, was first published in *Letters of Robert Louis Stevenson to his Family and Friends*, selected and edited with Notes and Introductions by Sidney Colvin, London, 1899.
"Requiem" was first published in *Underwoods*, London, 1887.
"I will make you brooches and toys for your delight," "Bright is the ring of words," and "In the highlands, in the country places" were first published in *The Works of Robert Louis Stevenson,* Volume XIV, Edinburgh, 1895.

A Note on the Illustrations

Many of the plates are drawn from early illustrated editions of Stevenson's works; these are the kinds of illustration that accompanied Stevenson's stories when they were presented to their earliest readers. Some of them are by considerable illustrators whose reputations remain high today – like Walter Crane, Charles Robinson, and Millicent Sowerby. Others, though, are by artist-craftsmen who, although popular in their own day, and producers of a very considerable body of work, are now less well remembered – like William Hole, W. L. Metcalf, and H. M. Paget. These, and men like them, provided the solid backbone to late-Victorian illustrated books; their work is of a consistently high standard of skill and technique and, unlike some modern jacket illustrators, they seem always to have read and understood the text they were illustrating. If they lack the imagination and the use of symbolic imagery that distinguished their predecessors in the earlier part of the nineteenth century, this is more because of the changing demands of the book-buying public than because of lack of competence in the illustrators.

Other plates show the work of later illustrators; it is entertaining, and perhaps even instructive, to compare the two frontispieces – separated by almost ninety years – drawn by Walter Crane and Edward Ardizzone for *Travels with a Donkey* (Plates 7, 8) and the spare clean outlines cut by W. A. Dwiggins in the 1920s (Plate 25) with the more cursive line of, for example, H. M. Paget in the 1890s (Plates 26, 27).

Three illustrations (Plates 2–4) are included to give an impression of the Edinburgh that Stevenson knew in his youth and another (Plate 5) is an example of Stevenson's own work from his sketchbook – it is a drawing of part of the countryside he walked through on his *Travels with a Donkey*.

Two curiosities are also included; Plates 30 and 31 show two translations of Stevenson's work to the stage.

Finally, there is a section of film stills from some of the many adaptations of Stevenson's stories to the screen; these will, it is hoped, revive some pleasant film-going memories; they should also be seen as illustrations accompanying the detailed Filmography that concludes this anthology.

The Illustrated

ROBERT LOUIS

STEVENSON

The Strange Case of Dr. Jekyll and Mr. Hyde

1. Story of the Door

MR. UTTERSON the lawyer was a man of a rugged countenance, that was never lighted by a smile; cold, scanty and embarrassed in discourse; backward in sentiment; lean, long, dusty, dreary, and yet somehow lovable. At friendly meetings, and when the wine was to his taste, something eminently human beaconed from his eye; something indeed which never found its way into his talk, but which spoke not only in these silent symbols of the after-dinner face, but more often and loudly in the acts of his life. He was austere with himself; drank gin when he was alone, to mortify a taste for vintages; and though he enjoyed the theatre, had not crossed the doors of one for twenty years. But he had an approved tolerance for others; sometimes wondering, almost with envy, at the high pressure of spirits involved in their misdeeds; and in any extremity inclined to help rather than to reprove. "I incline to Cain's heresy," he used to say quaintly: "I let my brother go to the devil in his own way." In this character it was frequently his fortune to be the last reputable acquaintance and the last good influence in the lives of down-going men. And to such as these, so long as they came about his chambers, he never marked a shade of change in his demeanour.

No doubt the feat was easy to Mr. Utterson; for he was undemonstrative at the best, and even his friendships seemed to be founded in a similar catholicity of good-nature. It is the mark of a modest man to accept his friendly circle ready made from the hands of opportunity; and that was the lawyer's way. His friends were those of his own blood, or those whom he had known the longest; his affections, like ivy, were the growth of time, they implied no aptness in the object. Hence, no doubt, the bond that united him to Mr. Richard Enfield, his distant kinsman, the well-known man about town. It was a nut to crack for many, what these two could see in each other, or what subject they could find in common. It was reported by those who encountered them in their Sunday walks, that they said nothing, looked singularly dull, and would hail with obvious relief the appearance of a friend. For all that, the two men put the greatest store by these excursions, counted them the chief jewel of each week, and not only set aside occasions of pleasure, but even resisted the calls of business, that they might enjoy them uninterrupted.

It chanced on one of these rambles that their way led them down a by-street in a busy quarter of London. The street was small and what is called quiet, but it drove a thriving trade on the week-days. The inhabitants were all doing well, it seemed, and all emulously hoping to do better still, and laying out the surplus of their gains in coquetry; so that the shop fronts stood along that thoroughfare with an air of invitation, like rows of smiling saleswomen. Even on Sunday, when it veiled its more florid charms and lay comparatively empty of passage, the street shone out in contrast to its dingy neighbourhood, like a fire in a forest; and with its freshly painted shutters, well-polished brasses, and general cleanliness and gaiety of note, instantly caught and pleased the eye of the passenger.

Two doors from one corner, on the left hand going east, the line was broken by the entry of a court; and just at that point, a certain sinister block of building thrust forward its gable on the street. It was two storeys high; showed no window, nothing but a door on the lower storey and a blind forehead of discoloured wall on the upper; and bore in every feature the marks of prolonged and sordid negligence. The door, which was equipped with neither bell nor knocker, was blistered and distained. Tramps slouched into the recess and struck matches on the panels; children kept shop upon the steps; the schoolboy had tried his knife on the mouldings; and for close on a generation no one had appeared to drive away these random visitors or to repair their ravages.

Mr. Enfield and the lawyer were on the other side of the by-street; but when they came abreast of the entry, the former lifted up his cane and pointed.

"Did you ever remark that door?" he asked; and when his companion had replied in the affirmative, "It is connected in my mind," added he, "with a very odd story."

"Indeed!" said Mr. Utterson, with a slight change of voice, "and what was that?"

"Well, it was this way," returned Mr. Enfield: "I was coming home from some place at the end of the world, about three o'clock of a black winter morning, and my way lay through a part of town where there was literally nothing to be seen but lamps. Street after street, and all the folks asleep—street after street, all lighted up as if for a procession, and all as empty as a church—till at last I got into that state of mind when a man listens and listens and begins to long for the sight of a policeman. All at once, I saw two figures: one a little man who was stumping along eastward at a good walk, and the other a girl of maybe eight or ten who was running as hard as she was able down a cross-street. Well, sir, the two ran into one another naturally enough at the corner; and then came the horrible part of the thing; for the man trampled calmly over the child's body and left her screaming on the ground. It sounds nothing to hear, but it was hellish to see. It wasn't like a man; it was like some damned Juggernaut. I gave a view halloa, took to my heels, collared my gentleman, and brought him back to where there was already quite a group about the screaming child. He was perfectly cool and made no resistance, but gave me one look, so ugly that it brought out the sweat on me like running. The people who had turned out were the girl's own family; and pretty soon the doctor, for whom someone had been sent, put in his appearance. Well, the child was not much the worse, more frightened, according to the Sawbones; and there you might have supposed would be an end to it. But there was one curious circumstance. I had taken a loathing to my gentleman at first sight. So had the child's family, which was only natural. But the doctor's case was what struck me. He was the usual cut-and-dry apothecary, of no particular age and colour, with a strong Edinburgh accent, and about as emotional as a bagpipe. Well, sir, he was like the rest of us: every time he looked at my prisoner, I saw that Sawbones turned sick and white with the desire to kill him. I knew what was in his mind, just as he knew what was in mine; and killing being out of the question, we did the next best. We told the man we could and would make such a scandal out of this, as should make his name stink from one end of London to the other. If he had any friends or any credit, we undertook that he should lose them. And all the time, as we were pitching it in red hot, we were keeping the women off him as best we could, for they were as wild as harpies. I never saw a circle of such hateful faces; and there was the man in the middle, with a kind of black sneering coolness—frightened too, I could see that—but carrying it off, sir, really like Satan. 'If you choose to make capital out of this accident,' he said, 'I am naturally helpless. No gentleman but wishes to avoid a scene,' says he. 'Name your figure.' Well, we screwed him up to a hundred pounds for the child's family; he would have clearly liked to stick out; but there was something about the lot of us that meant mischief, and at last he struck. The next thing was to get the money; and where do you think he carried us but to that place with the door?—whipped out a key, went in, and presently came back with the matter of ten pounds in gold and a cheque for the balance on Coutts's, drawn payable to bearer, and signed with a name that I can't mention, though it's one of the points of my story, but it was a name at least very well known and often printed. The figure was stiff; but the signature was good for more than that, if it was only genuine. I took the liberty of pointing out to my gentleman that the whole business looked apocryphal; and that a man does not, in real life, walk into a cellar door at four in the morning and come out of it with another man's cheque for close upon a hundred pounds. But he was quite easy and sneering. 'Set your mind at rest,' says he; 'I will stay with you till the banks open, and cash the cheque myself.' So we all set off, the doctor, and the child's father, and our friend and myself, and passed the rest of the night in my chambers; and next day, when we had breakfasted, went in a body to the bank. I gave in the cheque myself, and said I had every reason to believe it was a forgery. Not a bit of it. The cheque was genuine."

"Tut-tut!" said Mr. Utterson.

"I see you feel as I do," said Mr. Enfield. "Yes, it's a bad story. For my man was a fellow that nobody could have to do with, a really damnable man; and the person that drew the cheque is the very pink of the proprieties, celebrated too, and (what makes it worse) one of you fellows who do what they call good. Blackmail, I suppose; an honest man paying through the nose for some of the capers of his youth. Blackmail House is what I call that place with the door, in consequence. Though even that, you know, is far from explaining all," he added; and with the words fell into a vein of musing.

From this he was recalled by Mr. Utterson asking rather suddenly: "And you don't know if the drawer of the cheque lives there?"

"A likely place, isn't it?" returned Mr. Enfield. "But I happen to have noticed his address; he lives in some square or other."

"And you never asked about—the place with the door?" said Mr. Utterson.

"No, sir: I had a delicacy," was the reply. "I feel very strongly about putting questions; it partakes too much of the style of the day of judgment. You start a question, and it's like starting a stone. You sit quietly on the top of a hill; and away the stone goes, starting others; and presently some bland old bird (the last you would have thought of) is knocked on the head in his own back garden, and the family have to change their name. No, sir, I make it a rule of mine: the more it looks like Queer Street, the less I ask."

"A very good rule, too," said the lawyer.

"But I have studied the place for myself," continued Mr. Enfield. "It seems scarcely a house. There is no other door, and nobody goes in or out of that one, but, once in a great while, the gentleman of my adventure. There are three windows looking on the court on the first floor; none below; the windows are always shut, but they're clean. And then there is a chimney, which is generally smoking; so somebody must live there. And yet it's not so sure; for the buildings are so packed together about that court, that it's hard to say where one ends and another begins."

The pair walked on again for a while in silence; and then—"Enfield," said Mr. Utterson, "that's a good rule of yours."

"Yes, I think it is," returned Enfield.

"But for all that," continued the lawyer, "there's one point I want to ask: I want to ask the name of that man who walked over the child."

"Well," said Mr. Enfield, "I can't see what harm it would do. It was a man of the name of Hyde."

"Hm," said Mr. Utterson. "What sort of a man is he to see?"

"He is not easy to describe. There is something wrong with his appearance; something displeasing, something downright detestable. I never saw a man I so disliked, and yet I scarce know why. He must be deformed somewhere; he gives a strong feeling of deformity, although I couldn't specify the point. He's an extraordinary-looking man, and yet I really can name nothing out of the way. No, sir; I can make no hand of it; I can't describe him. And it's not want of memory; for I declare I can see him this moment."

Mr. Utterson again walked some way in silence, and obviously under a weight of consideration. "You are sure he used a key?" he inquired at last.

"My dear sir . . ." began Enfield, surprised out of himself.

"Yes, I know," said Utterson; "I know it must seem strange. The fact is, if I do ask you the name of the other party, it is because I know it already. You see, Richard, your tale has gone home. If you have been inexact in any point, you had better correct it."

"I think you might have warned me," returned the other, with a touch of sullenness. "But I have been pedantically exact, as you call it. The fellow had a key; and, what's more, he has it still. I saw him use it, not a week ago."

Mr. Utterson sighed deeply, but said never a word; and the young man presently resumed. "Here is another lesson to say nothing," said he. "I am ashamed of my long tongue. Let us make a bargain never to refer to this again."

"With all my heart," said the lawyer. "I shake hands on that, Richard."

2. Search for Mr. Hyde

THAT EVENING Mr. Utterson came home to his bachelor house in sombre spirits, and sat down to dinner without relish. It was his custom of a Sunday, when this meal was over, to sit close by the fire, a volume of some dry divinity on his reading-desk, until the clock of the neighbouring church rang out the hour of twelve, when he would go soberly and gratefully to bed. On this night, however, as soon as the cloth was taken away, he took up a candle and went into his business room. There he opened his safe, took from the most private part of it a document endorsed on the envelope as Dr. Jekyll's Will, and sat down with a clouded brow to study its contents. The will was holograph; for Mr. Utterson, though he took charge of it now that it was made, had refused to lend the least assistance in the making of it; it provided not only that, in case of the decease of Henry Jekyll, M.D., D.C.L., LL.D., F.R.S., &c., all his possessions were to pass into the hands of his "friend and benefactor Edward Hyde"; but that in case of Dr. Jekyll's "disappearance or unexplained absence for any period exceeding three calendar months," the said Edward Hyde should step into the said Henry Jekyll's shoes without further delay, and free from any burthen or obligation, beyond the payment of a few small sums to the members of the doctor's household. This document had long been the lawyer's eyesore. It offended him both as a lawyer and as a lover of the sane and customary sides of life, to whom the fanciful was the immodest. And hitherto it was his ignorance of Mr. Hyde that had swelled his indignation; now, by a sudden turn, it was his knowledge. It was already bad enough when the name was but a name of which he could learn no more. It was worse when it began to be clothed upon with detestable attributes; and out of the shifting, insubstantial mists that had so long baffled his eye, there leaped up the sudden definite presentment of a fiend.

"I thought it was madness," he said, as he replaced the obnoxious paper in the safe; "and now I begin to fear it is disgrace."

With that he blew out his candle, put on a great-coat, and set forth in the direction of Cavendish Square, that citadel of medicine, where his friend, the great Dr. Lanyon, had his house and received his crowding patients. "If any one knows, it will be Lanyon," he thought.

The solemn butler knew and welcomed him; he was subjected to no stage of delay, but ushered direct from the door to the dining-room, where Dr. Lanyon sat alone over his wine. This was a hearty, healthy, dapper, red-faced gentleman, with a shock of hair prematurely white, and a boisterous and decided manner. At sight of Mr. Utterson, he sprang up from his chair and welcomed him with both hands. The geniality, as was the way of the man, was somewhat theatrical to the eye; but it reposed on genuine feeling. For these two were old friends, old mates both at school and college, both thorough respecters of themselves and of each other, and, what does not always follow, men who thoroughly enjoyed each other's company.

After a little rambling talk, the lawyer led up to the subject which so disagreeably preoccupied his mind.

"I suppose, Lanyon," he said, "you and I must be the two oldest friends that Henry Jekyll has?"

"I wish the friends were younger," chuckled Dr. Lanyon. "But I suppose we are. And what of that? I see little of him now."

"Indeed!" said Utterson. "I thought you had a bond of common interest."

"We had," was his reply. "But it is more than ten years since Henry Jekyll became too fanciful for me. He began to go wrong, wrong in mind; and though, of course, I continue to take an interest in him for old sake's sake as they say, I see and I have seen devilish little of the man. Such unscientific balderdash," added the doctor, flushing suddenly purple, "would have estranged Damon and Pythias."

This little spirt of temper was somewhat of a relief to Mr. Utterson. "They have only differed on some point of science," he thought; and being a man of no scientific passions (except in the matter of conveyancing), he even added: "It is nothing worse than that!" He gave his friend a few seconds to recover his composure, and then approached the question he had come to put.

"Did you ever come across a *protégé* of his—one Hyde?" he asked.

"Hyde?" repeated Lanyon. "No. Never heard of him. Since my time."

That was the amount of information that the lawyer carried back with him to the great, dark bed on which he tossed to and fro until the small hours of the morning began to grow large. It was a night of little ease to his toiling mind, toiling in mere darkness and besieged by questions.

Six o'clock struck on the bells of the church that was so conveniently near to Mr. Utterson's dwelling, and still he was digging at the problem. Hitherto it had touched him on the intellectual side alone; but now his imagination also was engaged, or rather enslaved; and as he lay and tossed in the gross darkness of the night and the curtained room, Mr. Enfield's tale went by before his mind in a scroll of lighted pictures. He would be aware of the great field of lamps of a nocturnal city; then of the figure of a man walking swiftly; then of a child running from the doctor's; and then these met, and that human Juggernaut trod the child down and passed on regardless of her screams. Or else he would see a room in a rich house, where his friend lay asleep, dreaming and smiling at his dreams; and then the door of that room would be opened, the curtains of the bed plucked apart, the sleeper recalled, and, lo! there would stand by his side a figure to whom power was given, and even at that dead hour he must rise and do its bidding. The figure in these two phases haunted the lawyer all night; and if at any time he dozed over, it was but to see it glide more stealthily through sleeping houses, or move the more swiftly, and still the more swiftly, even to dizziness, through wider labyrinths of lamp-lighted city, and at every street corner crush a child and leave her screaming. And still the figure had no face by which he might know it; even in his dreams it had no face, or one that baffled him and melted before his eyes; and thus it was that there sprang up and grew apace in the lawyer's mind a singularly strong, almost an inordinate, curiosity to behold the features of the real Mr. Hyde. If he could but once set eyes on him, he thought the mystery would lighten and perhaps roll altogether away, as was the habit of mysterious things when well examined. He might see a reason for his friend's strange preference or bondage (call it which you please), and even for the startling clauses of the will. And at least it would be a face worth seeing: the face of a man who was without bowels of mercy: a face which had but to show itself to raise up, in the mind of the unimpressionable Enfield, a spirit of enduring hatred.

From that time forward, Mr. Utterson began to haunt the door in the by-street of shops. In the morning before office hours, at noon when business was plenty and time scarce, at night under the face of the fogged city moon, by all lights and at all hours of solitude or concourse, the lawyer was to be found on his chosen post.

"If he be Mr. Hyde," he had thought, "I shall be Mr. Seek."

And at last his patience was rewarded. It was a fine dry night; frost in the air; the streets as clean as a ball-room floor; the lamps, unshaken by any wind, drawing a regular pattern of light and shadow. By ten o'clock, when the shops were closed, the by-street was very solitary, and in spite of the low growl of London from all round, very silent. Small sounds carried far; domestic sounds out of the houses were clearly audible on either side of the roadway: and the rumour of any approach of any passenger preceded him by a long time. Mr. Utterson had been some minutes at his post when he was aware of an odd light footstep drawing near. In the course of his nightly patrols he had long grown accustomed to the quaint effect with which the footfalls of a single person, while he is still a great way off, suddenly spring out distinct from the vast hum and clatter of the city. Yet his attention had never before been so sharply and decisively arrested; and it was with a strong, superstitious prevision of success that he withdrew into the entry of the court.

The steps drew swiftly nearer, and swelled out suddenly louder as they turned the end of the street. The lawyer, looking forth from the entry, could soon see what manner of man he had to deal with. He was small, and very plainly dressed; and the look of him, even at that distance, went somehow strongly against the watcher's inclination. But he made straight for the door, crossing the roadway to save time; and as he came, he drew a key from his pocket, like one approaching home.

Mr. Utterson stepped out and touched him on the shoulder as he passed. "Mr. Hyde, I think?"

Mr. Hyde shrank back with a hissing intake of the breath. But his fear was only momentary; and though he did not look the lawyer in the face, he answered coolly enough: "That is my name. What do you want?"

"I see you are going in," returned the lawyer. "I am an old friend of Dr. Jekyll's—Mr. Utterson, of Gaunt Street—you must have heard my name; and meeting you so conveniently, I thought you might admit me."

"You will not find Dr. Jekyll; he is from home," replied Mr.

Hyde, blowing in the key. And then suddenly, but still without looking up, "How did you know me?" he asked.

"On your side," said Mr. Utterson, "will you do me a favour?"

"With pleasure," replied the other. "What shall it be?"

"Will you let me see your face?" asked the lawyer.

Mr. Hyde appeared to hesitate; and then, as if upon some sudden reflection, fronted about with an air of defiance; and the pair stared at each other pretty fixedly for a few seconds. "Now I shall know you again," said Mr. Utterson. "It may be useful."

"Yes," returned Mr. Hyde, "it is as well we have met; and *à propos*, you should have my address." And he gave a number of a street in Soho.

"Good God!" thought Mr. Utterson, "can he too have been thinking of the will?" But he kept his feelings to himself, and only grunted in acknowledgment of the address.

"And now," said the other, "how did you know me?"

"By description," was the reply.

"Whose description?"

"We have common friends," said Mr. Utterson.

"Common friends!" echoed Mr. Hyde, a little hoarsely. "Who are they?"

"Jekyll, for instance," said the lawyer.

"He never told you," cried Mr. Hyde, with a flush of anger. "I did not think you would have lied."

"Come," said Mr. Utterson, "that is not fitting language."

The other snarled aloud into a savage laugh; and the next moment, with extraordinary quickness, he had unlocked the door and disappeared into the house.

The lawyer stood awhile when Mr. Hyde had left him, the picture of disquietude. Then he began slowly to mount the street, pausing every step or two, and putting his hand to his brow like a man in mental perplexity. The problem he was thus debating as he walked was one of a class that is rarely solved. Mr. Hyde was pale and dwarfish; he gave an impression of deformity without any namable malformation, he had a displeasing smile, he had borne himself to the lawyer with a sort of murderous mixture of timidity and boldness, and he spoke with a husky whispering and somewhat broken voice,—all these were points against him; but not all of these together could explain the hitherto unknown disgust, loathing, and fear with which Mr. Utterson regarded him. "There must be something else," said the perplexed gentleman. "There *is* something more, if I could find a name for it. God bless me, the man seems hardly human! Something troglodytic, shall we say? or can it be the old story of Dr. Fell? or is it the mere radiance of a foul soul that thus transpires through, and transfigures, its clay continent? The last, I think; for, O my poor old Harry Jekyll, if ever I read Satan's signature upon a face, it is on that of your new friend!"

Round the corner from the by-street there was a square of ancient, handsome houses, now for the most part decayed from their high estate, and let in flats and chambers to all sorts and conditions of men: map-engravers, architects, shady lawyers, and the agents of obscure enterprises. One house, however, second from the corner, was still occupied entire; and at the door of this, which wore a great air of wealth and comfort, though it was now plunged in darkness except for the fan-light, Mr. Utterson stopped and knocked. A well-dressed, elderly servant opened the door.

"Is Dr. Jekyll at home, Poole?" asked the lawyer.

"I will see, Mr. Utterson," said Poole, admitting the visitor, as he spoke, into a large, low-roofed, comfortable hall, paved with flags, warmed (after the fashion of a country house) by a bright, open fire, and furnished with costly cabinets of oak. "Will you wait here by the fire, sir? or shall I give you a light in the dining-room?"

"Here, thank you," said the lawyer; and he drew near and leaned on the tall fender. This hall, in which he was now left alone, was a pet fancy of his friend the doctor's; and Utterson himself was wont to speak of it as the pleasantest room in London. But to-night there was a shudder in his blood; the face of Hyde sat heavy on his memory; he felt (what was rare with him) a nausea and distaste of life; and in the gloom of his spirits, he seemed to read a menace in the flickering of the firelight on the polished cabinets and the uneasy starting of the shadow on the roof. He was ashamed of his relief when Poole presently returned to announce that Dr. Jekyll was gone out.

"I saw Mr. Hyde go in by the old dissecting-room door, Poole," he said. "Is that right, when Dr. Jekyll is from home!"

"Quite right, Mr. Utterson, sir," replied the servant. "Mr. Hyde has a key."

"Your master seems to repose a great deal of trust in that young man, Poole," resumed the other, musingly.

"Yes, sir, he do indeed," said Poole. "We have all orders to obey him."

"I do not think I ever met Mr. Hyde?" asked Utterson.

"O dear no, sir. He never *dines* here," replied the butler. "Indeed, we see very little of him on this side of the house; he mostly comes and goes by the laboratory."

"Well, good-night, Poole."

"Good-night, Mr. Utterson."

And the lawyer set out homeward with a very heavy heart. "Poor Harry Jekyll," he thought, "my mind misgives me he is in deep waters! He was wild when he was young; a long while ago, to be sure; but in the law of God there is no statute of limitations. Ah, it must be that; the ghost of some old sin, the cancer of some concealed disgrace; punishment coming, *pede claudo*, years after memory has forgotten and self-love condoned the fault." And the lawyer, scared by the thought, brooded awhile on his own past, groping in all the corners of memory, lest by chance some Jack-in-the-Box of an old iniquity should leap to light there. His past was fairly blameless; few men could read the rolls of their life with less apprehension; yet he was humbled to the dust by the many ill things he had done, and raised up again into a sober and fearful gratitude by the many that he had come so near to doing, yet avoided. And then by a return on his former subject, he conceived a spark of hope. "This Master Hyde, if he were studied," thought he, "must have secrets of his own: black secrets, by the look of him; secrets compared to which poor Jekyll's worst would be like sunshine. Things cannot continue as they are. It turns me cold to think of this creature stealing like a thief to Harry's bedside; poor Harry, what a wakening! And the danger of it! for if this Hyde suspects the existence of the will, he may grow impatient to inherit. Ay, I must put my shoulder to the wheel—if Jekyll will but let me," he added, "if Jekyll will only let me." For once more he saw before his mind's eye, as clear as a transparency, the strange clauses of the will.

3. Dr. Jekyll was quite at ease

A FORTNIGHT later, by excellent good fortune, the doctor gave one of his pleasant dinners to some five or six old cronies, all intelligent reputable men, and all judges of good wine; and Mr. Utterson so contrived that he remained behind after the others had departed. This was no new arrangement, but a thing that had befallen many scores of times. Where Utterson was liked, he was liked well. Hosts loved to detain the dry lawyer, when the light-hearted and the loose-tongued had already their foot on the threshold; they liked to sit awhile in his unobtrusive company, practising for solitude, sobering their minds in the man's rich silence, after the expense and strain of gaiety. To this rule Dr. Jekyll was no exception; and as he now sat on the opposite side of the fire—a large, well-made, smooth-faced man of fifty, with something of a slyish cast perhaps, but every mark of capacity and kindness—you could see by his looks that he cherished for Mr. Utterson a sincere and warm affection.

"I have been wanting to speak to you, Jekyll," began the latter. "You know that will of yours?"

A close observer might have gathered that the topic was distasteful; but the doctor carried it off gaily. "My poor Utterson," said he, "you are unfortunate in such a client. I never saw a man so distressed as you were by my will; unless it were that hide-bound pedant, Lanyon, at what he called my scientific heresies. O, I know he's a good fellow—you needn't frown—an excellent fellow, and I always mean to see more of him; but a hide-bound pedant for all that; an ignorant, blatant pedant. I was never more disappointed in any man than Lanyon."

"You know I never approved of it," pursued Utterson, ruthlessly disregarding the fresh topic.

"My will? Yes, certainly, I know that," said the doctor, a trifle sharply. "You have told me so."

"Well, I tell you so again," continued the lawyer. "I have been learning something of young Hyde."

The large handsome face of Dr. Jekyll grew pale to the very lips, and there came a blackness about his eyes. "I do not care to hear more," said he. "This is a matter I thought we had agreed to drop."

"What I heard was abominable," said Utterson.

"It can make no change. You do not understand my position," returned the doctor, with a certain incoherency of manner. "I am painfully situated, Utterson; my position is a very strange—a very strange one. It is one of those affairs that cannot be mended by talking."

"Jekyll," said Utterson, "you know me: I am a man to be trusted. Make a clean breast of this in confidence; and I make no doubt I can get you out of it."

"My good Utterson," said the doctor, "this is very good of you, this is downright good of you, and I cannot find words to thank you in. I believe you fully; I would trust you before any man alive, ay, before myself, if I could make the choice; but indeed it isn't what you fancy; it is not so bad as that; and just to put your good heart at rest, I will tell you one thing: the moment I choose, I can be rid of Mr. Hyde. I give you my hand upon that; and I thank you again and again; and I will just add one little word, Utterson, that I'm sure you'll take in good part: this is a private matter, and I beg of you to let it sleep."

Utterson reflected a little, looking in the fire.

"I have no doubt you are perfectly right," he said at last, getting to his feet.

"Well, but since we have touched upon this business, and for the last time, I hope," continued the doctor, "there is one point I should like you to understand. I have really a very great interest in poor Hyde. I know you have seen him; he told me so; and I fear he was rude. But I do sincerely take a great, a very great interest in that young man; and if I am taken away, Utterson, I wish you to promise me that you will bear with him and get his rights for him. I think you would, if you knew all; and it would be a weight off my mind if you would promise."

"I can't pretend that I shall ever like him," said the lawyer.

"I don't ask that," pleaded Jekyll, laying his hand upon the other's arm; "I only ask for justice; I only ask you to help him for my sake, when I am no longer here."

Utterson heaved an irrepressible sigh. "Well," said he, "I promise."

4. The Carew Murder Case

NEARLY a year later, in the month of October, 18—, London was startled by a crime of singular ferocity, and rendered all the more notable by the high position of the victim. The details were few and startling. A maid-servant living alone in a house not far from the river had gone upstairs to bed about eleven. Although a fog rolled over the city in the small hours, the early part of the night was cloudless, and the lane, which the maid's window overlooked, was brilliantly lit by the full moon. It seems she was romantically given; for she sat down upon her box, which stood immediately under the window, and fell into a dream of musing. Never (she used to say, with streaming tears, when she narrated that experience), never had she felt more at peace with all men or thought more kindly of the world. And as she so sat she became aware of an aged and beautiful gentleman with white hair drawing near along the lane; and advancing to meet him, another and very small gentleman, to whom at first she paid less attention. When they had come within speech (which was just under the maid's eyes) the older man bowed and accosted the other with a very pretty manner of politeness. It did not seem as if the subject of his address were of great importance; indeed, from his pointing, it sometimes appeared as if he were only inquiring his way; but the moon shone on his face as he spoke, and the girl was pleased to watch it, it seemed to breathe such an innocent and old-world kindness of disposition, yet with something high too, as of a well-founded self-content. Presently her eye wandered to the other, and she was surprised to recognize in him a certain Mr. Hyde, who had once visited her master, and for whom she had conceived a dislike. He had in his hand a heavy cane, with which he was trifling; but he answered never a word, and seemed to listen with an ill-contained impatience. And then all of a sudden he broke out in a great flame of anger, stamping with his foot, brandishing the cane, and carrying on (as the maid described it) like a madman. The old gentleman took a step back, with the air of one very much surprised and a trifle hurt; and at that Mr. Hyde broke out of all bounds, and clubbed him to the earth. And next moment, with ape-like fury, he was trampling his victim under foot, and hailing down a storm of blows, under which the bones were audibly shattered and the body jumped upon the roadway. At the horror of these sights and sounds the maid fainted.

It was two o'clock when she came to herself and called for the police. The murderer was gone long ago; but there lay his victim in the middle of the lane, incredibly mangled. The stick with which the deed had been done, although it was of some rare and very tough and heavy wood, had broken in the middle under the stress of this insensate cruelty; and one splintered half had rolled in the neighbouring gutter—the other, without doubt, had been carried away by the murderer. A purse and a gold watch were found upon the victim; but no card or papers, except a sealed and stamped envelope, which he had been probably carrying to the post, and which bore the name and address of Mr. Utterson.

This was brought to the lawyer the next morning, before he was out of bed; and he had no sooner seen it, and been told the circumstances, than he shot out a solemn lip. "I shall say nothing till I have seen the body," said he; "this may be very serious. Have the kindness to wait while I dress." And with the same grave countenance he hurried through his breakfast and drove to the police station, whither the body had been carried. As soon as he came into the cell, he nodded.

"Yes," said he, "I recognize him. I am sorry to say that this is Sir Danvers Carew."

"Good God, sir!" exclaimed the officer, "is it possible?" And the next moment his eye lighted up with professional ambition. "This will make a deal of noise," he said. "And perhaps you can help us to the man." And he briefly narrated what the maid had seen, and showed the broken stick.

Mr. Utterson had already quailed at the name of Hyde; but when the stick was laid before him, he could doubt no longer: broken and battered as it was, he recognized it for one that he had himself presented many years before to Henry Jekyll.

"Is this Mr. Hyde a person of small stature?" he inquired.

"Particularly small and particularly wicked-looking, is what the maid calls him," said the officer.

Mr. Utterson reflected; and then, raising his head, "If you will come with me in my cab," he said, "I think I can take you to his house."

It was by this time about nine in the morning, and the first fog of the season. A great chocolate-coloured pall lowered over heaven, but the wind was continually charging and routing these embattled vapours; so that as the cab crawled from street to street, Mr. Utterson beheld a marvellous number of degrees and hues of twilight; for here it would be dark like the back-end of evening; and there would be a glow of a rich, lurid brown, like the light of some strange conflagration; and here, for a moment, the fog would be quite broken up, and a haggard shaft of daylight would glance in between the swirling wreaths. The dismal quarter of Soho seen under these changing glimpses, with its muddy ways, and slatternly passengers, and its lamps, which had never been extinguished or had been kindled afresh to combat this mournful reinvasion of darkness, seemed, in the lawyer's eyes, like a district of some city in a nightmare. The thoughts of his mind, besides, were of the gloomiest dye; and when he glanced at the companion of his drive, he was conscious of some touch of that terror of the law and the law's officers which may at times assail the most honest.

As the cab drew up before the address indicated, the fog lifted a little and showed him a dingy street, a gin palace, a low French eating-house, a shop for the retail of penny numbers and twopenny salads, many ragged children huddled in the doorways, and many women of many different nationalities passing out, key in hand, to have a morning glass; and the next moment the fog settled down again upon that part, as brown as umber, and cut him off from his blackguardly surroundings. This was the home of Henry Jekyll's favourite; of a man who was heir to a quarter of a million sterling.

An ivory-faced and silvery-haired old woman opened the door. She had an evil face, smoothed by hypocrisy; but her manners were excellent. Yes, she said, this was Mr. Hyde's, but he was not at home; he had been in that night very late, but had gone away again in less than an hour: there was nothing strange in that; his habits were very irregular, and he was often absent; for instance, it was nearly two months since she had seen him till yesterday.

"Very well then, we wish to see his rooms," said the lawyer; and when the woman began to declare it was impossible, "I had better tell you who this person is," he added. "This is Inspector Newcomen, of Scotland Yard."

A flash of odious joy appeared upon the woman's face. "Ah!" said she, "he is in trouble! What has he done?"

Mr. Utterson and the inspector exchanged glances. "He don't seem a very popular character," observed the latter. "And now, my good woman, just let me and this gentleman have a look about us."

In the whole extent of the house, which but for the old woman remained otherwise empty, Mr. Hyde had only used a couple of rooms; but these were furnished with luxury and good taste. A closet was filled with wine; the plate was of silver, the napery elegant; a good picture hung upon the walls, a gift (as Utterson supposed) from Henry Jekyll, who was much of a connoisseur; and the carpets were of many plies and agreeable in colour. At this moment, however, the rooms bore every mark of having been recently and hurriedly ransacked; clothes lay about the floor, with their pockets inside out; lockfast drawers stood open; and on the earth lay a pile of gray ashes, as though many papers had been burned. From these embers the inspector disinterred the butt end of a green cheque book which had resisted the action of the fire; the other half of the stick was found behind the door; and as this clinched his suspicions, the officer declared himself delighted. A visit to the bank, where several thousand pounds were found to be lying to the murderer's credit, completed his gratification.

"You may depend upon it, sir," he told Mr. Utterson: "I have him in my hand. He must have lost his head, or he never would have left the stick, or, above all, burned the cheque book. Why, money's life to the man. We have nothing to do but wait for him at the bank, and get out the handbills."

This last, however, was not so easy of accomplishment; for Mr. Hyde had numbered few familiars—even the master of the servant-maid had only seen him twice; his family could nowhere be traced; he had never been photographed; and the few who could describe him differed widely, as common observers will. Only on one point were they agreed; and that was the haunting sense of unexpressed deformity with which the fugitive impressed his beholders.

5. Incident of the Letter

IT WAS late in the afternoon when Mr. Utterson found his way to Dr. Jekyll's door, where he was at once admitted by Poole, and carried down by the kitchen offices and across a yard which had once been a garden, to the building which was indifferently known as the laboratory or the dissecting-rooms. The doctor had bought the house from the heirs of a celebrated surgeon; and his own tastes being rather chemical than anatomical, had changed the destination of the block at the bottom of the garden. It was the first time that the lawyer had been received in that part of his friend's quarters; and he eyed the dingy windowless structure with curiosity, and gazed round with a distasteful sense of strangeness as he crossed the theatre, once crowded with eager students and now lying gaunt and silent, the tables laden with chemical apparatus, the floor strewn with crates and littered with packing straw, and the light falling dimly through the foggy cupola. At the further end, a flight of stairs mounted to a door covered with red baize; and through this Mr. Utterson was at last received into the doctor's cabinet. It was a large room, fitted round with glass presses, furnished, among other things, with a cheval-glass and a business table, and looking out upon the court by three dusty windows barred with iron. The fire burned in the grate; a lamp was set lighted on the chimney-shelf, for even in the houses the fog began to lie thickly; and there, close up to the warmth, sat Dr. Jekyll, looking deadly sick. He did not rise to meet his visitor, but held out a cold hand, and bade him welcome in a changed voice.

"And now," said Mr. Utterson, as soon as Poole had left them, "you have heard the news?"

The doctor shuddered. "They were crying it in the square," he said. "I heard them in my dining-room."

"One word," said the lawyer. "Carew was my client, but so are you; and I want to know what I am doing. You have not been mad enough to hide this fellow?"

"Utterson, I swear to God," cried the doctor, "I swear to God I will never set eyes on him again. I bind my honour to you that I am done with him in this world. It is all at an end. And indeed he does not want my help; you do not know him as I do; he is safe, he is quite safe; mark my words, he will never more be heard of."

The lawyer listened gloomily; he did not like his friend's feverish manner. "You seem pretty sure of him," said he; "and for your sake, I hope you may be right. If it came to a trial, your name might appear."

"I am quite sure of him," replied Jekyll; "I have grounds for certainty that I cannot share with any one. But there is one thing on which you may advise me. I have—I have received a letter; and I am at a loss whether I should show it to the police. I should like to leave it in your hands, Utterson; you would judge wisely, I am sure; I have so great a trust in you."

"You fear, I suppose, that it might lead to his detection?" asked the lawyer.

"No," said the other. "I cannot say that I care what becomes of Hyde; I am quite done with him. I was thinking of my own character, which this hateful business has rather exposed."

Utterson ruminated awhile; he was surprised at his friend's selfishness, and yet relieved by it. "Well," said he, at last, "let me see the letter."

The letter was written in an odd, upright hand, and signed "Edward Hyde"; and it signified, briefly enough, that the writer's benefactor, Dr. Jekyll, whom he had long so unworthily repaid for a thousand generosities, need labour under no alarm for his safety, as he had means of escape on which he placed a sure dependence. The lawyer liked this letter well enough: it put a better colour on the intimacy than he had looked for; and he blamed himself for some of his past suspicions.

"Have you the envelope?" he asked.

"I burned it," replied Jekyll, "before I thought what I was about. But it bore no postmark. The note was handed in."

"Shall I keep this and sleep upon it?" asked Utterson.

"I wish you to judge for me entirely," was the reply. "I have lost confidence in myself."

"Well, I shall consider," returned the lawyer. "And now one word more: it was Hyde who dictated the terms in your will about that disappearance?"

The doctor seemed seized with a qualm of faintness; he shut his mouth tight and nodded.

"I knew it," said Utterson. "He meant to murder you. You have had a fine escape."

"I have had what is far more to the purpose," returned the doctor solemnly: "I have had a lesson—O God, Utterson, what a lesson I have had!" And he covered his face for a moment with his hands.

On his way out, the lawyer stopped and had a word or two with Poole. "By the by," said he, "there was a letter handed in to-day: what was the messenger like?" But Poole was positive nothing had come except by post; "And only circulars by that," he added.

This news sent off the visitor with his fears renewed. Plainly the letter had come by the laboratory door; possibly, indeed, it had been written in the cabinet; and, if that were so, it must be differently judged, and handled with the more caution. The news-boys, as he went, were crying themselves hoarse along the footways: "Special edition. Shocking murder of an M.P." That was the funeral oration of one friend and client; and he could not help a certain apprehension lest the good name of another should be sucked down in the eddy of the scandal. It was, at least, a ticklish decision that he had to make; and, self-reliant as he was by habit, he began to cherish a longing for advice. It was not to be had directly; but perhaps, he thought, it might be fished for.

Presently after, he sat on one side of his own hearth, with Mr. Guest, his head clerk, upon the other, and midway between, at a nicely calculated distance from the fire, a bottle of a particular old wine that had long dwelt unsunned in the foundations of his house. The fog still slept on the wing above the drowned city, where the lamps glimmered like carbuncles; and through the muffle and smother of these fallen clouds, the procession of the town's life was still rolling in through the great arteries with a sound as of a mighty wind. But the room was gay with firelight. In the bottle the acids were long ago resolved; the imperial dye had softened with time, as the colour grows richer in stained windows; and the glow of hot autumn afternoons on hillside vineyards was ready to be set free and to disperse the fogs of London. Insensibly the lawyer melted. There was no man from whom he kept fewer secrets than Mr. Guest; and he was not always sure that he kept as many as he meant. Guest had often been on business to the doctor's: he knew Poole; he could scarce have failed to hear of Mr. Hyde's familiarity about the house; he might draw conclusions: was it not as well, then, that he should see a letter which put that mystery to rights? and, above all, since Guest, being a great student and critic of handwriting, would consider the step natural and obliging? The clerk, besides, was a man of counsel; he would scarce read so strange a document without dropping a remark; and by that remark Mr. Utterson might shape his future course.

"This is a sad business about Sir Danvers," he said.

"Yes, sir, indeed. It has elicited a great deal of public feeling," returned Guest. "The man, of course, was mad."

"I should like to hear your views on that," replied Utterson. "I have a document here in his handwriting; it is between ourselves, for I scarce know what to do about it; it is an ugly business at the best. But there it is; quite in your way: a murderer's autograph."

Guest's eyes brightened, and he sat down at once and studied it with passion. "No, sir," he said; "not mad; but it is an odd hand."

"And by all accounts a very odd writer," added the lawyer.

Just then the servant entered with a note.

"Is that from Dr. Jekyll, sir?" inquired the clerk. "I thought I knew the writing. Anything private, Mr. Utterson?"

"Only an invitation to dinner. Why? do you want to see it?"

"One moment. I thank you, sir"; and the clerk laid the two sheets of paper alongside and sedulously compared their contents. "Thank you, sir," he said at last, returning both; "it's a very interesting autograph."

There was a pause, during which Mr. Utterson struggled with himself. "Why did you compare them, Guest?" he inquired suddenly.

"Well, sir," returned the clerk, "there's a rather singular resemblance; the two hands are in many points identical; only differently sloped."

"Rather quaint," said Utterson.

"It is, as you say, rather quaint," returned Guest.

"I wouldn't speak of this note, you know," said the master.

"No, sir," said the clerk. "I understand."

But no sooner was Mr. Utterson alone that night than he locked the note into his safe, where it reposed from that time forward. "What?" he thought. "Henry Jekyll forge for a murderer!" And his blood ran cold in his veins.

6. Remarkable Incident of Dr. Lanyon

TIME ran on; thousands of pounds were offered in reward, for the death of Sir Danvers was resented as a public injury; but Mr. Hyde had disappeared out of the ken of the police as though he had never existed. Much of his past was unearthed, indeed, and all disreputable: tales came out of the man's cruelty, at once so callous and violent, of his vile life, of his strange associates, of the hatred that seemed to have surrounded his career; but of his present whereabouts, not a whisper. From the time he had left the house in Soho on the morning of the murder, he was simply blotted out; and gradually, as time drew on, Mr. Utterson began to recover from the hotness of his alarm, and to grow more at quiet with himself. The death of Sir Danvers was, to his way of thinking, more than paid for by the disappearance of Mr. Hyde. Now that the evil influence had been withdrawn, a new life began for Dr. Jekyll. He came out of his seclusion, renewed relations with his friends, became once more their familiar guest and entertainer; and whilst he had always been known for charities, he was now no less distinguished for religion. He was busy, he was much in the open air, he did good; his face seemed to open and brighten, as if with an inward consciousness of service; and for more than two months the doctor was at peace.

On the 8th of January Utterson had dined at the doctor's with a small party; Lanyon had been there; and the face of the host had looked from one to the other as in the old days when the trio were inseparable friends. On the 12th, and again on the 14th, the door was shut against the lawyer. "The doctor was confined to the house," Poole said, "and saw no one." On the 15th he tried again, and was again refused; and having now been used for the last two months to see his friend almost daily, he found this return of solitude to weigh upon his spirits. The fifth night he had in Guest to dine with him; and the sixth he betook himself to Dr. Lanyon's.

There at least he was not denied admittance; but when he came in, he was shocked at the change which had taken place in the doctor's appearance. He had his death-warrant written legibly upon his face.

The rosy man had grown pale; his flesh had fallen away; he was visibly balder and older; and yet it was not so much these tokens of a swift physical decay that arrested the lawyer's notice, as a look in the eye and quality of manner that seemed to testify to some deep-seated terror of the mind. It was unlikely that the doctor should fear death; and yet that was what Utterson was tempted to suspect. "Yes," he thought; "he is a doctor, he must know his own state and that his days are counted; and the knowledge is more than he can bear." And yet when Utterson remarked on his ill looks, it was with an air of great firmness that Lanyon declared himself a doomed man.

"I have had a shock," he said, "and I shall never recover. It is a question of weeks. Well, life has been pleasant; I liked it; yes, sir, I used to like it. I sometimes think if we knew all, we should be more glad to get away."

"Jekyll is ill, too," observed Utterson. "Have you seen him?"

But Lanyon's face changed, and he held up a trembling hand. "I wish to see or hear no more of Dr. Jekyll," he said, in a loud, unsteady voice. "I am quite done with that person; and I beg that you will spare me any allusion to one whom I regard as dead."

"Tut, tut!" said Mr. Utterson; and then, after a considerable pause, "Can't I do anything?" he inquired. "We are three very old friends, Lanyon; we shall not live to make others."

"Nothing can be done," returned Lanyon; "ask himself."

"He will not see me," said the lawyer.

"I am not surprised at that," was the reply. "Some day, Utterson, after I am dead, you may perhaps come to learn the right and wrong of this. I cannot tell you. And in the meantime, if you can sit and talk with me of other things, for God's sake, stay and do so; but if you cannot keep clear of this accursed topic, then, in God's name, go, for I cannot bear it."

As soon as he got home, Utterson sat down and wrote to Jekyll, complaining of his exclusion from the house, and asking the cause of this unhappy break with Lanyon; and the next day brought him a long answer, often very pathetically worded, and sometimes darkly mysterious in drift. The quarrel with Lanyon was incurable. "I do not blame our old friend," Jekyll wrote, "but I share his view that we must never meet. I mean from henceforth to lead a life of extreme seclusion; you must not be surprised, nor must you doubt my friendship, if my door is often shut even to you. You must suffer me to go my own dark way. I have brought on myself a punishment and a danger that I cannot name. If I am the chief of sinners, I am the chief of sufferers also. I could not think that this earth contained a place for sufferings and terrors so unmanning; and you can do but one thing, Utterson, to lighten this destiny, and that is to respect my silence." Utterson was amazed; the dark influence of Hyde had been withdrawn, the doctor had returned to his old tasks and amities; a week ago, the prospect had smiled with every promise of a cheerful and an honoured age; and now in a moment, friendship and peace of mind and the whole tenor of his life were wrecked. So great and unprepared a change pointed to madness; but in view of Lanyon's manner and words, there must lie for it some deeper ground.

A week afterwards Dr. Lanyon took to his bed, and in something less than a fortnight he was dead. The night after the funeral, at which he had been sadly affected, Utterson locked the door of his business room, and sitting there by the light of a melancholy candle, drew out and set before him an envelope addressed by the hand and sealed with the seal of his dead friend. "PRIVATE: for the hands of J. G. Utterson ALONE, and in case of his predecease *to be destroyed unread*," so it was emphatically superscribed; and the lawyer dreaded to behold the contents. "I have buried one friend to-day," he thought: "what if this should cost me another?" And then he condemned the fear as a disloyalty, and broke the seal. Within there was another enclosure, likewise sealed, and marked upon the cover as "not to be opened till the death or disappearance of Dr. Henry Jekyll." Utterson could not trust his eyes. Yes, it was disappearance; here again, as in the mad will, which he had long ago restored to its author, here again were the idea of a disappearance and the name of Henry Jekyll bracketed. But in the will, that idea had sprung from the sinister suggestion of the man Hyde; it was set there with a purpose all too plain and horrible. Written by the hand of Lanyon, what should it mean? A great curiosity came to the trustee, to disregard the prohibition and dive at once to the bottom of these mysteries; but professional honour and faith to his dead friend were stringent obligations; and the packet slept in the inmost corner of his private safe.

It is one thing to mortify curiosity, another to conquer it; and it may be doubted if, from that day forth, Utterson desired the society of his surviving friend with the same eagerness. He thought of him kindly; but his thoughts were disquieted and fearful. He went to call indeed; but he was perhaps relieved to be denied admittance; perhaps, in his heart, he preferred to speak with Poole upon the doorstep, and surrounded by the air and sounds of the open city, rather than to be admitted into that house of voluntary bondage, and to sit and speak with its inscrutable recluse. Poole had, indeed, no very pleasant news to communicate. The doctor, it appeared, now more than ever confined himself to the cabinet over the laboratory, where he would sometimes even sleep: he was out of spirits, he had grown very silent, he did not read; it seemed as if he had something on his mind. Utterson became so used to the unvarying character of these reports, that he fell off little by little in the frequency of his visits.

7. Incident at the Window

IT CHANCED on Sunday, when Mr. Utterson was on his usual walk with Mr. Enfield, that their way lay once again through the by-street; and that when they came in front of the door, both stopped to gaze on it.

"Well," said Enfield, "that story's at an end, at least. We shall never see more of Mr. Hyde."

"I hope not," said Utterson. "Did I ever tell you that I once saw him, and shared your feeling of repulsion?"

"It was impossible to do the one without the other," returned Enfield. "And, by the way, what an ass you must have thought me, not to know that this was a back way to Dr. Jekyll's? It was partly your own fault that I found it out even when I did."

"So you found it out, did you?" said Utterson. "But if that be so, we may step into the court and take a look at the windows. To tell you the truth, I am uneasy about poor Jekyll; and even outside, I feel as if the presence of a friend might do him good."

The court was very cool and a little damp, and full of premature twilight, although the sky, high up overhead, was still bright with sunset. The middle one of the three windows was half-way open; and sitting close beside it, taking the air with an infinite sadness of mien, like some disconsolate prisoner, Utterson saw Dr. Jekyll.

"What! Jekyll!" he cried. "I trust you are better."

"I am very low, Utterson," replied the doctor drearily; "very low. It will not last long, thank God."

"You stay too much indoors," said the lawyer. "You should be out, whipping up the circulation, like Mr. Enfield and me. (This is my cousin—Mr. Enfield—Dr. Jekyll.) Come, now; get your hat, and take a quick turn with us."

"You are very good," sighed the other. "I should like to very much; but no, no, no; it is quite impossible; I dare not. But indeed, Utterson, I am very glad to see you; this is really a great pleasure. I would ask you and Mr. Enfield up, but the place is really not fit."

"Why then," said the lawyer, good-naturedly, "the best thing we can do is to stay down here, and speak with you from where we are."

"That is just what I was about to venture to propose," returned the doctor, with a smile. But the words were hardly uttered, before the smile was struck out of his face and succeeded by an expression of such abject terror and despair, as froze the very blood of the two gentlemen below. They saw it but for a glimpse, for the window was instantly thrust down; but that glimpse had been sufficient, and they turned and left the court without a word. In silence, too, they traversed the by-street; and it was not until they had come into a neighbouring thoroughfare, where even upon a Sunday there were still some stirrings of life, that Mr. Utterson at last turned and looked at his companion. They were both pale; and there was an answering horror in their eyes.

"God forgive us! God forgive us!" said Mr. Utterson.

But Mr. Enfield only nodded his head very seriously, and walked on once more in silence.

8. The Last Night

MR. UTTERSON was sitting by his fireside one evening after dinner, when he was surprised to receive a visit from Poole.

"Bless me, Poole, what brings you here?" he cried; and then, taking a second look at him, "what ails you?" he added; "is the doctor ill?"

"Mr. Utterson," said the man, "there is something wrong."

"Take a seat, and here is a glass of wine for you," said the lawyer. "Now, take your time, and tell me plainly what you want."

"You know the doctor's ways, sir," replied Poole, "and how he shuts himself up. Well, he's shut up again in the cabinet; and I don't like it, sir—I wish I may die if I like it. Mr. Utterson, sir, I'm afraid."

"Now, my good man," said the lawyer, "be explicit. What are you afraid of?"

"I've been afraid for about a week," returned Poole, doggedly disregarding the question; "and I can bear it no more."

The man's appearance amply bore out his words; his manner was altered for the worse; and except for the moment when he had first announced his terror, he had not once looked the lawyer in the face. Even now, he sat with the glass of wine untasted on his knee, and his eyes directed to a corner of the floor. "I can bear it no more," he repeated.

"Come," said the lawyer, "I see you have some good reason, Poole; I see there is something seriously amiss. Try to tell me what it is."

"I think there's been foul play," said Poole hoarsely.

"Foul play!" cried the lawyer, a good deal frightened, and rather inclined to be irritated in consequence. "What foul play? What does the man mean?"

"I daren't say, sir," was the answer; "but will you come along with me and see for yourself?"

Mr. Utterson's only answer was to rise and get his hat and greatcoat; but he observed with wonder the greatness of the relief that appeared upon the butler's face, and perhaps with no less, that the wine was still untasted when he set it down to follow.

It was a wild, cold, seasonable night of March, with a pale moon, lying on her back as though the wind had tilted her, and a flying wrack of the most diaphanous and lawny texture. The wind made talking difficult, and flecked the blood into the face. It seemed to have swept the streets unusually bare of passengers, besides; for Mr. Utterson thought he had never seen that part of London so deserted. He could have wished it otherwise; never in his life had he been conscious of so sharp a wish to see and touch his fellow-creatures; for, struggle as he might, there was borne in upon his mind a crushing anticipation of calamity. The square, when they got there, was all full of wind and dust, and the thin trees in the garden were lashing themselves along the railing. Poole, who had kept all the way a pace or two ahead, now pulled up in the middle of the pavement, and in spite of the biting weather, took off his hat and mopped his brow with a red pocket-handkerchief. But for all the hurry of his coming, these were not the dews of exertion that he wiped away, but the moisture of some strangling anguish; for his face was white, and his voice, when he spoke, harsh and broken.

"Well, sir," he said, "here we are, and God grant there be nothing wrong."

"Amen, Poole," said the lawyer.

Thereupon the servant knocked in a very guarded manner; the door was opened on the chain; and a voice asked from within, "Is that you, Poole?"

"It's all right," said Poole. "Open the door."

The hall, when they entered it, was brightly lighted up; the fire was built high; and about the hearth the whole of the servants, men and women, stood huddled together like a flock of sheep. At the sight of Mr. Utterson, the housemaid broke into hysterical whimpering; and the cook, crying out, "Bless God! it's Mr. Utterson," ran forward as if to take him in her arms.

"What, what? Are you all here?" said the lawyer, peevishly. "Very irregular, very unseemly: your master would be far from pleased."

"They're all afraid," said Poole.

Blank silence followed, no one protesting; only the maid lifted up her voice, and now wept loudly.

"Hold your tongue!" Poole said to her, with a ferocity of accent that testified to his own jangled nerves; and indeed when the girl had so suddenly raised the note of her lamentation, they had all started and turned towards the inner door with faces of dreadful expectation. "And now," continued the butler, addressing the knife-boy, "reach me a candle, and we'll get this through hands at once." And then he begged Mr. Utterson to follow him, and led the way to the back garden.

"Now, sir," said he, "you come as gently as you can. I want you to hear, and I don't want you to be heard. And see here, sir, if by any chance he was to ask you in, don't go."

Mr. Utterson's nerves, at this unlooked-for termination, gave a jerk that nearly threw him from his balance; but he re-collected his courage and followed the butler into the laboratory building and through the surgical theatre, with its lumber of crates and bottles, to the foot of the stair. Here Poole motioned him to stand on one side and listen; while he himself, setting down the candle and making a great and obvious call on his resolution, mounted the steps, and knocked with a somewhat uncertain hand on the red baize of the cabinet door.

"Mr. Utterson, sir, asking to see you," he called; and even as he did so, once more violently signed to the lawyer to give ear.

A voice answered from within: "Tell him I cannot see any one," it said, complainingly.

"Thank you, sir," said Poole, with a note of something like triumph in his voice; and taking up his candle, he led Mr. Utterson back across the yard and into the great kitchen, where the fire was out and beetles were leaping on the floor.

"Sir," he said, looking Mr. Utterson in the eyes, "was that my master's voice?"

"It seems much changed," replied the lawyer, very pale, but giving look for look.

"Changed? Well, yes I think so," said the butler. "Have I been twenty years in this man's house, to be deceived about his voice? No, sir; master's made away with; he was made away with eight days ago, when we heard him cry out upon the name of God; and *who's* in there instead of him, and *why* it stays there, is a thing that cries to Heaven, Mr. Utterson!"

"This is a very strange tale, Poole; this is rather a wild tale, my man," said Mr. Utterson, biting his finger. "Suppose it were as you suppose, supposing Dr. Jekyll to have been—well, murdered, what could induce the murderer to stay? That won't hold water; it doesn't commend itself to reason."

"Well, Mr. Utterson, you are a hard man to satisfy, but I'll do it yet," said Poole. "All this last week (you must know), him, or it, or whatever it is that lives in that cabinet, has been crying night and day for some sort of medicine and cannot get it to his mind. It was sometimes his way—the master's, that is—to write his orders on a sheet of paper and throw it on the stair. We've had nothing else this week back; nothing but papers, and a closed door, and the very meals left there to be smuggled in when nobody was looking. Well, sir, every day, ay, and twice and thrice in the same day, there have been orders and complaints, and I have been sent flying to all the wholesale chemists in town. Every time I brought the stuff back, there would be another paper telling me to return it, because it was not pure, and another order to a different firm. This drug is wanted bitter bad, sir, whatever for."

"Have you any of these papers?" asked Mr. Utterson.

Poole felt in his pocket and handed out a crumpled note, which the lawyer, bending nearer to the candle, carefully examined. Its contents ran thus: "Dr. Jekyll presents his compliments to Messrs. Maw. He assures them that their last sample is impure and quite useless for his present purpose. In the year 18—, Dr. J. purchased a somewhat large quantity from Messrs. M. He now begs them to search with the most sedulous care, and should any of the same quality be left, to forward it to him at once. Expense is no consideration. The importance of this to Dr. J. can hardly be exaggerated." So far the letter had run composedly enough; but here, with a sudden splutter of the pen, the writer's emotion had broken loose. "For God's sake," he had added, "find me some of the old."

"This is a strange note," said Mr. Utterson and then sharply, "How do you come to have it open?"

"The man at Maw's was main angry, sir, and he threw it back to me like so much dirt," returned Poole.

"This is unquestionably the doctor's hand, do you know?" resumed the lawyer.

"I thought it looked like it," said the servant, rather sulkily; and then, with another voice, "But what matters hand of write?" he said. "I've seen him!"

"Seen him?" repeated Mr. Utterson. "Well?"

"That's it!" said Poole. "It was this way. I came suddenly into the theatre from the garden. It seems he had slipped out to look for this drug, or whatever it is; for the cabinet door was open, and there he was at the far end of the room, digging among the crates. He looked up when I came in, gave a kind of cry, and whipped upstairs into the cabinet. It was but for one minute that I saw him, but the hair stood upon my head like quills. Sir, if that was my master, why had he a mask upon his face? If it was my master, why did he cry out like a rat and run from me? I have served him long enough. And then . . ." the man paused, and passed his hand over his face.

"These are all very strange circumstances," said Mr. Utterson, "but I think I begin to see daylight. Your master, Poole, is plainly seized with one of those maladies that both torture and deform the sufferer, hence, for aught I know, the alteration of his voice; hence the mask and his avoidance of his friends; hence his eagerness to find this drug, by means of which the poor soul retains some hope of ultimate recovery—God grant that he be not deceived! There is my explanation; it is sad enough, Poole, ay, and appalling to consider; but it is plain and natural, hangs well together, and delivers us from all exorbitant alarms."

"Sir," said the butler, turning to a sort of mottled pallor, "that thing was not my master, and there's the truth. My master"—here he looked round him, and began to whisper—"is a tall fine build of a man, and this was more of a dwarf." Utterson attempted to protest. "O, sir," cried Poole, "do you think I do not know my master after twenty years? do you think I do not know where his head comes to in the cabinet door, where I saw him every morning of my life? No, sir, that thing in the mask was never Dr. Jekyll—God knows what it was, but it was never Dr. Jekyll; and it is the belief of my heart that there was murder done."

"Poole," replied the lawyer, "if you say that, it will become my duty to make certain. Much as I desire to spare your master's feelings, much as I am puzzled about this note, which seems to prove him to be still alive, I shall consider it my duty to break in that door."

"Ah, Mr. Utterson, that's talking!" cried the butler.

"And now comes the second question," resumed Utterson: "Who is going to do it?"

"Why, you and me, sir," was the undaunted reply.

"That is very well said," returned the lawyer; "and whatever comes of it, I shall make it my business to see you are no loser."

"There is an axe in the theatre," continued Poole; "and you might take the kitchen poker for yourself."

The lawyer took that rude but weighty instrument into his hand, and balanced it. "Do you know, Poole," he said, looking up, "that you and I are about to place ourselves in a position of some peril?"

"You may say so, sir, indeed," returned the butler.

"It is well, then, that we should be frank," said the other. "We both think more than we have said; let us make a clean breast. This masked figure that you saw, did you recognize it?"

"Well, sir, it went so quick, and the creature was so doubled up, that I could hardly swear to that," was the answer. "But if you mean, was it Mr. Hyde?—why, yes, I think it was! You see, it was much of the same bigness; and it had the same quick light way with it; and then who else could have got in by the laboratory door? You have not forgot, sir, that at the time of the murder he had still the key with him? But that's not all. I don't know, Mr. Utterson, if ever you met this Mr. Hyde?"

"Yes," said the lawyer, "I once spoke with him."

"Then you must know, as well as the rest of us, that there was something queer about that gentleman—something that gave a man a turn—I don't know rightly how to say it, sir, beyond this: that you felt it in your marrow—kind of cold and thin."

"I own I felt something of what you describe," said Mr. Utterson.

"Quite so, sir," returned Poole. "Well, when that masked thing like a monkey jumped from among the chemicals and whipped into the cabinet, it went down my spine like ice. O, I know it's not evidence, Mr. Utterson; I'm book-learned enough for that; but a man has his feelings; and I give you my bible-word it was Mr. Hyde!"

"Ay, ay," said the lawyer. "My fears incline to the same point. Evil, I fear, founded—evil was sure to come—of that connection. Ay, truly, I believe you; I believe poor Harry is killed; and I believe his murderer (for what purpose, God alone can tell) is still lurking in his victim's room. Well, let our name be vengeance. Call Bradshaw."

The footman came at the summons, very white and nervous.

"Pull yourself together, Bradshaw," said the lawyer. "This suspense, I know, is telling upon all of you; but it is now our intention to make an end of it. Poole, here, and I are going to force our way into the cabinet. If all is well, my shoulders are broad enough to bear the blame. Meanwhile, lest anything should really be amiss, or any malefactor seek to escape by the back, you and the boy must go round the corner with a pair of good sticks, and take your post at the laboratory door. We give you ten minutes to get to your stations."

As Bradshaw left, the lawyer looked at his watch. "And now, Poole, let us get to ours," he said; and taking the poker under his arm, he led the way into the yard. The scud had banked over the moon, and it was now quite dark. The wind, which only broke in puffs and draughts into that deep well of building, tossed the light of the candle to and fro about their steps, until they came into the shelter of the theatre, where they sat down silently to wait. London hummed solemnly all around; but nearer at hand, the stillness was only broken by the sound of a footfall moving to and fro along the cabinet floor.

"So it will walk all day, sir," whispered Poole; "ay, and the better part of the night. Only when a new sample comes from the chemist, there's a bit of a break. Ah, it's an ill conscience that's such an enemy to rest! Ah, sir, there's blood foully shed in every step of it! But hark again, a little closer—put your heart in your ears, Mr. Utterson, and tell me, is that the doctor's foot?"

The steps fell lightly and oddly, with a certain swing, for all they went so slowly; it was different indeed from the heavy creaking tread of Henry Jekyll. Utterson sighed. "Is there never anything else?" he asked.

Poole nodded. "Once," he said. "Once I heard it weeping!"

"Weeping? now that?" said the lawyer, conscious of a sudden chill of horror.

"Weeping like a woman or a lost soul," said the butler. "I came away with that upon my heart, that I could have wept too."

But now the ten minutes drew to an end. Poole disinterred the axe from under a stack of packing straw; the candle was set upon the nearest table to light them to the attack; and they drew near with bated breath to where that patient foot was still going up and down, up and down in the quiet of the night.

"Jekyll," cried Utterson, with a loud voice, "I demand to see you." He paused a moment, but there came no reply. "I give you fair warning, our suspicions are aroused, and I must and shall see you," he resumed; "if not by fair means, then by foul—if not of your consent, then by brute force!"

"Utterson," said the voice, "for God's sake, have mercy!"

"Ah, that's not Jekyll's voice—it's Hyde's!" cried Utterson. "Down with the door, Poole!"

Poole swung the axe over his shoulder; the blow shook the building, and the red baize door leaped against the lock and hinges. A dismal screech, as of mere animal terror, rang from the cabinet. Up went the axe again, and again the panels crashed and the frame bounded; four times the blow fell; but the wood was tough and the fittings were of excellent workmanship; and it was not until the fifth that the lock burst in sunder; and the wreck of the door fell inwards on the carpet.

The besiegers, appalled by their own riot and the stillness that had succeeded, stood back a little and peered in. There lay the cabinet before their eyes in the quiet lamplight, a good fire glowing and chattering on the hearth, the kettle singing its thin strain, a drawer or two open, papers neatly set forth on the business table, and nearer the fire, the things laid out for tea; the quietest room, you would have said, and, but for the glazed presses full of chemicals, the most commonplace that night in London.

Right in the midst there lay the body of a man sorely contorted and still twitching. They drew near on tiptoe, turned it on its back, and beheld the face of Edward Hyde. He was dressed in clothes far too large for him, clothes of the doctor's bigness; the cords of his face still moved with a semblance of life, but life was quite gone; and by the crushed phial in the hand and the strong smell of kernels that hung upon the air, Utterson knew that he was looking on the body of a self-destroyer.

"We have come too late," he said sternly, "whether to save or punish. Hyde is gone to his account; and it only remains for us to find the body of your master."

The far greater proportion of the building was occupied by the theatre, which filled almost the whole ground storey and was lighted from above, and by the cabinet, which formed an upper storey at one end and looked upon the court. A corridor joined the theatre to the door on the by-street; and with this, the cabinet communicated separately by a second flight of stairs. There were besides a few dark closets and a spacious cellar. All these they now thoroughly examined. Each closet needed but a glance, for all were empty, and all, by the dust that fell from their doors, had stood long unopened. The cellar, indeed, was filled with crazy lumber, mostly dating from the times of the surgeon who was Jekyll's predecessor; but even as they opened the door, they were advertised of the uselessness of further search by the fall of a perfect mat of cobweb which had for years sealed up the entrance. Nowhere was there any trace of Henry Jekyll, dead or alive.

Poole stamped on the flags of the corridor. "He must be buried here," he said, hearkening to the sound.

"Or he may have fled," said Utterson, and he turned to examine the door in the by-street. It was locked; and lying near by on the flags, they found the key, already stained with rust.

"This does not look like use," observed the lawyer.

"Use!" echoed Poole. "Do you not see, sir, it is broken? much as if a man had stamped on it."

"Ah," continued Utterson, "and the fractures, too, are rusty." The two men looked at each other with a scare. "This is beyond me, Poole," said the lawyer. "Let us go back to the cabinet."

They mounted the stair in silence, and, still with an occasional awe-struck glance at the dead body, proceeded more thoroughly to examine the contents of the cabinet. At one table there were traces of chemical work, various measured heaps of some white salt being laid on glass saucers, as though for an experiment in which the unhappy man had been prevented.

"That is the same drug that I was always bringing him," said Poole; and even as he spoke, the kettle with a startling noise boiled over.

This brought them to the fireside, where the easy chair was drawn cosily up, and the tea things stood ready to the sitter's elbow, the very sugar in the cup. There were several books on a shelf; one lay beside the tea things open, and Utterson was amazed to find it a copy of a pious work for which Jekyll had several times expressed a great esteem, annotated, in his own hand, with startling blasphemies.

Next, in the course of their review of the chamber, the searchers came to the cheval-glass, into whose depth they looked with an involuntary horror. But it was so turned as to show them nothing but the rosy glow playing on the roof, the fire sparkling in a hundred repetitions along the glazed front of the presses, and their own pale and fearful countenances stooping to look in.

"This glass has seen some strange things, sir," whispered Poole.

"And surely none stranger than itself," echoed the lawyer, in the same tone. "For what did Jekyll"—he caught himself up at the word with a start, and then conquering the weakness—"what could Jekyll want with it?" he said.

"You may say that!" said Poole.

Next they turned to the business table. On the desk, among the neat array of papers, a large envelope was uppermost, and bore, in the doctor's hand, the name of Mr. Utterson. The lawyer unsealed it, and several enclosures fell to the floor. The first was a will, drawn in the same eccentric terms as the one which he had returned six months before, to serve as a testament in case of death and as a deed of gift in case of disappearance; but in place of the name of Edward Hyde, the lawyer, with indescribable amazement, read the name of Gabriel John Utterson. He looked at Poole, and then back at the papers, and last of all at the dead malefactor stretched upon the carpet.

"My head goes round," he said. "He has been all these days in possession; he had no cause to like me; he must have raged to see himself displaced; and he has not destroyed this document."

He caught the next paper; it was a brief note in the doctor's hand, and dated at the top. "O Poole!" the lawyer cried, "he was alive and here this day. He cannot have been disposed of in so short a space; he must be still alive, he must have fled! And then, why fled? and how? and in that case can we venture to declare this suicide? O, we must be careful. I foresee that we may yet involve your master in some dire catastrophe."

"Why don't you read it, sir?" asked Poole.

"Because I fear," replied the lawyer, solemnly. "God grant I have no cause for it!" And with that he brought the paper to his eye, and read as follows:

MY DEAR UTTERSON,—When this shall fall into your hands, I shall have disappeared, under what circumstances I have not the penetration to foresee; but my instincts and all the circumstances of my nameless situation tell me that the end is sure and must be early. Go then, and first read the narrative which Lanyon warned me he was to place in your hands; and if you care to hear more, turn to the confession of

Your unworthy and unhappy friend,

HENRY JEKYLL.

"There was a third enclosure?" asked Utterson.

"Here, sir," said Poole, and gave into his hands a considerable packet sealed in several places.

The lawyer put it in his pocket. "I would say nothing of this paper. If your master has fled or is dead, we may at least save his credit. It is now ten; I must go home and read these documents in quiet; but I shall be back before midnight, when we shall send for the police."

They went out, locking the door of the theatre behind them; and Utterson, once more leaving the servants gathered about the fire in the hall, trudged back to his office to read the two narratives in which this mystery was now to be explained.

9. Dr. Lanyon's Narrative

On the ninth of January, now four days ago, I received by the evening delivery a registered envelope, addressed in the hand of my colleague and old school-companion, Henry Jekyll. I was a good deal surprised by this; for we were by no means in the habit of correspondence; I had seen the man, dined with him, indeed, the night before; and I could imagine nothing in our intercourse that should justify the formality of registration. The contents increased my wonder; for this is how the letter ran:

10*th December* 18—.

Dear Lanyon,—You are one of my oldest friends; and although we may have differed at times on scientific questions, I cannot remember, at least on my side, any break in our affection. There was never a day when, if you had said to me, "Jekyll, my life, my honour, my reason, depend upon you," I would not have sacrificed my fortune or my left hand to help you. Lanyon, my life, my honour, my reason, are all at your mercy; if you fail me to-night, I am lost. You might suppose, after this preface, that I am going to ask you for something dishonourable to grant. Judge for yourself.

I want you to postpone all other engagements for to-night—ay, even if you were summoned to the bedside of an emperor; to take a cab, unless your carriage should be actually at the door; and, with this letter in your hand for consultation, to drive straight to my house. Poole, my butler, has his order; you will find him waiting your arrival with a locksmith. The door of my cabinet is then to be forced; and you are to go in alone; to open the glazed press (letter E) on the left hand, breaking the lock if it be shut; and to draw out, *with all its contents as they stand*, the fourth drawer from the top or (which is the same thing) the third from the bottom. In my extreme distress of mind, I have a morbid fear of misdirecting you; but even if I am in error, you may know the right drawer by its contents: some powders, a phial, and a paper book. This drawer I beg of you to carry back with you to Cavendish Square exactly as it stands.

That is the first part of the service: now for the second. You should be back, if you set out at once on the receipt of this, long before midnight; but I will leave you that amount of margin, not only in the fear of one of those obstacles that can neither be prevented nor foreseen, but because an hour when your servants are in bed is to be preferred for what will then remain to do. At midnight, then, I have to ask you to be alone in your consulting-room, to admit with your own hand into the house a man who will present himself in my name, and to place in his hands the drawer that you will have brought with you from my cabinet. Then you will have played your part, and earned my gratitude completely. Five minutes afterwards, if you insist upon an explanation, you will have understood that these arrangements are of capital importance; and that by the neglect of one of them, fantastic as they must appear, you might have charged your conscience with my death or the shipwreck of my reason.

Confident as I am that you will not trifle with this appeal, my heart sinks and my hand trembles at the bare thought of such a possibility. Think of me at this hour, in a strange place, labouring under a blackness of distress that no fancy can exaggerate, and yet well aware that, if you will but punctually serve me, my troubles will roll away like a story that is told. Serve me, my dear Lanyon, and save

Your friend,
H. J.

P.S.—I had already sealed this up when a fresh terror struck upon my soul. It is possible that the post office may fail me, and this letter not come into your hands until to-morrow morning. In that case, dear Lanyon, do my errand when it shall be most convenient for you in the course of the day; and once more expect my messenger at midnight. It may then already be too late; and if that night passes without event, you will know that you have seen the last of Henry Jekyll.

Upon the reading of this letter, I made sure my colleague was insane; but till that was proved beyond the possibility of doubt, I felt bound to do as he requested. The less I understood of this farrago, the less I was in a position to judge of its importance; and an appeal so worded could not be set aside without a grave responsibility. I rose accordingly from table, got into a hansom, and drove straight to Jekyll's house. The butler was awaiting my arrival; he had received by the same post as mine a registered letter of instruction, and had sent at once for a locksmith and a carpenter. The tradesmen came while we were yet speaking; and we moved in a body to old Dr. Denman's surgical theatre, from which (as you are doubtless aware) Jekyll's private cabinet is most conveniently entered. The door was very strong, the lock excellent; the carpenter avowed he would have great trouble, and have to do much damage, if force were to be used; and the locksmith was near despair. But this last was a handy fellow, and after two hours' work, the door stood open. The press marked E was unlocked; and I took out the drawer, had it filled up with straw and tied in a sheet, and returned with it to Cavendish Square.

Here I proceeded to examine its contents. The powders were neatly enough made up, but not with the nicety of the dispensing chemist; so that it was plain they were of Jekyll's private manufacture; and when I opened one of the wrappers, I found what seemed to me a simple crystalline salt of a white colour. The phial, to which I next turned my attention, might have been about half full of a blood-red liquor, which was highly pungent to the sense of smell, and seemed to me to contain phosphorus and some volatile ether. At the other ingredients I could make no guess. The book was an ordinary version book, and contained little but a series of dates. These covered a period of many years; but I observed that the entries ceased nearly a year ago, and quite abruptly. Here and there a brief remark was appended to a date, usually no more than a single word: "double" occurring perhaps six times in a total of several hundred entries; and once very early in the list, and followed by several marks of exclamation, "total failure!!!" All this, though it whetted my curiosity, told me little that was definite. Here were a phial of some tincture, a paper of some salt, and the record of a series of experiments that had led (like too many of Jekyll's investigations) to no end of practical usefulness. How could the presence of these articles in my house affect either the honour, the sanity, or the life of my flighty colleague? If his messenger could go to one place, why could he not go to another? And even granting some impediment, why was this gentleman to be received by me in secret? The more I reflected, the more convinced I grew that I was dealing with a case of cerebral disease; and though I dismissed my servants to bed, I loaded an old revolver, that I might be found in some posture of self-defence.

Twelve o'clock had scarce rung out over London, ere the knocker sounded very gently on the door. I went myself at the summons, and found a small man crouching against the pillars of the portico.

"Are you from Dr. Jekyll?" I asked.

He told me "yes" by a constrained gesture; and when I had bidden him enter, he did not obey me without a searching backward glance into the darkness of the square. There was a policeman not far off, advancing with his bull's-eye open; and at the sight, I thought my visitor started and made greater haste.

These particulars struck me, I confess, disagreeably; and as I followed him into the bright light of the consulting-room, I kept my hand ready on my weapon. Here, at last, I had a chance of clearly seeing him. I had never set eyes on him before, so much was certain. He was small, as I have said; I was struck besides with the shocking expression of his face, with his remarkable combination of great muscular activity and great apparent debility of constitution, and—last but not least—with the odd, subjective disturbance caused by his neighbourhood. This bore some resemblance to incipient rigor, and was accompanied by a marked sinking of the pulse. At the time, I set it down to some idiosyncratic, personal distaste, and merely wondered at the acuteness of the symptoms; but I have since had reason to believe the cause to lie much deeper in the nature of man, and to turn on some nobler hinge than the principle of hatred.

This person (who had thus, from the first moment of his entrance, struck in me what I can only describe as a disgustful curiosity) was dressed in a fashion that would have made an ordinary person laughable; his clothes, that is to say, although they were rich and sober fabric, were enormously too large for him in every measurement—the trousers hanging on his legs and rolled up to keep them from the ground, the waist of the coat below his haunches, and the collar sprawling wide upon his shoulders. Strange to relate, this ludicrous accoutrement was far from moving me to laughter. Rather, as there was something abnormal and misbegotten in the very essence of the creature that now faced me—something seizing, surprising, and revolting—this fresh disparity seemed but to fit in with and to reinforce it; so that to my interest in the man's nature and character there was added a curiosity as to his origin, his life, his fortune and status in the world.

These observations, though they have taken so great a space to be set down in, were yet the work of a few seconds. My visitor was, indeed, on fire with sombre excitement.

"Have you got it?" he cried. "Have you got it?" And so lively was his impatience that he even laid his hand upon my arm and sought to shake me.

I put him back, conscious at this touch of a certain icy pang along my blood. "Come, sir," said I. "You forget that I have not yet the pleasure of your acquaintance. Be seated, if you please." And I showed him an example, and sat down myself in my customary seat and with as fair an imitation of my ordinary manner to a patient as the lateness of the hour, the nature of my pre-occupations, and the horror I had of my visitor would suffer me to muster.

"I beg your pardon, Dr. Lanyon," he replied, civilly enough. "What you say is very well founded; and my impatience has sown its heel to my politeness. I come here at the instance of your colleague, Dr. Henry Jekyll, on a piece of business of some moment; and I understood . . ." he paused and put his hand to his throat, and I could see, in spite of his collected manner, that he was wrestling against the approaches of the hysteria—"I understood, a drawer . . ."

But here I took pity on my visitor's suspense, and some perhaps on my own growing curiosity.

"There it is, sir," said I, pointing to the drawer, where it lay on the floor behind a table, and still covered with the sheet.

He sprang to it, and then paused, and laid his hand upon his heart; I could hear his teeth grate with the convulsive action of his jaws; and his face was so ghastly to see that I grew alarmed both for life and reason.

"Compose yourself," said I.

He turned a dreadful smile to me, and, as if with the decision of despair, plucked away the sheet. At the sight of the contents, he uttered one loud sob of such immense relief that I sat petrified. And the next moment, in a voice that was already fairly well under control, "Have you a graduated glass?" he asked.

I rose from my place with something of an effort, and gave him what he asked.

He thanked me with a smiling nod, measured out a few minims of the red tincture and added one of the powders. The mixture, which was at first of a reddish hue, began, in proportion as the crystals melted, to brighten in colour, to effervesce audibly, and to throw off small fumes of vapour. Suddenly, and at the same moment, the ebullition ceased, and the compound changed to a dark purple, which faded again more slowly to a watery green. My visitor, who had watched these metamorphoses with a keen eye, smiled, set down the glass upon the table, and then turned and looked upon me with an air of scrutiny.

"And now," said he, "to settle what remains. Will you be wise? will you be guided? will you suffer me to take this glass in my hand, and to go forth from your house without further parley? or has the greed of curiosity too much command of you? Think before you answer, for it shall be done as you decide. As you decide, you shall be left as you were before, and neither richer nor wiser, unless the sense of service rendered to a man in mortal distress may be counted as a kind of riches of the soul. Or, if you shall so prefer to choose, a new province of knowledge and new avenues to fame and power shall be laid open to you, here, in this room, upon the instant; and your sight shall be blasted by a prodigy to stagger the unbelief of Satan."

"Sir," said I, affecting a coolness that I was far from truly possessing, "you speak enigmas, and you will perhaps not wonder that I hear you with no very strong impression of belief. But I have gone too far in the way of inexplicable services to pause before I see the end."

"It is well," replied my visitor. "Lanyon, you may remember your vows: what follows is under the seal of our profession. And now, you who have so long been bound to the most narrow and material views, you who have denied the virtue of transcendental medicine, you who have derided your superiors—behold!"

He put the glass to his lips, and drank at one gulp. A cry followed; he reeled, staggered, clutched at the table and held on, staring with injected eyes, gasping with open mouth; and as I looked, there came, I thought, a change—he seemed to swell—his face became suddenly black, and the features seemed to melt and alter—and the next moment I had sprung to my feet and leaped back against the wall, my arm raised to shield me from that prodigy, my mind submerged in terror.

"O God!" I screamed, and "O God!" again and again; for there before my eyes—pale and shaken, and half-fainting, and groping before him with his hands, like a man restored from death—there stood Henry Jekyll!

What he told me in the next hour I cannot bring my mind to set on paper. I saw what I saw, I heard what I heard, and my soul sickened at it; and yet, now when that sight has faded from my eyes, I ask myself if I believe it, and I cannot answer. My life is shaken to its roots; sleep has left me; the deadliest terror sits by me at all hours of the day and night; I feel that my days are numbered, and that I must die; and yet I shall die incredulous. As for the moral turpitude that man unveiled to me, even with tears of penitence, I cannot, even in memory, dwell on it without a start of horror. I will say but one thing, Utterson, and that (if you can bring your mind to credit it) will be more than enough. The creature who crept into my house that night was, on Jekyll's own confession, known by the name of Hyde and hunted for in every corner of the land as the murderer of Carew.

HASTIE LANYON.

10. Henry Jekyll's Full Statement of the Case

I WAS born in the year 18— to a large fortune, endowed besides with excellent parts, inclined by nature to industry, fond of the respect of the wise and good among my fellow-men, and thus, as might have been supposed, with every guarantee of an honourable and distinguished future. And indeed, the worst of my faults was a certain impatient gaiety of disposition, such as has made the happiness of many, but such as I found it hard to reconcile with my imperious desire to carry my head high, and wear a more than commonly grave countenance before the public. Hence it came about that I concealed my pleasures; and that when I reached years of reflection, and began to look round me, and take stock of my progress and position in the world, I stood already committed to a profound duplicity of life. Many a man would have even blazoned such irregularities as I was guilty of; but from the high views that I had set before me, I regarded and hid them with an almost morbid sense of shame. It was thus rather the exacting nature of my aspirations, than any particular degradation in my faults, that made me what I was, and, with even a deeper trench than in the majority of men, severed in me those provinces of good and ill which divide and compound man's dual nature. In this case, I was driven to reflect deeply and inveterately on that hard law of life which lies at the root of religion, and is one of the most plentiful springs of distress. Though so profound a double-dealer, I was in no sense a hypocrite; both sides of me were in dead earnest; I was no more myself when I laid aside restraint and plunged in shame, than when I laboured, in the eye of day, at the furtherance of knowledge or the relief of sorrow and suffering. And it chanced that the direction of my scientific studies, which led wholly towards the mystic and the transcendental, reacted and shed a strong light on this consciousness of the perennial war among my members. With every day, and from both sides of my intelligence, the moral and the intellectual, I thus drew steadily nearer to that truth by whose partial discovery I have been doomed to such a dreadful shipwreck: that man is not truly one, but truly two. I say two, because the state of my own knowledge does not pass beyond that point. Others will follow, others will outstrip me on the same lines; and I hazard the guess that man will be ultimately known for a mere polity of multifarious, incongruous, and independent denizens. I, for my part, from the nature of my life, advanced infallibly in one direction, and in one direction only. It was on the moral side, and in my own person, that I learned to recognize the thorough and primitive quality of man; I saw that, of the two natures that contended in the field of my consciousness, even if I could rightly be said to be either, it was only because I was radically both; and from an early date, even before the course of my scientific discoveries had begun to suggest the most naked possibility of such a miracle, I had learned to dwell with pleasure, as a beloved day-dream, on the thought of the separation of these elements. If each, I told myself, could but be housed in separate identities, life would be relieved of all that was unbearable; the unjust might go his way, delivered from the aspirations and remorse of his more upright twin; and the just could walk steadfastly and securely on his upward path, doing the good things in which he found his pleasure, and no longer exposed to disgrace and penitence by the hands of this extraneous evil. It was the curse of mankind that these incongruous faggots were thus bound together—that in the agonized womb of consciousness these polar twins should be continuously struggling. How, then, were they dissociated?

I was so far in my reflections, when, as I have said, a side light began to shine upon the subject from the laboratory table. I began to perceive more deeply than it has ever yet been stated, the trembling immateriality, the mist-like transience, of this seemingly so solid body in which we walk attired. Certain agents I found to have the power to shake and to pluck back that fleshly vestment, even as a wind might toss the curtains of a pavilion. For two good reasons, I will not enter deeply into this scientific branch of my confession. First, because I have been made to learn that the doom and burthen of our life is bound for ever on man's shoulders; and when the attempt is made to cast it off, it but returns upon us with more unfamiliar and more awful pressure. Second, because, as my narrative will make, alas! too evident, my discoveries were incomplete. Enough, then, that I not only recognized my natural body for the mere aura and effulgence of certain of the powers that made up my spirit, but managed to compound a drug by which these powers should be dethroned from their supremacy, and a second form and countenance substituted, none the less natural to me because they were the expression, and bore the stamp, of lower elements in my soul.

I hesitated long before I put this theory to the test of practice. I knew well that I risked death; for any drug that so potently controlled and shook the very fortress of identity, might by the least scruple of an overdose or at the least inopportunity in the moment of exhibition, utterly blot out that immaterial tabernacle which I looked to it to change. But the temptation of a discovery so singular and profound at last overcame the suggestions of alarm. I had long since prepared my tincture; I purchased at once, from a firm of wholesale chemists, a large quantity of a particular salt, which I knew, from my experiments, to be the last ingredient required; and, late one accursed night, I compounded the elements, watched them boil and smoke together in the glass, and when the ebullition had subsided, with a strong blow of courage, drank off the potion.

The most racking pangs succeeded: a grinding in the bones, deadly nausea, and a horror of the spirit that cannot be exceeded at the hour of birth or death. Then these agonies began swiftly to subside, and I came to myself as if out of a great sickness. There was something strange in my sensations, something indescribably new, and, from its very novelty, incredibly sweet. I felt younger, lighter, happier in body; within I was conscious of a heady recklessness, a current of disordered sensual images running like a mill race in my fancy, a solution of the bonds of obligation, an unknown but not an innocent freedom of the soul. I knew myself, at the first breath of this new life, to be more wicked, tenfold more wicked, sold a slave to my original evil; and the thought, in that moment, braced and delighted me like wine. I stretched out my hands, exulting in the freshness of these sensations; and in the act, I was suddenly aware that I had lost in stature.

There was no mirror, at that date, in my room; that which stands beside me as I write was brought there later on, and for the very purpose of those transformations. The night, however, was far gone into the morning—the morning, black as it was, was nearly ripe for the conception of the day—the inmates of my house were locked in the most rigorous hours of slumber; and I determined, flushed as I was with hope and triumph, to venture in my new shape as far as to my bedroom. I crossed the yard, wherein the constellations looked down upon me, I could have been, I thought, with wonder, the first creature of that sort that their unsleeping vigilance had yet disclosed to them; I stole through the corridors, a stranger in my own house; and coming to my room, I saw for the first time the appearance of Edward Hyde.

I must here speak by theory alone, saying not that which I know, but that which I suppose to be most probable. The evil side of my nature, to which I had now transferred the stamping efficacy, was less robust and less developed than the good which I had just deposed. Again, in the course of my life, which had been, after all, nine-tenths a life of effort, virtue and control, it had been much less exercised and much less exhausted. And hence, as I think, it came about that Edward Hyde was so much smaller, slighter, and younger than Henry Jekyll. Even as good shone upon the countenance of the one, evil was written broadly and plainly on the face of the other. Evil besides (which I must still believe to be the lethal side of man) had left on that body an imprint of deformity and decay. And yet when I looked upon that ugly idol in the glass, I was conscious of no repugnance, rather of a leap of welcome. This, too, was myself. It seemed natural and human. In my eyes it bore a livelier image of the spirit, it seemed more express and single, than the imperfect and divided countenance I had been hitherto accustomed to call mine. And in so far I was doubtless right. I have observed that when I wore the semblance of Edward Hyde, none could come near to me at first without a visible misgiving of the flesh. This, as I take it, was because all human beings, as we meet them, are commingled out of good and evil: and Edward Hyde, alone, in the ranks of mankind, was pure evil.

I lingered but a moment at the mirror: the second and conclusive experiment had yet to be attempted; it yet remained to be seen if I had lost my identity beyond redemption and must flee before daylight from a house that was no longer mine: and hurrying back to my cabinet, I once more prepared and drank the cup, once more suffered the pangs of dissolution, and came to myself once more with the character, the stature, and the face of Henry Jekyll.

That night I had come to the fatal cross-roads. Had I approached my discovery in a more noble spirit, had I risked the experiment while under the empire of generous or pious aspirations, all must have been otherwise, and from these agonies of death and birth I had come forth an angel instead of a fiend. The drug had no discriminating action; it was neither diabolical nor divine; it but shook the doors of the prison-house of my disposition; and like the captives of Philippi, that which stood within ran forth. At that time my virtue slumbered; my evil, kept awake by ambition, was alert and swift to seize the occasion; and the thing that was projected was Edward Hyde. Hence, although I had now two characters as well as two appearances, one was wholly evil, and the other was still the old Henry Jekyll, that incongruous compound of whose reformation and improvement I had already learned to despair. The movement was thus wholly toward the worse.

Even at that time, I had not yet conquered my aversion to the dryness of a life of study. I would still be merrily disposed at times; and as my pleasures were (to say the least) undignified, and I was not only well known and highly considered, but growing towards the elderly man, this incoherency of my life was daily growing more unwelcome. It was on this side that my new power tempted me until I fell in slavery. I had but to drink the cup, to doff at once the body of the noted professor, and to assume, like a thick cloak, that of Edward Hyde. I smiled at the notion; it seemed to me at the time to be humorous; and I made my preparations with the most studious care. I took and furnished that house in Soho to which Hyde was tracked by the police; and engaged as housekeeper a creature whom I well knew to be silent and unscrupulous. On the other side, I announced to my servants that a Mr. Hyde (whom I described) was to have full liberty and power about my house in the square; and, to parry mishaps, I even called and made myself a familiar object in my second character. I next drew up that will to which you so much objected; so that if anything befell me in the person of Dr. Jekyll, I could enter on that of Edward Hyde without pecuniary loss. And thus fortified, as I supposed, on every side, I began to profit by the strange immunities of my position.

Men have before hired bravos to transact their crimes, while their person and reputation sat under shelter. I was the first that ever did so for his pleasures. I was the first that could thus plod in the public eye with a load of genial respectability, and in a moment, like a schoolboy, strip off these lendings and spring headlong into the sea of liberty.

But for me, in my impenetrable mantle, the safety was complete. Think of it—I did not even exist! Let me but escape into my laboratory door, give me but a second or two to mix and swallow the draught that I had always standing ready, and whatever he had done, Edward Hyde would pass away like the stain of breath upon a mirror; and there in his stead, quietly at home, trimming the midnight lamp in his study, a man who could afford to laugh at suspicion, would be Henry Jekyll.

The pleasures which I made haste to seek in my disguise were, as I have said, undignified; I would scarce use a harder term. But in the hands of Edward Hyde they soon began to turn towards the monstrous. When I would come back from these excursions, I was often plunged into a kind of wonder at my vicarious depravity. This familiar that I called out of my own soul, and sent forth alone to do his good pleasure, was a being inherently malign and villainous; his every act and thought centred on self; drinking pleasure with bestial avidity from any degree of torture to another; relentless like a man of stone. Henry Jekyll stood at times aghast before the acts of Edward Hyde; but the situation was apart from ordinary laws, and insidiously relaxed the grasp of conscience. It was Hyde, after all, and Hyde alone, that was guilty. Jekyll was no worse; he woke again to his good qualities seemingly unimpaired; he would even make haste, where it was possible, to undo the evil done by Hyde. And thus his conscience slumbered.

Into the details of the infamy at which I thus connived (for even now I can scarce grant that I committed it) I have no design of entering. I mean but to point out the warnings and the successive steps with which my chastisement approached. I met with one accident which, as it brought on no consequence, I shall no more than mention. An act of cruelty to a child aroused against me the anger of a passer-by, whom I recognized the other day in the person of your kinsman; the doctor and the child's family joined him; there were moments when I feared for my life; and at last, in order to pacify their too just resentment, Edward Hyde had to bring them to the door, and pay them in a cheque drawn in the name of Henry Jekyll. But this danger was easily eliminated from the future by opening an account at another bank in the name of Edward Hyde himself; and when, by sloping my own hand backwards, I had supplied my double with a signature, I thought I sat beyond the reach of fate.

Some two months before the murder of Sir Danvers, I had been out for one of my adventures, had returned at a late hour, and woke the next day in bed with somewhat odd sensations. It was in vain I looked about me; in vain I saw the decent furniture and tall proportions of my room in the square; in vain that I recognized the pattern of the bed curtains and the design of the mahogany frame; something still kept insisting that I was not where I was, that I had not wakened where I seemed to be, but in the little room in Soho where I was accustomed to sleep in the body of Edward Hyde. I smiled to myself, and, in my psychological way, began lazily to inquire into the elements of this illusion, occasionally, even as I did so, dropping back into a comfortable morning doze. I was still so engaged when, in one of my more wakeful moments, my eye fell upon my hand. Now, the hand of Henry Jekyll (as you have often remarked) was professional in shape and size; it was large, firm, white and comely. But the hand which I now saw, clearly enough in the yellow light of a mid-London morning, lying half shut on the bed-clothes, was lean, corded, knuckly, of a dusky pallor, and thickly shaded with a swart growth of hair. It was the hand of Edward Hyde.

I must have stared upon it for near half a minute, sunk as I was in the mere stupidity of wonder, before terror woke up in my breast as sudden and startling as the crash of cymbals; and bounding from my bed, I rushed to the mirror. At the sight that met my eyes, my blood was changed into something exquisitely thin and icy. Yes, I had gone to bed Henry Jekyll, I had awakened Edward Hyde. How was this to be explained? I asked myself; and then, with another bound of terror —how was it to be remedied? It was well on in the morning; the servants were up; all my drugs were in the cabinet—a long journey, down two pairs of stairs, through the back passage, across the open court and through the anatomical theatre, from where I was then standing horror-struck. It might indeed be possible to cover my face; but of what use was that, when I was unable to conceal the alteration in my stature? And then, with an overpowering sweetness of relief, it came back upon my mind that the servants were already used to the coming and going of my second self. I had soon dressed, as well as I was able, in clothes of my own size; had soon passed through the house, where Bradshaw stared and drew back at seeing Mr. Hyde at such an hour and in such a strange array; and ten minutes later, Dr. Jekyll had returned to his own shape, and was sitting down, with a darkened brow, to make a feint of breakfasting.

Small indeed was my appetite. This inexplicable incident, this reversal of my previous experience, seemed, like the Babylonian finger on the wall, to be spelling out the letters of my judgment; and I began to reflect more seriously than ever before on the issues and possibilities of my double existence. That part of me which I had the power of projecting had lately been much exercised and nourished; it had seemed to me of late as though the body of Edward Hyde had grown in stature, as though (when I wore that form) I were conscious of a more generous tide of blood; and I began to spy a danger that, if this were much prolonged, the balance of my nature might be permanently overthrown, the power of voluntary change be forfeited, and the character of Edward Hyde become irrevocably mine. The power of the drug had not been always equally displayed. Once, very early in my career, it had totally failed me; since then I had been obliged on more than one occasion to double, and once, with infinite risk of death, to treble the amount; and these rare uncertainties had cast hitherto the sole shadow on my contentment. Now, however, and in the light of that morning's accident, I was led to remark that whereas, in the beginning, the difficulty had been to throw off the body of Jekyll, it had of late gradually but decidedly transferred itself to the other side. All things therefore seemed to point to this: that I was slowly losing hold of my original and better self, and becoming slowly incorporated with my second and worse.

Between these two I now felt I had to choose. My two natures had memory in common, but all other faculties were most unequally shared between them. Jekyll (who was composite), now with the most sensitive apprehensions, now with a greedy gusto, projected and shared in the pleasures and adventures of Hyde; but Hyde was indifferent to Jekyll, or but remembered him as the mountain bandit remembers the cavern in which he conceals himself from pursuit. Jekyll had more than a father's interest; Hyde had more than a son's indifference. To cast in my lot with Jekyll was to die to those appetities which I had long secretly indulged and had of late begun to pamper. To cast it in with Hyde was to die to a thousand interests and aspirations, and to become, at a blow and for ever, despised and friendless. The bargain might appear unequal; but there was still another consideration in the scales; for while Jekyll would suffer smartingly in the fires of abstinence, Hyde would be not even conscious of all that he had lost. Strange as my circumstances were, the terms of this debate are as old and commonplace as man; much the same inducements and alarms cast the die for any tempted and trembling sinner; and it fell out with me, as it falls with so vast a majority of my fellows, that I chose the better part, and was found wanting in the strength to keep to it.

Yes, I preferred the elderly and discontented doctor, surrounded by friends, and cherishing honest hopes; and bade a resolute farewell to the liberty, the comparative youth, the light step, leaping pulses and secret pleasures, that I had enjoyed in the disguise of Hyde. I made this choice perhaps with some unconscious reservation, for I neither gave up the house in Soho, nor destroyed the clothes of Edward Hyde, which still lay ready in my cabinet. For two months, however, I was true to my determination; for two months I led a life of such severity as I had never before attained to, and enjoyed the compensations of an approving conscience. But time began at last to obliterate the freshness of my alarm; the praises of conscience began to grow into a thing of course; I began to be tortured with throes and longings, as of Hyde struggling after freedom; and at last, in an hour of moral weakness, I once again compounded and swallowed the transforming draught.

I do not suppose that when a drunkard reasons with himself upon his vice, he is once out of five hundred times affected by the dangers that he runs through his brutish physical insensibility; neither had I, long as I had considered my position, made enough allowance for the complete moral insensibility and insensate readiness to evil which were the leading characters of Edward Hyde. Yet it was by these that I was punished. My devil had been long caged, he came out roaring. I was conscious, even when I took the draught, of a more unbridled, a more furious propensity to ill. It must have been this, I suppose, that stirred in my soul that tempest of impatience with which I listened to the civilities of my unhappy victim; I declare at least, before God, no man morally sane could have been guilty of that crime upon so pitiful a provocation; and that I struck in no more reasonable spirit than that in which a sick child may break a plaything. But I had voluntarily stripped myself of all those balancing instincts by which even the worst of us continues to walk with some degree of steadiness among temptations; and in my case, to be tempted, however slightly, was to fall.

Instantly the spirit of hell awoke in me and raged. With a transport of glee, I mauled the unresisting body, tasting delight from every blow; and it was not till weariness had begun to succeed that I was suddenly, in the top fit of my delirium, struck through the heart by a cold thrill of terror. A mist dispersed; I saw my life to be forfeit; and fled from the scene of these excesses, at once glorying and trembling, my lust of evil gratified and stimulated, my love of life screwed to the topmost peg. I ran to the house in Soho, and (to make assurance doubly sure) destroyed my papers; thence I set out through the lamplit streets, in the same divided ecstasy of mind, gloating on my crime, lightheadedly devising others in the future, and yet still hastening and still harkening in my wake for the steps of the avenger. Hyde had a song upon his lips as he compounded the draught, and as he drank it pledged the dead man. The pangs of transformation had not done tearing him, before Henry Jekyll, with streaming tears of gratitude and remorse, had fallen upon his knees and lifted his clasped hands to God. The veil of self-indulgence was rent from head to foot, I saw my life as a whole: I followed it up from the days of childhood, when I had walked with my father's hand, and through the self-denying toils of my professional life, to arrive again and again, with the same sense of unreality, at the damned horrors of the evening. I could have screamed aloud; I sought with tears and prayers to smother down the crowd of hideous images and sounds with which my memory swarmed against me; and still, between the petitions, the ugly face of my iniquity stared into my soul. As the acuteness of this remorse began to die away, it was succeeded by a sense of joy. The problem of my conduct was solved. Hyde was thenceforth impossible; whether I would or not, I was now confined to the better part of my existence; and, oh, how I rejoiced to think it! with what willing humility I embraced anew the restrictions of natural life! with what sincere renunciation I locked the door by which I had so often gone and come, and ground the key under my heel!

The next day came the news that the murder had been overlooked, that the guilt of Hyde was patent to the world, and that the victim was a man high in public estimation. It was not only a crime, it had been a tragic folly. I think I was glad to know it; I think I was glad to have my better impulses thus buttressed and guarded by the terrors of the scaffold. Jekyll was now my city of refuge; let but Hyde peep out an instant, and the hands of all men would be raised to take and slay him.

I resolved in my future conduct to redeem the past; and I can say with honesty that my resolve was fruitful of some good. You know yourself how earnestly in the last months of last year I laboured to relieve suffering; you know that much was done for others, and that the days passed quietly, almost happily for myself. Nor can I truly say that I wearied of this beneficent and innocent life; I think instead that I daily enjoyed it more completely; but I was still cursed with my duality of purpose; and as the first edge of my penitence wore off, the lower side of me, so long indulged, so recently chained down, began to growl for licence. Not that I dreamed of resuscitating Hyde; the bare idea of that would startle me to frenzy; no, it was in my own person that I was once more tempted to trifle with my conscience; and it was as an ordinary secret sinner that I at last fell before the assaults of temptation.

There comes an end to all things; the most capacious measure is filled at last; and this brief condescension to my evil finally destroyed the balance of my soul. And yet I was not alarmed; the fall seemed natural, like a return to the old days before I had made my discovery. It was a fine, clear January day, wet under foot where the frost had melted, but cloudless overhead; and the Regent's Park was full of winter chirrupings and sweet with spring odours. I sat in the sun on a bench; the animal within me licking the chops of memory; the spiritual side a little drowsed, promising subsequent penitence, but not yet moved to begin. After all, I reflected, I was like my neighbours; and then I smiled, comparing myself with other men, comparing my active goodwill with the lazy cruelty of their neglect. And at the very moment of that vainglorious thought, a qualm came over me, a horrid nausea and the most deadly shuddering. These passed away, and left me faint; and then as in its turn the faintness subsided, I began to be aware of a change in the temper of my thoughts, a greater boldness, a contempt of danger, a solution of the bonds of obligation. I looked down; my clothes hung formlessly on my shrunken limbs; the hand that lay on my knee was corded and hairy. I was once more Edward Hyde. A moment before I had been safe of all men's respect, wealthy, beloved—the cloth laying for me in the dining-room at home; and now I was the common quarry of mankind, hunted, houseless, a known murderer, thrall to the gallows.

My reason wavered, but it did not fail me utterly. I have more than once observed that, in my second character, my faculties seemed sharpened to a point and my spirits more tensely elastic; thus it came about that, where Jekyll perhaps might have succumbed, Hyde rose to the moment. My drugs were in one of the presses of my cabinet: how was I to reach them? That was the problem that (crushing my temples in my hands) I set myself to solve. The laboratory door I had closed. If I sought to enter by the house, my own servants would consign me to the gallows. I saw I must employ another hand, and thought of Lanyon. How was he to be reached? how persuaded? Supposing that I escaped capture in the streets, how was I to make my way into his presence? and how should I, an unknown and displeasing visitor, prevail on the famous physician to rifle the study of his colleague, Dr. Jekyll? Then I remembered that of my original character, one part remained to me: I could write my own hand; and once I had conceived the kindling spark, the way that I must follow became lighted up from end to end.

Thereupon, I arranged my clothes as best I could, and summoning a passing hansom, drove to an hotel in Portland Street, the name of which I chanced to remember. At my appearance (which was indeed comical enough, however tragic a fate these garments covered) the driver could not conceal his mirth. I gnashed my teeth upon him with a gust of devilish fury; and the smile withered from his face—happily for him—yet more happily for myself, for in another instant I had certainly dragged him from his perch. At the inn, as I entered, I looked about me with so black a countenance as made the attendants tremble; not a look did they exchange in my presence; but obsequiously took my orders, led me to a private room, and brought me wherewithal to write. Hyde in danger of his life was a creature new to me: shaken with inordinate anger, strung to the pitch of murder, lusting to inflict pain. Yet the creature was astute; mastered his fury with a great effort of the will; composed his two important letters, one to Lanyon and one to Poole, and, that he might receive actual evidence of their being posted, sent them out with directions that they should be registered.

Thenceforward, he sat all day over the fire in the private room, gnawing his nails; there he dined, sitting alone with his fears, the waiter visibly quailing before his eye; and thence, when the night was fully come, he set forth in the corner of a closed cab, and was driven to and fro about the streets of the city. He, I say—I cannot say, I. That child of Hell had nothing human; nothing live in him but fear and hatred. And when at last, thinking the driver had begun to grow suspicious, he discharged the cab and ventured on foot, attired in his misfitting clothes, an object marked out for observation, into the midst of the nocturnal passengers, these two base passions raged within him like a tempest. He walked fast, hunted by his fears, chattering to himself, skulking through the less frequented thoroughfares, counting the minutes that still divided him from midnight. Once a woman spoke to him, offering, I think, a box of lights. He smote her in the face, and she fled.

When I came to myself at Lanyon's, the horror of my old friend perhaps affected me somewhat: I do not know; it was at least but a drop in the sea to the abhorrence with which I looked back upon these hours. A change had come over me. It was no longer the fear of the gallows, it was the horror of being Hyde that racked me. I received Lanyon's condemnation partly in a dream; it was partly in a dream that I came home to my own house and got into bed. I slept after the prostration of the day, with a stringent and profound slumber which not even the nightmares that wrung me could avail to break. I awoke in the morning shaken, weakened, but refreshed. I still hated and feared the thought of the brute that slept within me, and I had not of course forgotten the appalling dangers of the day before; but I was once more at home, in my own house and close to my drugs; and gratitude for my escape shone so strong in my soul that it almost rivalled the brightness of hope.

I was stepping leisurely across the court after breakfast, drinking the chill of the air with pleasure, when I was seized again with those indescribable sensations that heralded the change; and I had but the time to gain the shelter of my cabinet, before I was once again raging and freezing with the passions of Hyde. It took on this occasion a double dose to recall me to myself; and, alas! six hours after, as I sat looking sadly in the fire, the pangs returned, and the drug had to be re-administered. In short, from that day forth it seemed only by a great effort as of gymnastics, and only under the immediate stimulation of the drug, that I was able to wear the countenance of Jekyll. At all hours of the day and night I would be taken with the premonitory shudder; above all, if I slept, or even dozed for a moment in my chair, it was always as Hyde that I awakened. Under the strain of this continually impending doom and by the sleeplessness to which I now condemned myself, ay, even beyond what I had thought possible to man, I became, in my own person, a creature eaten up and emptied by fever, languidly weak both in body and mind, and solely occupied by one thought: the horror of my other self. But when I slept, or when the virtue of the medicine wore off, I would leap almost without transition (for the pangs of transformation grew daily less marked) into the possession of a fancy brimming with images of terror, a soul boiling with causeless hatreds, and a body that seemed not strong enough to contain the raging energies of life. The powers of Hyde seemed to have grown with the sickliness of Jekyll. And certainly the hate that now divided them was equal on each side. With Jekyll, it was a thing of vital instinct. He had now seen the full deformity of that creature that shared with him some of the phenomena of consciousness, and was co-heir with him to death: and beyond these links of community, which in themselves made the most poignant part of his distress, he thought of Hyde, for all his energy of life, as of something not only hellish but inorganic. This was the shocking thing; that the slime of the pit seemed to utter cries and voices; that the amorphous dust gesticulated and sinned; that what was dead, and had no shape, should usurp the offices of life. And this again, that that insurgent horror was knit to him closer than a wife, closer than an eye; lay caged in his flesh, where he heard it mutter and felt it struggle to be born; and at every hour of weakness, and in the confidence of slumber, prevailed against him, and deposed him out of life. The hatred of Hyde for Jekyll was of a different order. His terror of the gallows drove him continually to commit temporary suicide, and return to his subordinate station of a part instead of a person; but he loathed the necessity, he loathed the despondency into which Jekyll was now fallen, and he resented the dislike with which he was himself regarded. Hence the apelike tricks that he would play me, scrawling in my own hand blasphemies on the pages of my books, burning the letters and destroying the portrait of my father; and indeed, had it not been for his fear of death, he would long ago have ruined himself in order to involve me in the ruin. But his love of life is wonderful; I go further: I, who sicken and freeze at the mere thought of him, when I recall the abjection and passion of this attachment, and when I know how he fears my power to cut him off by suicide, I find it in my heart to pity him.

It is useless, and the time awfully fails me, to prolong this description; no one has ever suffered such torments, let that suffice; and yet even to these, habit brought—no, not alleviation—but a certain callousness of soul, a certain acquiescence of despair; and my punishment might have gone on for years, but for the last calamity which has now fallen, and which has finally severed me from my own face and nature. My provision of the salt, which had never been renewed since the date of the first experiment, began to run low. I sent out for a fresh supply, and mixed the draught; the ebullition followed, and the first change of colour, not the second; I drank it, and it was without efficiency. You will learn from Poole how I have had London ransacked; it was in vain; and I am now persuaded that my first supply was impure, and that it was that unknown impurity which lent efficacy to the draught.

About a week has passed, and I am now finishing this statement under the influence of the last of the old powders. This, then, is the last time, short of a miracle, that Henry Jekyll can think his own thoughts or see his own face (now how sadly altered!) in the glass. Nor must I delay too long to bring my writing to an end; for if my narrative has hitherto escaped destruction, it has been by a combination of great prudence and great good luck. Should the throes of change take me in the act of writing it, Hyde will tear it in pieces; but if some time shall have elapsed after I have laid it by, his wonderful selfishness and circumscription to the moment will probably save it once again from the action of his apelike spite. And indeed the doom that is closing on us both has already changed and crushed him. Half an hour from now, when I shall again and for ever reindue that hated personality, I know how I shall sit shuddering and weeping in my chair, or continue, with the most strained and fear-struck ecstasy of listening, to pace up and down this room (my last earthly refuge) and give ear to every sound of menace. Will Hyde die upon the scaffold? or will he find the courage to release himself at the last moment? God knows; I am careless; this is my true hour of death, and what is to follow concerns another than myself. Here, then, as I lay down the pen, and proceed to seal up my confession, I bring the life of that unhappy Henry Jekyll to an end.

Thrawn Janet

THE REVEREND Murdoch Soulis was long minister of the moorland parish of Balweary, in the vale of Dule. A severe, bleakfaced old man, dreadful to his hearers, he dwelt in the last years of his life, without relative or servant or any human company, in the small and lonely manse under the Hanging Shaw. In spite of the iron composure of his features, his eye was wild, scared, and uncertain; and when he dwelt, in private admonitions, on the future of the impenitent, it seemed as if his eye pierced through the storms of time to the terrors of eternity. Many young persons coming to prepare themselves against the season of the Holy Communion were dreadfully affected by his talk. He had a sermon on 1 Peter v. 8, "The devil as a roaring lion", on the Sunday after every seventeenth of August, and he was accustomed to surpass himself upon that text both by the appalling nature of the matter and the terror of his bearing in the pulpit. The children were frightened into fits, and the old looked more than usually oracular, and were, all that day, full of those hints that Hamlet deprecated. The manse itself, where it stood by the water of Dule among some thick trees, with the Shaw overhanging it on the one side, and on the other many cold, moorish hill-tops rising towards the sky, had begun, at a very early period of Mr. Soulis's ministry, to be avoided in the dusk hours by all who valued themselves upon their prudence; and guidmen sitting at the clachan alehouse shook their heads together at the thought of passing late by that uncanny neighbourhood. There was one spot, to be more particular, which was regarded with especial awe. The manse stood between the high-road and the water of Dule, with a gable to each; its back was towards the kirk-town of Balweary, nearly half a mile away; in front of it, a bare garden, hedged with thorn, occupied the land between the river and the road. The house was two storeys high, with two large rooms on each. It opened not directly on the garden, but on a causewayed path or passage, giving on the road on the one hand, and closed on the other by the tall willows and elders that bordered on the stream. And it was this strip of causeway that enjoyed among the young parishioners of Balweary so infamous a reputation. The minister walked there often after dark, sometimes groaning aloud in the instancy of his unspoken prayers; and when he was from home, and the manse door was locked, the more daring schoolboys ventured, with beating hearts, to "follow my leader" across that legendary spot.

This atmosphere of terror, surrounding, as it did, a man of God of spotless character and orthodoxy, was a common cause of wonder and subject of inquiry among the few strangers who were led by chance or business into that unknown, outlying country. But many even of the people of the parish were ignorant of the strange events which had marked the first year of Mr. Soulis's ministrations; and among those who were better informed, some were naturally reticent, and others shy of that particular topic. Now and again, only, one of the older folk would warm into courage over his third tumbler, and recount the cause of the minister's strange looks and solitary life.

Fifty years syne, when Mr. Soulis cam' first into Ba'weary, he was still a young man—a callant, the folk said—fu' o' book learnin' and grand at the exposition, but, as was natural in sae young a man, wi' nae leevin' experience in religion. The younger sort were greatly taken wi' his gifts and his gab; but auld, concerned, serious men and women were moved even to prayer for the young man, whom they took to be a self-deceiver, and the parish that was like to be sae ill-supplied. It was before the days o' the Moderates—weary fa' them; but ill things are like guid—they baith come bit by bit, a pickle at a time; and there were folk even then that said the Lord had left the college professors to their ain devices, an' the lads that went to study wi' them wad hae done mair and better sittin' in a peat-bog, like their forebears of the persecution, wi' a Bible under their oxter and a speerit o' prayer in their heart. There was nae doubt, onyway, but that Mr. Soulis had been ower lang at the college. He was careful and troubled for mony things besides the ae thing needful. He had a feck o' books wi' him—mair than had ever been seen before in a' that presbytery; and a sair wark the carrier had wi' them, for they were a' like to have smoored in the Deil's Hag between this and Kilmackerlie. They were books o' divinity, to be sure, or so they ca'd them; but the serious were o' opinion there was little service for sae mony, when the hail o' God's Word would gang in the neuk of a plaid. Then he wad sit half the day and half the nicht forbye, which was scant decent—writin', nae less; and first, they were feared he wad read his sermons; and syne it was proved he was writin' a book himsel', which was surely no fittin' for ane of his years an' sma' experience.

Onyway it behoved him to get an auld, decent wife to keep the manse for him an' see to his bit denners; and he was recommended to an auld limmer—Janet M'Clour, they ca'd her—and sae far left to himsel' as to be ower persuaded. There was mony advised him to the contrar, for Janet was mair than suspeckit by the best folk in Ba'weary. Lang or that, she had had a wean to a dragoon; she hadnae come forrit for maybe thretty year; and bairns had seen her mumblin' to hersel' up on Key's Loan in the gloamin', whilk was an unco time an' place for a God-fearin' woman. Howsoever, it was the laird himsel' that had first tauld the minister o' Janet; and in thae days he wad have gane a far gate to pleesure the laird. When folk tauld him that Janet was sib to the deil, it was a' superstition by his way of it; an' when they cast up the Bible to him an' the witch of Endor, he wad threep it doun their thrapples that thir days were a' gane by, and the deil was mercifully restrained.

Weel, when it got about the clachan that Janet M'Clour was to be servant at the manse, the folk were fair mad wi' her an' him thegether; and some of the guidwives had nae better to dae than get round her door cheeks and chairge her wi' a' that was ken't again her, frae the sodger's bairn to John Tamson's twa kye. She was nae great speaker; folk usually let her gang her ain gate, an' she let them gang theirs, wi' neither Fair-guid-een nor Fair-guid-day; but when she buckled to, she had a tongue to deave the miller. Up she got, an' there wasnae an auld story in Ba'weary but she gart somebody lowp for it that day; they couldnae say ae thing but she could say twa to it; till, at the hinder end, the guidwives up and claught haud of her, and clawed the coats aff her back, and pu'd her doun the clachan to the water o' Dule, to see if she were a witch or no, soum or droun. The carline skirled till ye could hear her at the Hangin' Shaw, and she focht like ten; there was mony a guidwife bure the mark of her neist day an' mony a lang day after; and just in the hettest o' the collie-shangie, wha suld come up (for his sins) but the new minister.

"Women," said he (and he had a grand voice), "I charge you in the Lord's name to let her go."

Janet ran to him—she was fair wud wi' terror—an' clang to him, an' prayed him, for Christ's sake, save her frae the cummers; an' they, for their pairt, tauld him a' that was ken't, and maybe mair.

"Woman," says he to Janet, "is this true?"

"As the Lord sees me," says she, "as the Lord made me, no a word o't. Forbye the bairn," says she, "I've been a decent woman a' my days."

"Will you," says Mr. Soulis, "in the name of God, and before me, His unworthy minister, renounce the devil and his works?"

Weel, it wad appear that when he askit that, she gave a girn that fairly frichtit them that saw her, an' they could hear her teeth play dirl thegether in her chafts; but there was naething for it but the ae way or the ither; an' Janet lifted up her hand and renounced the deil before them a'.

"And now," says Mr. Soulis to the guidwives, "home with ye, one and all, and pray to God for His forgiveness."

And he gied Janet his arm, though she had little on her but a sark, and took her up the clachan to her ain door like a leddy of the land; an' her screighin' and laughin' as was a scandal to be heard.

There were mony grave folk lang ower their prayers that nicht; but when the morn cam' there was sic a fear fell upon a' Ba'weary that the bairns hid theirsels, and even the men folk stood and keekit frae their doors. For there was Janet comin' doun the clachan—her or her likeness, nane could tell—wi' her neck thrawn and her heid on ae side, like a body that has been hangit, and a girn on her face like an unstreakit corp. By-an'-by they got used wi' it, and even speered at her to ken what was wrang; but frae that day forth she couldnae speak like a Christian woman, but slavered and played click wi' her teeth like a pair o' shears; and frae that day forth the name o' God cam' never on her lips. Whiles she would try to say it, but it michtnae be. Them that kenned best said least; but they never gied that Thing the name o' Janet M'Clour; for the auld Janet, by their way o't, was in

9. This and the following three plates are from *A Child's Garden of Verses* (London, 1908) and are by Millicent Sowerby, the illustrator who best pictured the rather coy whimsy of Stevenson's poems for children. On this page: *Auntie's Skirts.*

Whenever Auntie moves around,
Her dresses make a curious sound;
They trail behind her up the floor,
And trundle after through the door.

10. *A Child's Garden of Verses*, Millicent Sowerby: *System.*

Every night my prayers I say,
And get my dinner every day;
And every day that I've been good,
I get an orange after food.

11. *A Child's Garden of Verses,* Millicent Sowerby: *Time to Rise.*

A birdie with a yellow bill
Hopped upon the window sill,
Cocked his shining eye and said:
"Ain't you 'shamed, you sleepy-head?"

12. *A Child's Garden of Verses*, Millicent Sowerby: *Happy Thought.*

The world is so full of a number of things,
I'm sure we should all be as happy as kings.

13. This and the following three plates are from the first illustrated edition of *A Child's Garden of Verses*, published in London in 1885. The illustrator-designer was Charles Robinson (brother of the better-remembered William Heath Robinson), whose career as a popular book illustrator was launched by the success of this book. The New York journal *The Bookman* said of it, "It is Stevenson's exquisite Children's Garden with still more childhood put into it." On this page: *Rain*.

14. *A Child's Garden of Verses*, Charles Robinson: *Happy Thought*.

15. *A Child's Garden of Verses*, Charles Robinson: *Up the mountainside of dreams.*

16. *A Child's Garden of Verses*, Charles Robinson: *The moon has a face like the clock in the hall.*

muckle hell that day. But the minister was neither to haud nor to bind; he preached about naething but the folk's cruelty that had gi'en her a stroke of the palsy; he skelpt the bairns that meddled her; and he had her up to the manse the same nicht, and dwalled there a' his lane wi' her under the Hangin' Shaw.

Weel, time gaed by; and the idler sort commenced to think mair lichtly o' that black business. The minister was weel thocht o'; he was aye late at the writing, folk wad see his can'le doun by the Dule water after twal' at e'en; and he seemed pleased wi' himsel' and upsitten as at first, though a' body could see that he was dwining. As for Janet she cam' an' she gaed; if she didnae speak muckle afore, it was reason she should speak less then; she meddled naebody; but she was an eldritch thing to see, an' nane wad hae mistrysted wi' her for Ba'weary glebe.

About the end o' July there cam' a spell o' weather, the like o't never was in that countryside; it was lown an' het an' heartless; the herds couldnae win up the Black Hill, the bairns were ower weariet to play; an' yet it was gousty too, wi' claps o' het wund that rumm'led in the glens, and bits o' shouers that slockened naething. We aye thocht it but to thun'er on the morn; but the morn cam', an' the morn's morning, and it was aye the same uncanny weather, sair on folks and bestial. Of a' that were the waur, nane suffered like Mr. Soulis; he could neither sleep, nor eat, he tauld his elders; an' when he wasnae writin' at his weary book, he wad be stravaguin' ower a' the countryside like a man possessed, when a' body else was blythe to keep caller ben the house.

Abune Hangin' Shaw, in the bield o' the Black Hill, there's a bit enclosed grund wi' an iron yett; and it seems, in the auld days, that was the kirkyaird o' Ba'weary, and consecrated by the Papists before the blessed licht shone upon the kingdom. It was a great howff o' Mr. Soulis's onyway; there he would sit an' consider his sermons; and indeed it's a bieldy bit. Weel, as he cam' ower the wast end o' the Black Hill, ae day, he saw first twa, an' syne fower, an' syne seeven corbie craws fleein' round an' round abune the auld kirkyaird. They flew laigh and heavy, an' squawked to ither as they gaed; and it was clear to Mr. Soulis that something had put them frae their ordinair. He wasnae easy fleyed, an' gaed straucht up to the wa's; an' what suld he find there but a man, or the appearance of a man, sittin' in the inside upon a grave. He was of a great stature, an' black as hell, and his e'en were singular to see. Mr. Soulis had heard tell o' black men, mony's the time; but there was something unco about this black man that daunted him. Het as he was, he took a kind o' cauld grue in the marrow o' his banes; but up he spak for a' that; an' says he: "My friend, are you a stranger in this place?" The black man answered never a word; he got upon his feet, an' begude to hirsle to the wa' on the far side; but he aye lookit at the minister; an' the minister stood an' lookit back; till a' in a meenute the black man was ower the wa' an' rinnin' for the bield o' the trees. Mr. Soulis, he hardly kenned why, ran after him; but he was sair forjaskit wi' his walk an' the het, unhalesome weather; and rin as he likit, he got nae mair than a glisk o' the black man amang the birks, till he won doun to the foot o' the hill-side, an' there he saw him ance mair, gaun, hap, step, an' lowp, ower Dule water to the manse.

Mr. Soulis wasnae weel pleased that this fearsome gangrel suld mak' sae free wi' Ba'weary manse; an' he ran the harder, an', wet shoon, ower the burn, an' up the walk; but the deil a black man was there to see. He stepped out upon the road, but there was naebody there; he gaed a' ower the gairden, bu na, nae black man. At the hinder end, and a bit feared as was but natural, he lifted the hasp and into the manse; and there was Janet M'Clour before his een, wi' her thrawn craig, and nane sae pleased to see him. And he aye minded sinsyne, when first he set his een upon her, he had the same cauld and deidly grue.

"Janet," says he, "have you seen a black man?"

"A black man?" quo' she. "Save us a'! Ye're no wise, minister. There's nae black man in a' Ba'weary."

But she didnae speak plain, ye maun understand; but yam-yammered, like a powney wi' the bit in its moo.

"Weel," says he, "Janet, if there was nae black man, I have spoken with the Accuser of the Brethren."

And he sat down like ane wi' a fever, an' his teeth chittered in his heid.

"Hoots," says she, "think shame to yoursel', minister"; an' gied him a drap brandy that she kept aye by her.

Syne Mr. Soulis gaed into his study amang a' his books. It's a lang, laigh, mirk chalmer, perishin' cauld in winter, an' no very dry even in the tap o' the simmer, for the manse stands near the burn. Sae doun he sat, and thocht of a' that had come an' gane since he was in Ba'weary, an' his hame, an' the days when he was a bairn an' ran daffin' on the braes; and that black man aye ran in his heid like the owercome of a sang. Aye the mair he thocht, the mair he thocht o' the black man. He tried the prayer, an' the words wouldnae come to him; an' he tried, they say, to write at his book, but he could nae mak' nae mair o' that. There was whiles he thocht the black man was at his oxter, an' the swat stood upon him cauld as well-water; and there was other whiles, when he cam' to himsel' like a christened bairn and minded naething.

The upshot was that he gaid to the window an' stood glowrin' at Dule Water. The trees are unco thick, an' the water lies deep an' black under the manse; an' there was Janet washin' the cla'es wi' her coats kilted. She had her back to the minister, an' he, for his pairt, hardly kenned what he was lookin' at. Syne she turned round, an' shawed her face; Mr. Soulis had the same cauld grue as twice that day afore, an' it was borne in upon him what folk said, that Janet was deid lang syne, an' this was a bogle in her clay-cauld flesh. He drew back a pickle and he scanned her narrowly. She was tramp-trampin' in the cla'es, croonin' to hersel'; and eh! Gude guide us, but it was a fearsome face. Whilės she sang louder, but there was nae man born o' woman that could tell the words o' her sang; an' whiles she lookit side-lang doun, but there was naething there for her to look at. There gaed a scunner through the flesh upon his banes; and that was Heeven's advertisement. But Mr. Soulis just blamed himsel', he said, to think sae ill of a puir auld afflicted wife that hadnae a freend forbye himsel'; an' he put up a bit prayer for him and her, an' drank a little caller water—for his heart rose again the meat—an' gaed up to his naked bed in the gloaming.

That was a nicht that has never been forgotten in Ba'weary, the nicht o' the seventeenth of August, seventeen hun'er' an' twal'. It had been het afore, as I hae said, but that nicht it was hetter than ever. The sun gaed doun among unco-lookin' clouds; it fell as mirk as the pit; no a star, no a breath o' wund; ye couldnae see your han' afore your face, and even the auld folk cuist the covers frae their beds and lay pechin' for their breath. Wi' a' that he had upon his mind, it was gey and unlikely Mr. Soulis wad get muckle sleep. He lay an' he tummled; the gude, caller bed that he got into brunt his very banes; whiles he slept, and whiles he waukened; whiles he heard the time o' nicht, and whiles a tyke yowlin' up the muir, as if somebody was deid; whiles he thocht he heard bogles claverin' in his lug, an' whiles he saw spunkies in the room. He behoved, he judged, to be sick; an' sick he was—little he jaloosed the sickness.

At the hinder end, he got a clearness in his mind, sat up in his sark on the bedside, and fell thinkin' ance mair o' the black man an' Janet. He couldnae weel tell how—maybe it was the cauld to his feet—but it cam' in upon him wi' a spate that there was some connection between thir twa, an' that either or baith o' them were bogles. And just at that moment, in Janet's room, which was neist to his, there cam' a stramp o' feet as if men were wars'lin', an' than a loud bang; an' then a wund gaed reishling round the fower quarters of the house; an' then a' was aince mair as seelent as the grave.

Mr. Soulis was feared for neither man nor deevil. He got his tinder-box, an' lit a can'le, an' made three steps o't ower to Janet's door. It was on the hasp, an' he pushed it open, an' keeked bauldly in. It was a big room, as big as the minister's ain, an plenished wi' grand, auld solid gear, for he had naething else. There was a fower posted bed wi' auld tapestry; and a braw cabinet of aik, that was fu' o' the minister's divinity books, an' put there to be out o' the gate; an' a wheen duds o' Janet's lying here and there about the floor. But nae Janet could Mr. Soulis see; nor ony sign of a contention. In he gaed (an' there's few that wad ha'e followed him) an' lookit a' round, an' listened. But there was naethin' to be heard, neither inside the manse nor in a' Ba'weary parish, an' naethin' to be seen but the muckle shadows turnin' round the can'le. An' then a' at aince, the minister's heart played dunt an' stood stock-still; an' a cauld wund blew amang the hairs o' his heid. Whaten a weary sicht was that for the puir man's een! For there was Janet hangin' frae a nail beside the auld aik cabinet: her heid aye lay on her shoother, her een were steeked, the tongue projekit frae her mouth, and her heels were twa feet clear abune the floor.

"God forgive us all!" thocht Mr. Soulis; "poor Janet's dead."

He cam' a step nearer to the corp; an' then his heart fair whammled in his inside. For by what cantrip it wad ill-beseem a man to judge, she was hingin' frae a single nail an' by a single wursted thread for darnin' hose.

It's an awfu' thing to be your lane at nicht wi' siccan prodigies o' darkness; but Mr. Soulis was strong in the Lord. He turned an' gaed his ways oot o' that room, and lockit the door ahint him; and step by step, down the stairs, as heavy as leed; and set doon the can'le on the table at the stairfoot. He couldnae pray, he couldnae think, he was dreepin' wi' caul' swat, an' naething could he hear but the dunt-dunt-duntin' o' his ain heart. He micht maybe have stood there an hour, or maybe twa, he minded sae little; when a' o' a sudden, he heard a laigh, uncanny steer upstairs; a foot gaed to an' fro in the cha'mer whaur the corp was hingin'; syne the door was opened, though he minded weel that he had lockit it; an' syne there was a step upon the landin', an' it seemed to him as if the corp was lookin' ower the rail and doun upon him whaur he stood.

He took up the can'le again (for he couldnae want the licht), and as saftly as ever he could, gaed straucht out o' the manse an' to the far end o' the causeway. It was aye pit-mirk; the flame o' the can'le, when he set it on the grund, brunt steedy and clear as in a room; naething moved, but the Dule water seepin' and sabbin' doon the glen, an' yon unhaly footstep that cam' plodding' doun the stairs inside the manse. He kenned the foot over weel, for it was Janet's; and at ilka step that cam' a wee thing nearer, the cauld got deeper in his vitals. He commended his soul to Him that made an' keepit him; "and O Lord," said he, "give me strength this night to war against the powers of evil."

By this time the foot was comin' through the passage for the door; he could hear a hand skirt alang the wa', as if the fearsome thing was feelin' for its way. The saughs tossed an' maned thegether, a lang sigh cam' ower the hills, the flame o' the can'le was blawn aboot; an' there stood the corp of Thrawn Janet, wi' her grogram goun an' her black mutch, wi' the heid aye upon the shouther, an' the girn still upon the face o't—leevin', ye wad hae said—deid, as Mr. Soulis weel kenned—upon the threshold o' the manse.

It's a strange thing that the saul of man should be that thirled into his perishable body; but the minister saw that, an' his heart didnae break.

She didnae stand there lang; she began to move again an' cam' slowly towards Mr. Soulis whaur he stood under the saughs. A' the life o' his body, a' the strength o' his speerit, were glowerin' frae his een. It seemed she was gaun to speak, but wanted words, an' made a sign wi' the left hand. There cam' a clap o' wund like a cat's fuff; oot gaed the can'le, the saughs skreighed like folk; an' Mr. Soulis kenned that, live or die, this was the end o't.

"Witch, beldame, devil!" he cried, "I charge you, by the power of God, begone—if you be dead, to the grave—if you be damned, to hell."

An' at that moment the Lord's ain hand out o' the Heevens struck the Horror whaur it stood; the auld, deid, desecrated corp o' the witch-wife, sae lang keepit frae the grave and hirsled round by deils, lowed up like a brunstane spunk and fell in ashes to the grund; the thunder followed, peal on dirling peal, the rairing rain upon the back o' that; and Mr. Soulis lowped through the garden hedge, and ran, wi' skelloch upon skelloch, for the clachan.

That same mornin', John Christie saw the Black Man pass the Muckle Cairn as it was chappin' six; before eicht, he gaed by the change-house at Knockdow; an' no lang after, Sandy M'Lellan saw him gaun linkin' doun the braes frae Kilmackerlie. There's little doubt but it was him that dwalled sae lang in Janet's body; but he was awa' at last; and sinsyne the deil has never fashed us in Ba'weary.

But it was a sair dispensation for the minster; lang, lang he lay ravin' in his bed; and frae that hour to this, he was the man ye ken the day.

The Merry Men

1. Eilean Aros

It was a Beautiful morning in late July when I set forth on foot for the last time for Aros. A boat had put me ashore the night before at Grisapol; I had such breakfast as the little inn afforded, and, leaving all my baggage till I had an occasion to come round for it by sea, struck right across the promontory with a cheerful heart.

I was far from being a native of these parts, springing, as I did, from an unmixed lowland stock. But an uncle of mine, Gordon Darnaway, after a poor, rough youth, and some years at sea, had married a young wife in the islands; Mary Maclean she was called, the last of her family; and when she died in giving birth to a daughter, Aros, the sea-girt farm, had remained in his possession. It brought him in nothing but the means of life, as I was well aware; but he was a man whom ill-fortune had pursued; he feared, cumbered as he was with the young child, to make a fresh adventure upon life; and remained in Aros, biting his nails at destiny. Years passed over his head in that isolation, and brought neither help nor contentment. Meantime out family was dying out in the lowlands; there is little luck for any of that race; and perhaps my father was the luckiest of all, for not only was he one of the last to die, but he left a son to his name and a little money to support it. I was a student of Edinburgh University, living well enough at my own charges, but without kith or kin; when some news of me found its way to Uncle Gordon on the Ross of Grisapol; and he, as he was a man who held blood thicker than water, wrote to me the day he heard of my existence, and taught me to count Aros as my home. Thus it was that I came to spend my vacations in that part of the country, so far from all society and comfort, between the codfish and the moorcocks; and thus it was that now, when I had done with my classes, I was returning thither with so light a heart that July day.

The Ross, as we call it, is a promontory neither wide nor high, but as rough as God made it to this day; the deep sea on either hand of it, full of rugged isles and reefs most perilous to seamen—all overlooked from the eastward by some very high cliffs and the great peak of Ben Kyaw. *The Mountain of the Mist*, they say the words signify in the Gaelic tongue; and it is well named. For that hill-top, which is more than three thousand feet in height, catches all the clouds that come blowing from the seaward; and, indeed, I used often to think that it must make them for itself; since when all heaven was clear to the sea level, there would be a streamer on Ben Kyaw. It brought water, too, and was mossy to the top in consequence. I have seen us sitting in broad sunshine on the Ross, and the rain falling black like crape upon the mountain. But the wetness of it made it often appear more beautiful to my eyes; for when the sun struck upon the hill sides, there were many wet rocks and watercourses that shone like jewels even as far as Aros, fifteen miles away.

The road that I followed was a cattle-track. It was twisted so as nearly to double the length of my journey; it went over rough boulders so that a man had to leap from one to another, and through soft bottoms where the moss came nearly to the knee. There was no cultivation anywhere, and not one house in the ten miles from Grisapol to Aros. Houses of course there were—three at least; but they lay so far on the one side or the other that no stranger could have found them from the track. A large part of the Ross is covered with big granite rocks, some of them larger than a two-roomed house, one beside another, with fern and deep heather in between them where the vipers breed. Any way the wind was, it was always sea air, as salt as on a ship; the gulls were as free as moorfowl over all the Ross; and whenever the way rose a little, your eye would kindle with the brightness of the sea. From the very midst of the land, on a day of wind and a high spring, I have heard the Roost roaring like a battle where it runs by Aros, and the great and fearful voices of the breakers that we call the Merry Men.

Aros itself—Aros Jay, I have heard the natives call it, and they say it means *The House of God*—Aros itself was not properly a piece of the

Ross, nor was it quite an islet. It formed the south-west corner of the land, fitted close to it, and was in one place only separated from the coast by a little gut of the sea not forty feet across the narrowest. When the tide was full, this was clear and still, like a pool on a land river; only there was a difference in the weeds and fishes, and the water itself was green instead of brown; but when the tide went out, in the bottom of the ebb, there was a day or two in every month when you could pass dryshod from Aros to the mainland. There was some good pasture, where my uncle fed the sheep he lived on; perhaps the feed was better because the ground rose higher on the islet than the main level of the Ross, but this I am not skilled enough to settle. The house was a good one for that country, two storeys high. It looked westward over a bay, with a pier hard by for a boat, and from the door you could watch the vapours blowing on Ben Kyaw.

On all this part of the coast, and especially near Aros, these great granite rocks that I have spoken of go down together in troops into the sea, like cattle on a summer's day. There they stand, for all the world like their neighbours ashore; only the salt water sobbing between them instead of the quiet earth, and clots of sea-pink blooming on their sides instead of heather; and the great sea conger to wreathe about the base of them instead of the poisonous viper of the land. On calm days you can go wandering between them in a boat for hours, echoes following you about the labyrinth; but when the sea is up, Heaven help the man that hears that cauldron boiling.

Off the south-west end of Aros these blocks are very many, and much greater in size. Indeed, they must grow monstrously bigger out to sea, for there must be ten sea miles of open water sown with them as thick as a country place with houses, some standing thirty feet above the tides, some covered, but all perilous to ships; so that on a clear, westerly blowing day I have counted from the top of Aros, the great rollers breaking white and heavy over as many as six-and-forty buried reefs. But it is nearer in shore that the danger is worst; for the tide, here running like a mill race, makes a long belt of broken water—a *Roost* we call it—at the tail of the land. I have often been out there in a dead calm at the slack of the tide; and a strange place it is, with the sea swirling and combing up and boiling like the cauldrons of a linn, and now and again a little dancing mutter of sound as though the *Roost* were talking to itself. But when the tide begins to run again, and above all in heavy weather, there is no man could take a boat within half a mile of it, nor a ship afloat that could either steer or live in such a place. You can hear the roaring of it six miles away. At the seaward end there comes the strongest of the bubble; and it's here that these big breakers dance together—the dance of death, it may be called—that have got the name, in these parts, of the Merry Men. I have heard it said that they run fifty feet high; but that must be the green water only, for the spray runs twice as high as that. Whether they got the name from their movements, which are swift and antic, or from the shouting they make about the turn of the tide, so that all Aros shakes with it, is more than I can tell.

The truth is, that in a south-westerly wind, that part of our archipelago is no better than a trap. If a ship got through the reefs, and weathered the Merry Men, it would be to come ashore on the south coast of Aros, in Sandag Bay, where so many dismal things befell our family, as I propose to tell. The thought of all these dangers, in the place I knew so long, makes me particularly welcome the works now going forward to set lights upon the headlands and buoys along the channels of our iron-bound, inhospitable islands.

The country people had many a story about Aros, as I used to hear from my uncle's man, Rorie, an old servant of the Macleans, who had transferred his services without afterthought on the occasion of the marriage. There was some tale of an unlucky creature, a sea-kelpie, that dwelt and did business in some fearful manner of his own among the boiling breakers of the Roost. A mermaid had once met a piper on Sandag beach, and there sang to him a long bright midsummer's night, so that in the morning he was found stricken crazy, and from thenceforward, till the day he died, said only one form of words; what they were in the original Gaelic I cannot tell, but they were thus translated: "Ah, the sweet singing out of the sea." Seals that haunted on that coast have been known to speak to man in his own tongue, presaging great disasters. It was here that a certain saint first landed on his voyage out of Ireland to convert the Hebrideans. And, indeed, I think he had some claim to be called saint; for, with the boats of that past to make so rough a passage, and land on such a ticklish coast, was surely not far short of the miraculous. It was to him, or to some of his monkish underlings who had a cell there, that the islet owes its holy and beautiful name, the House of God.

Among these old wives' stories there was one which I was inclined to hear with more credulity. As I was told, in that tempest which scattered the ships of the Invincible Armada over all the north and west of Scotland, one great vessel came ashore on Aros, and before the eyes of some solitary people on a hill-top, went down in a moment with all hands, her colours flying even as she sank. There was some likelihood in this tale; for another of that fleet sunk on the north side, twenty miles from Grisapol. It was told, I thought, with more detail and gravity than its companion stories, and there was one particularity which went far to convince me of its truth: the name, that is, of the ship was still remembered, and sounded, in my ears, Spanishly. The *Espirito Santo* they called it, a great ship of many decks of guns, laden with treasure and grandees of Spain, and fierce soldadoes, that now lay fathoms deep to all eternity, done with her wars and voyages, in Sandbag Bay, upon the west of Aros. No more salvoes of ordnance for that tall ship, the "Holy Spirit," no more fair winds or happy ventures; only to rot there deep in the sea-tangle and hear the shoutings of the Merry Men as the tide ran high about the island. It was a strange thought to me first and last, and only grew stranger as I learned the more of Spain, from which she had set sail with so proud a company, and King Philip, the wealthy king, that sent her on that voyage.

And now I must tell you, as I walked from Grisapol that day, the *Espirito Santo* was very much in my reflection. I had been favourably remarked by our then Principal in Edinburgh College, that famous writer, Dr. Robertson, and by him had been set to work on some papers of an ancient date to rearrange and sift of what was worthless; and in one of these, to my great wonder, I found a note of this very ship, the *Espirito Santo*, with her captain's name, and how she carried a great part of the Spaniard's treasure, and had been lost upon the Ross of Grisapol; but in what particular spot, the wild tribes of that place and period would give no information to the king's inquiries. Putting one thing with another, and taking our island tradition together with this note of old King Jamie's perquisitions after wealth, it had come strongly on my mind that the spot for which he sought in vain could be no other than the small bay of Sandag on my uncle's land; and being a fellow of a mechanical turn, I had ever since been plotting how to weigh that good ship up again with all her ingots, ounces, and doubloons, and bring back our house of Darnaway to its long-forgotten dignity and wealth.

This was a design of which I soon had reason to repent. My mind was sharply turned on different reflections; and since I became the witness of a strange judgment of God's, the thought of dead men's treasures had been intolerable to my conscience. But even at that time I must acquit myself of sordid greed; for if I desired riches, it was not for their own sake, but for the sake of a person who was dear to my heart—my uncle's daughter, Mary Ellen. She had been educated well, and had been a time to school upon the mainland; which, poor girl, she would have been happier without. For Aros was no place for her, with old Rorie the servant, and her father, who was one of the unhappiest men in Scotland, plainly bred up in a country place among Cameronians, long a skipper sailing out of the Clyde about the islands, and now, with infinite discontent, managing his sheep and a little 'long-shore fishing for the necessary bread. If it was sometimes weariful to me, who was there but a month or two, you may fancy what it was to her who dwelt in that same desert all the year round, with the sheep and flying sea-gulls, and the Merry Men singing and dancing in the Roost!

2. What the Wreck had brought to Aros

IT WAS half-flood when I got the length of Aros; and there was nothing for it but to stand on the far shore and whistle for Rorie with the boat. I had no need to repeat the signal. At the first sound, Mary was at the door flying a handkerchief by way of answer, and the old long-legged serving-man was shambling down the gravel to the pier. For all his hurry, it took him a long while to pull across the bay; and I observed him several times to pause, go into the stern, and look over curiously into the wake. As he came nearer, he seemed to me aged and haggard, and I thought he avoided my eye. The coble had been repaired, with two new thwarts and several patches of some rare and beautiful foreign wood, the name of it unknown to me.

"Why, Rorie," said I, as we began the return voyage, "this is fine wood. How came you by that?"

"It will be hard to chessel," Rorie opined reluctantly; and just then, dropping the oars, he made another of those dives into the stern which I had remarked as he came across to fetch me, and, leaning his hand on my shoulder, stared with an awful look into the waters of the bay.

"What is wrong?" I asked, a good deal startled.

"It will be a great feesh," said the old man, returning to his oars; and nothing more could I get out of him, but strange glances and an ominous nodding of the head. In spite of myself, I was infected with a measure of uneasiness; I turned also, and studied the wake. The water was still and transparent, but, out here in the middle of the bay, exceeding deep. For some time I could see naught; but at last it did seem to me as if something dark—a great fish, or perhaps only a shadow—followed studiously in the track of the moving coble. And then I remembered one of Rorie's superstitions: how in a ferry in Morven, in some great, exterminating feud among the clans, a fish, the like of it unknown in all our waters, followed for some years the passage of the ferry-boat, until no man dared to make the crossing.

"He will be waiting for the right man," said Rorie.

Mary met me on the beach, and led me up the brae and into the house of Aros. Outside and inside there were many changes. The garden was fenced with the same wood that I had noted in the boat; there were chairs in the kitchen covered with strange brocade; curtains of brocade hung from the window; a clock stood silent on the dresser; a lamp of brass was swinging from the roof; the table was set for dinner with the finest linen and silver; and all these new riches were displayed in the plain old kitchen that I knew so well, with the high-backed settle, and the stools, and the closet bed for Rorie; with the wide chimney the sun shone into, and the clear-smouldering peats; with the pipes on the mantelshelf and the three-cornered spittoons, filled with sea-shells instead of sand, on the floor; with the bare stone walls and bare wooden floor, and the three patchwork rugs that were of yore its sole adornment—poor man's patchwork, the like of it unknown in cities, woven with homespun, and Sunday black, and sea-cloth polished on the bench of rowing. The room, like the house, had been a sort of wonder in that countryside, it was so neat and habitable; and to see it now, shamed by these incongruous additions, filled me with indignation and a kind of anger. In view of the errand I had come upon to Aros, the feeling was baseless and unjust; but it burned high, at the first moment, in my heart.

"Mary, girl," said I, "this is the place I had learned to call my home, and I do not know it."

"It is my home by nature, not by the learning," she replied; "the place I was born and the place I'm like to die in; and I neither like these changes, nor the way they came, nor that which came with them. I would have liked better, under God's pleasure, they had gone down into the sea, and the Merry Men were dancing on them now."

Mary was always serious; it was perhaps the only trait that she shared with her father; but the tone with which she uttered these words was even graver than of custom.

"Ay," said I, "I feared it came by wreck, and that's by death; yet when my father died, I took his goods without remorse."

"Your father died a clean strae death, as the folk say," said Mary.

"True," I returned; "and a wreck is like a judgment. What was she called?"

"They ca'd her, the *Christ-Anna*," said a voice behind me; and turning round, I saw my uncle standing in the doorway.

He was a sour, small, bilious man, with a long face and very dark eyes; fifty-six years old, sound and active in body, and with an air somewhat between that of a shepherd and that of a man following the sea. He never laughed, that I heard; read long at the Bible; prayed much, like the Cameronians he had been brought up among; and indeed, in many ways, used to remind me of one of the hill-preachers in the killing times before the Revolution. But he never got much comfort, nor even, as I used to think, much guidance, by his piety. He had his black fits when he was afraid of hell; but he had led a rough life, to which he would look back with envy, and was still a rough, cold, gloomy man.

As he came in at the door out of the sunlight, with his bonnet on his head, and a pipe hanging in his button-hole, he seemed, like Rorie, to have grown older and paler, the lines were deeplier ploughed upon his face, and the whites of his eyes were yellow, like old stained ivory, or the bones of the dead.

"Ay," he repeated, dwelling upon the first part of the word, "the *Christ-Anna*. It's an awfu' name."

I made him my salutations, and complimented him upon his look of health; for I feared he had perhaps been ill.

"I'm in the body," he replied, ungraciously enough; "aye in the body and the sins of the body, like yoursel'. Denner," he said abruptly to Mary, and then ran on to me: "They're grand braws, thir that we hae gotten, are they no? Yon's a bonny knock, but it'll no gang; and the napery's by ordnar. Bonny, bairnly braws; it's for the like o' them folk sells the peace of God that passeth understanding; it's for the like o' them, an' maybe no even sae muckle worth, folk daunton God to His face and burn in muckle hell; and it's for that reason the Scripture ca's them, as I read the passage, the accursed thing, Mary, ye girzie," he interrupted himself to cry with some asperity, "what for hae ye no put out the twa candlesticks?"

"Why should we need them at high noon?" she asked.

But my uncle was not to be turned from his idea. "We'll bruik them while we may," he said; and so two massive candlesticks of wrought silver were added to the table equipage, already so unsuited to that rough sea-side farm.

"She cam' ashore Februar' 10, about ten at nicht," he went on to me. "There was nae wind, and a sair run o' sea; and she was in the sook o' the Roost, as I jaloose. We had seen her a' day, Rorie and me, beating to the wind. She was nae a handy craft, I'm thinking, that *Christ-Anna*;

for she would neither steer nor stey wi' them. A sair day they had of it; their hands was never off the sheets, and it perishin' cauld—ower cauld to snaw; and aye they would get a bit nip o' wind, and awa' again, to pit the emp'y hope into them. Eh, man! but they had a sair day for the last o't! He would have had a prood, prood heart that won ashore upon the back o' that."

"And were all lost?" I cried. "God help them!"

"Wheesht!" he said sternly. "Nane shall pray for the deid on my hearth-stone."

I disclaimed a Popish sense for my ejaculation; and he seemed to accept my disclaimer with unusual facility, and ran on once more upon what had evidently become a favourite subject.

"We fand her in Sandag Bay, Rorie an' me, and a' thae braws in the inside of her. There's a kittle bit, ye see, about Sandag; whiles the sook rins strong for the Merry Men; an' whiles again, when the tide's makin' hard an' ye can hear the Roost blawin' at the far-end of Aros, there comes a back-spang of current straucht into Sandag Bay. Weel, there's the thing that got the grip on the *Christ-Anna*. She but to have come in ram-stam an' stern forrit; for the bows of her are aften under, and the back-side of her is clear at hie-water o' neaps. But, man! the dunt that she cam' doon wi' when she struck! Lord save us a'! but it's an unco life to be sailor—a cauld, wanchancy life. Mony's the gliff I got mysel' in the great deep; and why the Lord should hae made yon unco water is mair than ever I could win to understand. He made the vales and the pastures, the bonny green yaird, the halesome, canty land—

And now they shout and sing to Thee,
For Thou hast made them glad,

as the Psalms say in the metrical version. No that I would preen my faith to that clink neither; but it's bonny, and easier to mind. 'Who go to sea in ships,' they hae't again—

And in
Great waters trading be,
Within the deep these men God's works
And His great wonders see.

Weel, it's easy sayin' sae. Maybe Dauvit wasnae very weel acquaint wi' the sea. But, troth, if it wasnae prentit in the Bible, I wad whiles be temp'it to think it wasnae the Lord, but the muckle, black deil that made the sea. There's naething good comes oot o't but the fish; an' the spetacle o' God riding on the tempest, to be shüre, whilk would be what Dauvit was likely ettling at. But, man, they were sair wonders that God showed to the *Christ-Anna*—wonders, do I ca' them? Judgments, rather: judgments in the mirk nicht among the draygons o' the deep. And their souls—to think o' that—their souls, man maybe no prepared! The sea—a muckle yett to hell!"

I observed, as my uncle spoke, that his voice was unnaturally moved and his manner unwontedly demonstrative. He leaned forward at these last words, for example, and touched me on the knee with his spread fingers, looking up into my face with a certain pallor, and I could see that his eyes shone with a deep-seated fire, and that the lines about his mouth were drawn and tremulous.

Even the entrance of Rorie, and the beginning of our meal, did not detach him from his train of thought beyond a moment. He condescended, indeed, to ask me some questions as to my success at college, but I thought it was with half his mind; and even in his extempore grace, which was, as usual, long and wandering, I could find the trace of his preoccupation, praying, as he did, that God would "remember in mercy fower puir, feckless fiddling, sinful creatures here by their lee-lane beside the great and dowie waters."

Soon there came an interchange of speeches between him and Rorie.

"Was it there?" asked my uncle.

"Ou, ay!" said Rorie.

I observed that they both spoke in a manner of aside, and with some show of embarrassment, and that Mary herself appeared to colour, and looked down on her plate. Partly to show my knowledge, and so relieve the party from awkward strain, partly because I was curious, I pursued the subject.

"You mean the fish?" I asked.

"Whatten fish?" cried my uncle. "Fish, quo' he! Fish! Your een are fu' o' fatness, man; your heid dozened wi' carnal leir. Fish! it's a bogle!"

He spoke with great vehemence, as though angry; and perhaps I was not very willing to be put down so shortly, for young men are disputatious. At least I remember I retorted hotly, crying out upon childish superstitions.

"And ye come frae the College!" sneered Uncle Gordon. "Gude kens what they learn folk there; it's no muckle service onyway. Do ye think, man, that there's naething in a' yon saut wilderness o' a world oot wast there, wi' the sea grasses growin', an' the sea beasts fechtin', an' the sun glintin' down into it, day by day? Na: the sea's like the land, but fearsomer. If there's folk ashore, there's folk in the sea—deid they may be, but they're folk whatever; and as for deils, there's nane that's like the sea deils. There's no sae muckle harm in the land deils, when a's said and done. Lang syne, when I was a callant in the south country, I mind there was an auld, bald bogle in the Peewie Moss. I got a glisk' o' him mysel' sittin' on his hunkers in a hag, as gray's a tombstane. An', troth, he was a fearsome-like taed. But he steered naebody. Nae doobt, if ane that was a reprobate, ane the Lord hated, had gane by there wi' his sin still upon his stamach, nae doobt the creature would hae lowped upo' the likes o' him. But there's deils in the deep sea would yoke on a communicant! Eh, sirs, if ye had gine doon wi' the puir lads in the *Christ-Anna*, ye would ken by now the mercy o' the seas. If ye had sailed it for as lang as me, ye would hate the thocht of it as I do. If ye had but used the een God gave ye, ye would hae learned the wickedness o' that fause, saut, cauld, bullering creature, and of a' that's in it by the Lord's permission: labsters an' partans, an' sic like, howking in the deid; muckle gutsy, blawing whales; an' fish—the hale clan o' them—cauld-wamed, blindeed uncanny ferlies. O, sirs," he cried, "the horror—the horror o' the sea!"

We were all somewhat staggered by this outburst; and the speaker himself, after that last hoarse apostrophe, appeared to sink gloomily into his own thoughts. But Rorie, who was greedy of superstitious lore, recalled him to the subject by a question.

"You will not ever have seen a teevil of the sea?" he asked.

"No clearly," replied the other. "I misdoobt if a mere man could see ane clearly and conteenue in the body. I hae sailed wi' a lad—they ca'd him Sandy Gabart; he saw ane, shüre eneuch, an' shüre eneuch it was the end of him. We were seeven days oot frae the Clyde,—a sair wark we had had—gaun north wi' seeds an' braws an' things for the Macleod. We had got in ower near under the Cutchull'ns, an' had just gane about by Soa, an' were off on a lang tack, we thocht would maybe hauld as far's Copnahow. I mind the nicht weel; a mune smoored wi' mist; a fine gaun breeze upon the water, but no steedy; an'—what nane o' us likit to hear—anither wund gurlin' owerheid, amang thae fearsome, auld stane craigs o' the Cutchull'ns. Weel, Sandy was forrit wi' the jib sheet; we couldnae see him for the mains'l, that had just begude to draw, when a' at ance he gied a skirl. I luffed for my life, for I thocht we were ower near Soa; but na, it wasnae that, it was puir Sandy Gabart's deid skeigh, or near hand, for he was deid in half an hour. A't he could tell was that a sea deil, or sea bogle, or sea spenster, or sic-like, had clum up by the bowsprit, an' gi'en him ae cauld, uncanny look. An', or the life was oot o' Sandy's body, we kent weel what the thing betokened, and why the wund gurled in the taps o' the Cutchull'ns; for doon it cam'—a wund do I ca' it! it was the wund o' the Lord's anger—an' a' that nicht we foucht like men dementit, and the niest we kenned we were ashore in Loch Uskevagh, an' the cocks were crawing in Benbecula."

"It will have been a merman," Rorie said.

"A merman!" screamed my uncle with immeasurable scorn. "Auld wives' clavers! There's nae sic things as mermen."

"But what was the creature like?" I asked.

"What like was it? Gude forbid that we suld ken what like it was! It had a kind of a heid upon it—man could say nae mair."

Then Rorie, smarting under the affront, told several tales of mermen, mermaids, and sea-horses that had come ashore upon the islands and attacked the crews of boats upon the sea; and my uncle, in spite of his incredulity, listened with uneasy interest.

"Aweel, aweel," he said, "it may be sae; I may be wrang; but I find nae word o' mermen in the Scriptures."

"And you will find nae word of Aros Roost, maybe," objected Rorie, and his argument appeared to carry weight.

When dinner was over, my uncle carried me forth with him to a bank behind the house. It was a very hot and quiet afternoon; scarce a ripple anywhere upon the sea, nor any voice but the familiar voice of sheep and gulls; and perhaps in consequence of this repose in nature, my kinsman showed himself more rational and tranquil than before. He spoke evenly and almost cheerfully of my career, with every now and then a reverence to the lost ship or the treasures it had brought to Aros. For my part, I listened to him in a sort of trance, gazing with all my heart on that remembered scene, and drinking gladly the sea-air and the smoke of peats that had been lit by Mary.

Perhaps an hour had passed when my uncle, who had all the while been covertly gazing on the surface of the little bay, rose to his feet and bade me follow his example. Now I should say that the great run of tide at the south-west end of Aros exercises a perturbing influence round all the coast. In Sandag Bay, to the south, a strong current runs at certain periods of the flood and ebb respectively; but in this northern bay—Aros Bay, as it is called—where the house stands and on which my uncle was now gazing, the only sign of disturbance is towards the end of the ebb, and even then it is too slight to be remarkable. When there is any swell, nothing can be seen at all; but when it is calm, as it often is, there appear certain strange, undecipherable marks—sea-runes, as we may name them—on the glassy surface of the bay. The like is common in a thousand places on the coast; and many a boy must have amused himself as I did, seeking to read in them some reference to himself or those he loved. It was to these marks that my uncle now directed my attention, struggling, as he did so, with an evident reluctance.

"Do ye see yon scart upo' the water?" he inquired; "yon ane wast the gray stane? Ay? Weel, it'll no be like a letter, wull it?"

"Certainly it is," I replied. "I have often remarked it. It is like a C."

He heaved a sigh as if heavily disappointed with my answer, and then added below his breath: "Ay, for the *Christ-Anna*."

"I used to suppose, sir, it was for myself," said I; "for my name is Charles."

"And so ye saw't afore?" he ran on, not heeding my remark. "Weel, weel, but that's unco strange. Maybe, it's been there waitin', as a man wad say, through a' the weary ages. Man, but that's awfu'." And then, breaking off: "Ye'll no see anither, will ye?" he asked.

"Yes," said I. "I see another very plainly, near the Ross side, where the road comes down—an M."

"An M," he repeated, very low; and then, again after another pause: "An' what wad ye make o' that?" he inquired.

"I had always thought it to mean Mary, sir," I answered, growing somewhat red, convinced as I was in my own mind that I was on the threshold of a decisive explanation.

But we were each following his own train of thought to the exclusion of the other's. My uncle once more paid no attention to my words; only hung his head and held his peace; and I might have been led to fancy that he had not heard me, if his next speech had not contained a kind of echo from my own.

"I would say naething o' thae clavers to Mary," he observed, and began to walk forward.

There is a belt of turf along the side of Aros Bay where walking is easy; and it was along this that I silently followed my silent kinsman. I was perhaps a little disappointed at having lost so good an opportunity to declare my love; but I was at the same time far more deeply exercised at the change that had befallen my uncle. He was never an ordinary, never, in the strict sense, an amiable, man; but there was nothing in even the worst that I had known of him before, to prepare me for so strange a transformation. It was impossible to close the eyes against one fact; that he had, as the saying goes, something on his mind, and as I mentally ran over the different words which might be represented by the letter M—misery, mercy, marriage, money, and the like—I was arrested with a sort of start by the word murder. I was still considering the ugly sound and fatal meaning of the word, when the direction of our walk brought us to a point from which a view was to be had to either side, back towards Aros Bay and homestead, and forward on the ocean, dotted to the north with isles, and lying to the southward blue and open to the sky. There my guide came to a halt, and stood staring for a while on that expanse. Then he turned to me and laid a hand on my arm.

"Ye think there's naething there?" he said, pointing with his pipe; and then cried out aloud, with a kind of exultation: "I'll tell ye, man! The deid are down there—thick like rattons!"

He turned at once, and, without another word, we retraced our steps to the house of Aros.

I was eager to be alone with Mary; yet it was not till after supper, and then but for a short while, that I could have a word with her. I lost no time beating about the bush, but spoke out plainly what was on my mind.

"Mary," I said, "I have not come to Aros without a hope. If that should prove well founded, we may all leave and go somewhere else, secure of daily bread and comfort; secure, perhaps, of something far beyond that, which it would seem extravagant in me to promise. But there's a hope that lies nearer to my heart than money." And at that I paused. "You can guess fine what that is, Mary," I said. She looked away from me in silence, and that was small encouragement, but I was not to be put off. "All my days I have thought the world of you," I continued; "the time goes on and I think always the more of you; I could not think to be happy or hearty in my life without you: you are the apple of my eye." Still she looked away, and said never a word; but I thought I saw that her hands shook. "Mary," I cried in fear, "do ye no like me?"

"O, Charlie man," she said, "is this a time to speak of it? Let me be, a while; let me be the way I am; it'll not be you that loses by the waiting!"

I made out by her voice that she was nearly weeping, and this put me out of any thought but to compose her. "Mary Ellen," I said, "say no more: I did not come to trouble you: your way shall be mine, and your time too; and you have told me all I wanted. Only just this one thing more: what ails you?"

She owned it was her father, but would enter into no particulars, only shook her head, and said he was not well and not like himself, and it was a great pity. She knew nothing of the wreck. "I havenae been near it," said she. "What for would I go near it, Charlie lad? The poor souls are gone to their account long syne; and I would just have wished they had ta'en their gear with them—poor souls!"

This was scarcely any great encouragement for me to tell her of the *Espirito Santo*; yet did I so, and at the very first word she cried out in surprise. "There was a man at Grisapol," she said, "in the month of May—a little, yellow, black-avised body, they tell me, with gold rings upon his fingers, and a beard; and he was speiring high and low for that same ship."

It was towards the end of April that I had been given these papers to sort out by Dr. Robertson: and it came suddenly back upon my mind that they were thus prepared for a Spanish historian, or a man calling himself such, who had come with high recommendations to the Principal, on a mission of inquiry as to the dispersion of the great Armada. Putting one thing with another, I fancied that the visitor "with the gold rings upon his fingers" might be the same with Dr. Robertson's historian from Madrid. If that were so, he would be more likely after treasure for himself than information for a learned society. I made up my mind, I should lose no time over my undertaking; and if the ship lay sunk in Sandag Bay, as perhaps both he and I supposed, it should not be for the advantage of this ringed adventurer, but for Mary and myself, and for the good, old, honest, kindly family of the Darnaways.

3. Land and Sea in Sandag Bay

I WAS early afoot next morning; and as soon as I had a bite to eat, set forth upon a tour of exploration. Something in my heart distinctly told me that I should find the ship of the Armada; and although I did not give way entirely to such hopeful thoughts, I was still very light in spirits and walked upon air. Aros is a very rough islet, its surface strewn with great rocks and shaggy with fern and heather, and my way lay almost north and south across the highest knoll, and though the whole distance was inside of two miles, it took more time and exertion than four upon a level road. Upon the summit I paused. Although not very high—not three hundred feet, as I think—it yet out-tops all the neighbouring lowlands of the Ross, and commands a great view of sea and islands. The sun, which had been up some time, was already hot upon my neck; the air was listless and thundery, although purely clear; away over the north-west, where the isles lie thickliest congregated, some half-a-dozen small and ragged clouds hung together in a covey; and the head of Ben Kyaw wore, not merely a few streamers, but a solid hood of vapour. There was a threat in the weather. The sea, it is true, was smooth like glass: even the Roost was but a seam on that wide mirror, and the Merry Men no more than caps of foam; but to my eye and ear, so long familiar with these places, the sea also seemed to lie uneasily; a sound of it, like a long sigh, mounted to where I stood; and, quiet as it was, the Roost itself appeared to be revolving mischief. For I ought to say that all we dwellers in these parts attributed, if not prescience, at least a quality of warning, to that strange and dangerous creature of the tides.

I hurried on, then, with the greater speed, and had soon descended the slope of Aros to the part that we call Sandag Bay. It is a pretty large piece of water compared with the size of the isle; well sheltered from all but the prevailing wind; sandy and shoal and bounded by low sand-hills to the west, but to the eastward lying several fathoms deep along a ledge of rocks. It is upon that side that, at a certain time each flood, the current mentioned by my uncle sets so strong into the bay; a little later, when the Roost begins to work higher, an undertow runs still more strongly in the reverse direction; and it is the action of this last, as I suppose, that has scoured that part so deep. Nothing is to be seen out of Sandag Bay but one small segment of the horizon and, in heavy weather, the breakers flying high over a deep sea reef.

From half-way down the hill, I had perceived the wreck of February last, a brig of considerable tonnage, lying, with her back broken, high and dry on the east corner of the sands; and I was making directly towards it, and already almost on the margin of the turf, when my eyes were suddenly arrested by a spot, cleared of fern and heather, and marked by one of those long, low, and almost human-looking mounds that we see so commonly in graveyards. I stopped like a man shot. Nothing had been said to me of any dead man or interment on the island; Rorie, Mary, and my uncle had all equally held their peace; of her at least, I was certain that she must be ignorant; and yet here, before my eyes, was proof indubitable of the fact. Here was a grave; and I had to ask myself, with a chill, what manner of man lay there in his last sleep, awaiting the signal of the Lord in that solitary sea-beat resting-place? My mind supplied no answer but what I feared to entertain. Shipwrecked, at least, he must have been; perhaps, like the old Armada mariners, from some far and rich land overseas; or perhaps one of my own race, perishing within eyesight of the smoke of home. I stood a while uncovered by his side, and I could have desired that it had lain in our religion to put up some prayer for that unhappy stranger, or, in the old classic way, outwardly to honour his misfortune. I knew, although his bones lay there, a part of Aros, till the trumpet sounded, his imperishable soul was forth and far away, among the raptures of the everlasting Sabbath or the pangs of hell; and yet my mind misgave me even with a fear, that perhaps he was near me where I stood, guarding his sepulchre, and lingering on the scene of his unhappy fate.

Certainly it was with a spirit somewhat overshadowed that I turned away from the grave to the hardly less melancholy spectacle of the wreck. Her stern was above the first arc of the flood; she was broken in two a little abaft the foremast—though indeed she had none, both masts having broken short in her disaster; and as the pitch of the beach was very sharp and sudden, and the bows lay many feet below the stern, the fracture gaped widely open, and you could see right through her poor hull upon the farther side. Her name was much defaced, and I could not make out clearly whether she was called *Christiania*, after the Norwegian city, or *Christiana*, after the good woman, Christian's wife, in that old book the *Pilgrim's Progress*. By her build she was a foreign ship, but I was not certain of her nationality. She had been painted green, but the colour was faded and weathered, and the paint peeling off in strips. The wreck of the mainmast lay alongside, half buried in sand. She was a forlorn sight, indeed, and I could not look without emotion at the bits of rope that still hung about her, so often handled of yore by shouting seamen; or the little scuttle where they had passed up and down to their affairs; or that poor noseless angel of a figure-head that had dipped into so many running billows.

I do not know whether it came most from the ship or from the grave, but I fell into some melancholy scruples, as I stood there, leaning with one hand against the battered timbers. The homelessness of men and even of inanimate vessels, cast away upon strange shores, came strongly in upon my mind. To make a profit of such pitiful misadventures seemed an unmanly and a sordid act; and I began to think of my quest as of something sacrilegious in its nature. But when I remembered Mary, I took heart again. My uncle would never consent to an imprudent marriage, nor would she, as I was persuaded, wed without his full approval. It behoved me, then, to be up and doing for my wife; and I thought with a laugh how long it was since that great sea-castle, the *Espirito Santo*, had left her bones in Sandag Bay, and how weak it would be to consider rights so long extinguished and misfortunes so long forgotten in the process of time.

I had my theory of where to seek for her remains. The set of the current and the soundings both pointed to the east side of the bay under the ledge of rocks. If she had been lost in Sandag Bay, and if, after these centuries, any portion of her held together, it was there that I should find it. The water deepens, as I have said, with great rapidity, and even close alongside the rocks several fathoms may be found. As I walked upon the edge I could see far and wide over the sandy bottom of the bay; the sun shone clear and green and steady in the deeps; the bay seemed rather like a great transparent crystal, as one sees them in a lapidary's shop; there was naught to show that it was water but an internal trembling, a hovering within of sunglints and netted shadows, and now and then a faint lap and a dying bubble round the edge. The shadows of the rocks lay out for some distance at their feet, so that my own shadow, moving, pausing, and stooping on the top of that, reached sometimes half across the bay. It was above all in this belt of shadows that I hunted for the *Espirito Santo*, since it was there the undertow ran strongest, whether in or out. Cool as the whole water seemed this broiling day, it looked, in that part, yet cooler, and had a mysterious invitation for the eyes. Peer as I pleased, however, I could see nothing but a few fishes or a bush of sea-tangle, and here and there a lump of rock that had fallen from above and now lay separate on the sandy floor. Twice did I pass from one end to the other of the rocks, and in the whole distance I could see nothing of the wreck, nor any place but one where it was possible for it to be. This was a large terrace in five fathoms of water, raised off the surface of the sand to a considerable height, and looking from above like a mere outgrowth of the rocks on which I walked. It was one mass of great sea-tangles like a grove, which prevented me judging of its nature, but in shape and size it bore some likeness to a vessel's hull. At least it was my best chance. If the *Espirito Santo* lay not there under the tangles, it lay nowhere at all in Sandag Bay; and I prepared to put the question to the proof, once for all, and either go back to Aros a rich man or cured for ever of my dreams of wealth.

I stripped to the skin, and stood on the extreme margin with my hands clasped, irresolute. The bay at that time was utterly quiet; there was no sound but from a school of porpoises somewhere out of sight behind the point; yet a certain fear withheld me on the threshold of my venture. Sad sea-feelings, scraps of my uncle's superstitions, thoughts of the dead, of the grave, of the old broken ships, drifted through my mind. But the strong sun upon my shoulders armed me to the heart, and I stooped forward and plunged into the sea.

It was all that I could do to catch a trail of the sea-tangle that grew so thickly on the terrace; but once so far anchored I secured myself by grasping a whole armful of these thick and slimy stalks, and, planting my feet against the edge, I looked around me. On all sides the clear sand stretched forth unbroken; it came to the foot of the rocks, scoured into the likeness of an alley in a garden by the action of the tides; and before me, for as far as I could see, nothing was visible but upon the sun-bright bottom of the bay. Yet the terrace to which I was then holding was as thick with strong sea-growths as a tuft of heather, and the cliff from which it bulged hung draped below the water-line with brown lianas. In this complexity of forms, all swaying together in the current, things were hard to be distinguished; and I was still uncertain whether my feet were pressed upon the natural rock or upon the timbers of the Armada treasure-ship, when the whole tuft of tangle came away in my hand, and in an instant I was on the surface, and the shores of the bay and the bright water swam before my eyes in a glory of crimson.

I clambered back upon the rocks, and threw the tangle of plant at my feet. Something at the same moment rang sharply, like a falling coin. I stooped, and there, sure enough, crusted with red rust, there lay an iron shoe-buckle. The sight of this poor human relic thrilled me to the heart, but not with hope nor fear, only with a desolate melancholy. I held it in my hand, and the thought of its owner appeared before me like the presence of an actual man. His weather-beaten face, his sailor's hands, his sea-voice hoarse with singing at the capstan, the very foot that had once worn that buckle and trod so much along the swerving decks—the whole human fact of him, as a creature like myself, with hair and blood and seeing eyes, haunted me in that sunny, solitary place, not like a spectre, but like some friend whom I had basely injured. Was the great treasure ship indeed below there, with her guns and chain and treasure, as she had sailed from Spain; her decks a garden for the seaweed, her cabin a breeding place for fish, soundless but for the dredging water, motionless but for the waving of the tangle upon her battlements—that old, populous, sea-riding castle, now a reef in Sandag Bay? Or, as I thought it likelier, was this a waif from the disaster of the foreign brig—was this shoe-buckle bought but the other day and worn by a man of my own period in the world's history, hearing the same news from day to day, thinking the same thoughts, praying, perhaps, in the same temple with myself? However it was, I was assailed with dreary thoughts; my uncle's words, "the dead are down there", echoed in my ears; and though I determined to dive once more, it was with a strong repugnance that I stepped forward to the margin of the rocks.

A great change passed at that moment over the appearance of the bay. It was no more that clear, visible interior, like a house roofed with glass, where the green, submarine sunshine slept so stilly. A breeze, I suppose, had flawed the surface, and a sort of trouble and blackness filled its bosom, where flashes of light and clouds of shadow tossed confusedly together. Even the terrace below obscurely rocked and quivered. It seemed a graver thing to venture on this place of ambushes; and when I leaped into the sea the second time it was with a quaking in my soul.

I secured myself as at first, and groped among the waving tangle. All that met my touch was cold and soft and gluey. The thicket was alive with crabs and lobsters, trundling to and fro lobsidedly, and I had to harden my heart against the horror of their carrion neighbourhood. On all sides I could feel the grain and the clefts of hard, living stone; no planks, no iron, not a sign of any wreck; the *Espirito Santo* was not there. I remember I had almost a sense of relief in my disappointment, and I was about ready to leave go, when something happened that sent me to the surface with my heart in my mouth. I had already stayed somewhat late over my explorations; the current was freshening with the change of the tide, and Sandag Bay was no longer a safe place for a single swimmer. Well, just at the last moment there came a sudden flush of current, dredging through the tangles like a wave. I lost one hold, was flung sprawling on my side, and, instinctively grasping for a fresh support, my fingers closed on something hard and cold. I think I knew at that moment what it was. At least I instantly left hold of the tangle, leaped for the surface, and clambered out next moment on the friendly rocks with the bone of a man's leg in my grasp.

Mankind is a material creature, slow to think and dull to perceive connections. The grave, the wreck of the brig, and the rusty shoe-buckle were surely plain advertisements. A child might have read their story, and yet it was not until I touched that actual piece of mankind that the full horror of the charnel ocean burst upon my spirit. I laid the bone beside the buckle, picked up my clothes, and ran as I was along the rocks towards the human shore. I could not be far enough from the spot; no fortune was vast enough to tempt me back again. The bones of the drowned dead should henceforth roll undisturbed by me, whether on tangle or minted gold. But as soon as I trod the good earth again, and had covered my nakedness against the sun, I knelt down over against the ruins of the brig, and out of the fulness of my heart prayed long and passionately for all poor souls upon the sea.

A generous prayer is never presented in vain; the petition may be refused, but the petitioner is always, I believe, rewarded by some gracious visitation. The horror, at least, was lifted from my mind; I could look with calm of spirit on that great bright creature, God's ocean; and as I set off homeward up the rough sides of Aros, nothing remained of my concern beyond a deep determination to meddle no more with the spoils of wrecked vessels or the treasures of the dead.

I was already some way up the hill before I paused to breathe and look behind me. The sight that met my eyes was doubly strange.

For, first, the storm that I had foreseen was now advancing with almost tropical rapidity. The whole surface of the sea had been dulled from its conspicuous brightness to an ugly hue of corrugated lead; already in the distance the white waves, the "skipper's daughters", had begun to flee before a breeze that was still insensible on Aros; and already along the curve of Sandag Bay there was a splashing run of sea that I could hear from where I stood. The change upon the sky was even more remarkable. There had begun to arise out of the south-west a huge and solid continent of scowling cloud; here and there, through rents in its contexture, the sun still poured a sheaf of spreading rays; and here and there, from all its edges, vast inky streamers lay forth along the yet unclouded sky. The menace was express and imminent. Even as I gazed, the sun was blotted out. At any moment the tempest might fall upon Aros in its might.

The suddenness of this change of weather so fixed my eyes on heaven that it was some seconds before they alighted on the bay, mapped out below my feet, and robbed a moment later of the sun. The knoll which I had just surmounted overflanked a little amphitheatre of lower hillocks sloping towards the sea, and beyond that the yellow arc of beach and the whole extent of Sandag Bay. It was a scene on which I had often looked down, but where I had never before beheld a human figure. I had but just turned my back upon it and left it empty, and my wonder may be fancied when I saw a boat and several men in that deserted spot. The boat was lying by the rocks. A pair of fellows, bareheaded, with their sleeves rolled up, and one with a boat-hook, kept her with difficulty to her moorings, for the current was growing brisker every moment. A little way off upon the ledge two men in black clothes, whom I judged to be superior in rank, laid their heads together over some task which at first I did not understand, but a second after I had made it out—they were taking bearings with the compass; and just then I saw one of them unroll a sheet of paper and lay his finger down, as though identifying features in a map. Meanwhile a third was walking to and fro, poking among the rocks and peering over the edge into the water. While I was still watching them with the stupefaction of surprise, my mind hardly yet able to work on what my eyes reported, this third person suddenly stopped and summoned his companions with a cry so loud that it reached my ears upon the hill. The others ran to him, even dropping the compass in their hurry, and I could see the bone and the shoe-buckle going from hand to hand, causing the most unusual gesticulations of surprise and interest. Just then I could hear the seamen crying from the boat, and saw them point westward to that cloud continent which was ever the more rapidly unfurling its blackness over heaven. The others seemed to consult; but the danger was too pressing to be braved, and they bundled into the boat, carrying my relics with them, and set forth out of the bay with all speed of oars.

I made no more ado about the matter, but turned and ran for the house. Whoever these men were, it was fit my uncle should be instantly informed. It was not then altogether too late in the day for a descent of the Jacobites; and maybe Prince Charlie, whom I knew my uncle to detest, was one of the three superiors whom I had seen upon the rocks. Yet as I ran, leaping from rock to rock, and turned the matter loosely in my mind, this theory grew ever the longer the less welcome to my reason. The compass, the map, the interest awakened by the buckle, and the conduct of that one among the strangers who had looked so often below him in the water, all seemed to point to a different explanation of their presence on that outlying, obscure islet of the western sea. The Madrid historian, the search instituted by Dr. Robertson, the bearded stranger with the rings, my own fruitless search that very morning in the deep water of Sandag Bay, ran together, piece by piece, in my memory, and I made sure that these strangers must be Spaniards in quest of ancient treasure and the lost ship of the Armada. But the people living in outlying islands, such as Aros, are answerable for their own security; there is none near by to protect or even to help them; and the presence in such a spot of a crew of foreign adventurers—poor, greedy, and most likely lawless—filled me with apprehensions for my uncle's money, and even for the safety of his daughter. I was still wondering how we were to get rid of them when I came, all breathless, to the top of Aros. The whole world was shadowed over; only in the extreme east, on a hill of the mainland, one last gleam of sunshine lingered like a jewel; rain had begun to fall, not heavily, but in great drops; the sea was rising with each moment, and already a band of white encircled Aros and the nearer coasts of Grisapol. The boat was still pulling seaward, but I now became aware of what had been hidden from me lower down—a large, heavily sparred, handsome schooner lying-to at the south end of Aros. Since I had not seen her in the morning when I had looked around so closely at the signs of the weather, and upon these lone waters where a sail was rarely visible, it was clear she must have lain last night behind the uninhabited Eilean Gour, and this proved conclusively that she was manned by strangers to our coast, for that anchorage, though good enough to look at, is little better than a trap for ships. With such ignorant sailors upon so wild a coast, the coming gale was not unlikely to bring death upon its wings.

4. The Gale

I FOUND my uncle at the gable end, watching the signs of the weather, with a pipe in his fingers.

"Uncle," said I, "there were men ashore at Sandag Bay—"

I had no time to go further; indeed, I not only forgot my words, but even my weariness, so strange was the effect on Uncle Gordon. He dropped his pipe and fell back against the end of the house with his jaw fallen, his eyes staring, and his long face as white as paper. We must have looked at one another silently for a quarter of a minute, before he made answer in this extraordinary fashion: "Had he a hair kep on?"

I knew as well as if I had been there that the man who now lay buried at Sandag had worn a hairy cap, and that he had come ashore alive. For the first and only time I lost toleration for the man who was my benefactor and the father of the woman I hoped to call my wife.

"These were living men," I said, "perhaps Jacobites, perhaps the French, perhaps pirates, perhaps adventurers come here to seek the Spanish treasure ship; but, whatever they may be, dangerous at least to your daughter and my cousin. And for your own guilty terrors, man, the dead sleeps well where you have laid him, I stood this morning by his grave; he will not wake before the trump of doom."

My kinsman looked upon me, blinking, while I spoke; then he fixed his eyes for a little on the ground, and pulled his fingers foolishly; but it was plain that he was past the power of speech.

"Come," said I. "You must think for others. You must come up the hill with me, and see this ship."

He obeyed without a word or a look, following slowly after my impatient strides. The spring seemed to have gone out of his body, and he scrambled heavily up and down the rocks, instead of leaping, as he was wont, from one to another. Nor could I, for all my cries, induce him to make better haste. Only once he replied to me complainingly, and like one in bodily pain: "Ay, ay, man, I'm coming." Long before we had reached the top, I had no other thought for him but pity. If the crime had been monstrous, the punishment was in proportion.

At last we emerged above the sky-line of the hill, and could see around us. All was black and stormy to the eye; the last gleam of sun had vanished; a wind had sprung up, not yet high, but gusty and unsteady to the point; the rain, on the other hand, had ceased. Short as was the interval, the sea already ran vastly higher than when I had stood there last; and already it had begun to break over some of the outward reef, and already it moaned aloud in the sea-caves of Aros. I looked, at first, in vain for the schooner.

"There she is," I said at last. But her new position, and the course she was now lying, puzzled me. "They cannot mean to beat to sea," I cried.

"That's what they mean," said my uncle, with something like joy; and just then the schooner went about and stood upon another tack, which put the question beyond the reach of doubt. These strangers, seeing a gale on hand, had thought first of sea-room. With the wind that threatened, in these reef-sown waters and contending against so violent a stream of tide, their course was certain death.

"Good God!" said I, "they are all lost."

"Ay," returned my uncle, "a'—a' lost. They hadnae a chance but to rin for Kyle Dona. The gate they're gaun the noo, they couldnae win through an the muckle deil were there to pilot them. Eh, man," he continued, touching me on the sleeve, "it's a braw nicht for a shipwreck! Twa in ae twalmonth! Eh, but the Merry Men 'll dance bonny!"

I looked at him, and it was then that I began to fancy him no longer in his right mind. He was peering up to me, as if for sympathy, a timid joy in his eyes. All that had passed between us was already forgotten in the prospect of this fresh disaster.

"If it were not too late," I cried with indignation, "I would take the coble and go out to warn them."

"Na, na," he protested, "ye maunnae interfere; ye maunnae meddle wi' the like o' that. It's His"—doffing his bonnet—"His wull. And, eh, man! but it's a braw nicht for't!"

Something like fear began to creep into my soul; and, reminding him that I had not yet dined, I proposed we should return to the house. But no; nothing would tear him from his place of outlook.

"I maun see the hail thing, man, Charlie," he explained; and then as the schooner went about a second time, "Eh, but they han'le her bonny!" he cried. "The *Christ-Anna* was naething to this."

Already the men on board the schooner must have begun to realize some part, but not yet the twentieth, of the dangers that environed their doomed ship. At every lull of the capricious wind they must have seen how fast the current swept them back. Every tack was made shorter, as they saw how little it prevailed. Every moment the rising swell began to boom and foam upon another sunken reef; and ever and again a breaker would fall in sounding ruin under the very bows of her, and the brown reef and streaming tangle appear in the hollow of the wave. I tell you, they had to stand to their tackle: there was no idle man aboard that ship, God knows. It was upon the progress of a scene so horrible to any human-hearted man that my misguided uncle now pored and gloated like a connoisseur. As I turned to go down the hill, he was lying on his belly on the summit, with his hands stretched forth and clutching in the heather. He seemed rejuvenated, mind and body.

When I got back to the house already dismally affected, I was still more sadly downcast at the sight of Mary. She had her sleeves rolled up over her strong arms, and was quietly making bread. I got a bannock from the dresser and sat down to eat it in silence.

"Are ye wearied, lad?" she asked after a while.

"I am not so much wearied, Mary," I replied, getting on my feet, "as I am weary of delay, and perhaps of Aros too. You know me well enough to judge me fairly, say what I like. Well, Mary, you may be sure of this: you had better be anywhere but here."

"I'll be sure of one thing," she returned: "I'll be where my duty is."

"You forget, you have a duty to yourself," I said.

"Ay, man?" she replied, pounding at the dough; "will you have found that in the Bible, now?"

"Mary," I said solemnly, "you must not laugh at me just now. God knows I am in no heart for laughing. If we could get your father with us, it would be best; but with him or without him, I want you far away from here, my girl; for your own sake, and for mine, ay, and for your father's too, I want you far—far away from here. I came with other thoughts; I came here as a man comes home; now it is all changed, and I have no desire nor hope but to flee—for that's the word—flee, like a bird out of the fowler's snare, from this accursed island."

She had stopped her work by this time.

"And do you think, now," said she, "do you think, now I have neither eyes nor ears? Do ye think I havenae broken my heart to have these braws (as he calls them, God forgive him!) thrown into the sea? Do ye think I have lived with him, day in, day out, and not seen what you saw in an hour or two? No," she said, "I know there is wrong in it; what wrong, I neither know nor want to know. There was never an ill thing made better by meddling, that I could hear of. But, my lad, you must never ask me to leave my father. While the breath is in his body, I'll be with him. And he's not long for here, either: that I can tell you. Charlie—he's not long for here. The mark is on his brow; and better so—maybe better so."

I was a while silent, not knowing what to say; and when I roused my head at last to speak, she got before me.

"Charlie," she said, "what's right for me, neednae be right for you. There's sin upon this house and trouble; you are a stranger; take your things upon your back and go your ways to better places and to better folk, and if you were ever minded to come back, though it were twenty years syne, you would find me aye waiting."

"Mary Ellen," I said, "I asked you to be my wife, and you said as good as yes. That's done for good. Wherever you are, I am; as I shall answer to my God."

As I said the words, the wind suddenly burst out raving, and then seemed to stand still and shudder round the house of Aros. It was the first squall, or prologue, of the coming tempest, and as we started and looked about us, we found that a gloom, like the approach of evening, had settled round the house.

"God pity all poor folks at sea!" she said. "We'll see no more of my father till the morrow's morning."

And then she told me, as we sat by the fire and hearkened to the rising gusts, of how this change had fallen upon my uncle. All last winter he had been dark and fitful in his mind. Whenever the Roost ran high, or, as Mary said, whenever the Merry Men were dancing, he would lie out for hours together on the Head, if it were at night, or on the top of Aros by day, watching the tumult of the sea, and sweeping the horizon for a sail. After February the tenth, when the wealth-bringing wreck was cast ashore at Sandag, he had been at first unnaturally gay, and his excitement had never fallen in degree, but only changed in kind from dark to darker. He neglected his work, and kept Rorie idle. They two would speak together by the hour at the gable end, in guarded tones and with an air of secrecy and almost of guilt; and if she questioned either, as at first she sometimes did, her inquiries were put aside with confusion. Since Rorie had first remarked the fish that hung about the ferry, his master had never set foot but once upon the mainland of the Ross. That once—it was in the height of the springs—he had passed dryshod while the tide was out; but, having lingered overlong on the far side, found himself cut off from Aros by the returning waters. It was with a shriek of agony that he had leaped across the gut, and he had reached home thereafter in a fever-fit of fear. A fear of the sea, a constant haunting thought of the sea, appeared in his talk and devotions, and even in his looks when he was silent.

Rorie alone came in to supper; but a little later my uncle appeared, took a bottle under his arm, put some bread in his pocket, and set forth again to his outlook, followed this time by Rorie. I heard that the schooner was losing ground, but the crew were still fighting every inch with hopeless ingenuity and courage; and the news filled my mind with blackness.

A little after sundown the full fury of the gale broke forth, such a gale as I have never seen in summer, nor, seeing how swiftly it had come, even in winter. Mary and I sat in silence, the house quaking overhead, the tempest howling without, the fire between us sputtering with raindrops. Our thoughts were far away with the poor fellows on the schooner, or my not less unhappy uncle, houseless on the promontory; and yet ever and again we were startled back to ourselves, when the wind would rise and strike the gable like a solid body, or suddenly fall and draw away, so that the fire leaped into flame and our hearts bounded in our sides. Now the storm in its might would seize and shake the four corners of the roof, roaring like Leviathan in anger. Anon, in a lull, cold eddies of tempest moved shudderingly in the room, lifting the hair upon our heads and passing between us as we sat. And again the wind would break forth in a chorus of melancholy sounds, hooting low in the chimney, wailing with flutelike softness round the house.

It was perhaps eight o'clock when Rorie came in and pulled me mysteriously to the door. My uncle, it appeared, had frightened even his constant comrade; and Rorie, uneasy at his extravagance, prayed me to come out and share the watch. I hastened to do as I was asked; the more readily as, with fear and horror, and the electrical tension of the night, I was myself restless and disposed for action. I told Mary to be under no alarm, for I should be a safeguard on her father; and wrapping myself warmly in a plaid, I followed Rorie into the open air.

The night, though we were so little past midsummer, was as dark as January. Intervals of a groping twilight alternated with spells of utter blackness; and it was impossible to trace the reason of these changes in the flying horror of the sky. The wind blew the breath out of a man's nostrils; all heaven seemed to thunder overhead like one huge sail; and when there fell a momentary lull on Aros, we could hear the gusts dismally sweeping in the distance. Over all the lowlands of the Ross, the wind must have blown as fierce as on the open sea; and God only knows the uproar that was raging round the head of Ben Kyaw. Sheets of mingled spray and rain were driven in our faces. All round the isle of Aros the surf, with an incessant, hammering thunder, beat upon the reefs and beaches. Now louder in one place, now lower in another, like the combinations of orchestral music, the constant mass of sound was hardly varied for a moment. And loud above all this hurly-burly I could hear the changeful voices of the Roost and the intermittent roaring of the Merry Men. At that hour, there flashed into my mind the reason of the name that they were called. For the noise of them seemed almost mirthful, as it outtopped the other noises of the night; or if not mirthful, yet instinct with a portentous joviality. Nay, and it seemed even human. As when savage men have drunk away their reason, and, discarding speech, bawl together in their madness by the hour; so, to my ears, these deadly breakers shouted by Aros in the night.

Arm in arm, and staggering against the wind, Rorie and I won every yard of ground with conscious effort. We slipped on the wet sod, we fell together sprawling on the rocks. Bruised, drenched, beaten, and breathless, it must have taken us near half an hour to get from the house down to the Head that overlooks the Roost. There, it seemed, was my uncle's favourite observatory. Right in the face of it, where the cliff is highest and most sheer, a hump of earth, like a parapet, makes a place of shelter from the common winds where a man may sit in quiet and see the tide and the mad billows contending at his feet. As he might look down from the window of a house upon some street disturbance, so, from this post, he looks down upon the tumbling of the Merry Men. On such a night, of course, he peers upon a world of blackness, where the waters wheel and boil, where the waves joust together with the noise of an explosion, and the foam towers and vanishes in the twinkling of an eye. Never before had I seen the Merry Men thus violent. The fury, height, and transiency of their spoutings was a thing to be seen and not recounted. High over our heads on the cliff rose their white columns in the darkness; and the same instant, like phantoms, they were gone. Sometimes three at a time would thus aspire and vanish; sometimes a gust took them, and the spray would fall about us, heavy as a wave. And yet the spectacle was rather maddening in its levity than impressive by its force. Thought was beaten down by the confounding uproar; a gleeful vacancy possessed the brains of men, a state akin to madness; and I found myself at times following the dance of the Merry Men as it were a tune upon a jigging instrument.

I first caught sight of my uncle when we were still some yards away in one of the flying glimpses of twilight that chequered the pitch darkness of the night. He was standing up behind the parapet, his head thrown back and the bottle to his mouth. As he put it down, he saw and recognized us with a toss of one hand fleeringly above his head.

"Has he been drinking?" shouted I to Rorie.

"He will aye be drunk when the wind blaws," returned Rorie in the same high key, and it was all that I could do to hear him.

"Then—was he so—in February?" I inquired.

Rorie's "Ay" was a cause of joy to me. The murder, then, had not sprung in cold blood from calculation; it was an act of madness no more to be condemned than to be pardoned. My uncle was a dangerous madman, if you will, but he was not cruel and base as I had feared. Yet what a scene for a carouse, what an incredible vice, was this that the poor man had chosen! I have always thought drunkenness a wild and almost fearful pleasure, rather demoniacal than human; but drunkenness, out here in the roaring blackness, on the edge of a cliff above that hell of waters, the man's head spinning like the Roost, his foot tottering on the edge of death, his ear watching for the signs of shipwreck, surely that, if it were credible in any one, was morally impossible in a man like my uncle, whose mind was set upon a damnatory creed and haunted by the darkest superstitions. Yet so it was; and, as we reached the bight of shelter and could breathe again, I saw the man's eyes shining in the night with an unholy glimmer.

"Eh, Charlie, man, it's grand!" he cried. "See to them!" he continued, dragging me to the edge of the abyss from whence arose that deafening clamour and those clouds of spray; "see to them dancin' man! Is that no wicked?"

He pronounced the word with gusto, and I thought it suited with the scene.

"They're yowlin' for thon schooner," he went on, his thin, insane voice clearly audible in the shelter of the bank, "an' she's comin' aye nearer, aye nearer, aye nearer an' nearer an' nearer; an' they ken't, the folk kens it, they ken weel it's wi' them. Charlie, lad, they're a' drunk in yon schooner, a' dozened wi' drink. They were a' drunk in the *Christ-Anna*, at the hinder end. There's nane could droon at sea wantin' the brandy. Hoot awa, what do you ken?" with a sudden blast of anger. "I tell ye, it cannae be; they daurnae droon withoot it. Ha'e," holding out the bottle, "tak' a sowp."

I was about to refuse, but Rorie touched me as if in warning; and indeed I had already thought better of the movement. I took the bottle, therefore, and not only drank freely myself, but contrived to spill even more as I was doing so. It was pure spirit, and almost strangled me to swallow. My kinsman did not observe the loss, but, once more throwing back his head, drained the remainder to the dregs. Then, with a loud laugh, he cast the bottle forth among the Merry Men, who seemed to leap up, shouting to receive it.

"Ha'e, bairns!" he cried, "ther's your han'sel. Ye'll get bonnier nor that, or morning."

Suddenly, out in the black night before us, and not two hundred yards away, we heard, at a moment when the wind was silent, the clear note of a human voice. Instantly the wind swept howling down upon the Head, and the Roost bellowed, and churned, and danced with a new fury. But we had heard the sound, and we knew, with agony, that this was the doomed ship now close on ruin, and that what we heard was the voice of her master issuing his last command.

Crouching together on the edge, we waited, straining every sense, for the inevitable end. It was long, however, and to us it seemed like ages, ere the schooner suddenly appeared for one brief instant relieved against a tower of glimmering foam. I still see her reefed mainsail flapping loose, as the boom fell heavily across the deck; I still see the black outline of the hull, and still think I can distinguish the figure of a man stretched upon the tiller. Yet the whole sight we had of her passed swifter than lightning; the very wave that disclosed her fell burying her for ever; the mingled cry of many voices at the point of death rose and was quenched in the roaring of the Merry Men. And with that the tragedy was at an end. The strong ship with all her gear, and the lamp perhaps still burning in the cabin, the lives of so many men, precious surely to others, dear, at least, as heaven to themselves, had all, in that one moment gone down into the surging waters. They were gone like a dream. And the wind still ran and shouted, and the senseless waters in the Roost still leaped and tumbled as before.

How long we lay there together, we three, speechless and motionless, is more than I can tell, but it must have been for long. At length, one by one, and almost mechanically, we crawled back into the shelter of the bank. As I lay against the parapet, wholly wretched and not entirely master of my mind, I could hear my kinsman maundering to himself in an altered and melancholy mood. Now he would repeat to himself with maudlin iteration, "Sic a fecht as they had—sic a sair fecht as they had, puir lads, puir lads!" and anon he would bewail that "a' the gear was as gude's tint," because the ship had gone down among the Merry Men instead of stranding on the shore; and throughout, the name—the *Christ-Anna*—would come and go in his divagations, pronounced with shuddering awe. The storm all this time was rapidly abating. In half an hour the wind had fallen to a breeze, and the change was accompanied or caused by a heavy, cold, and plumping rain. I must then have fallen asleep, and when I came to myself, drenched, stiff, and unrefreshed, day had already broken, grey, wet, discomfortable day; the wind blew in faint and shifting capfuls, the tide was out, the Roost was at its lowest, and only the strong beating surf round all the coasts of Aros remained to witness of the furies of the night.

5. A Man out of the Sea

RORIE set out for the house in search of warmth and breakfast; but my uncle was bent upon examining the shores of Aros, and I felt it a part of my duty to accompany him throughout. He was now docile and quiet, but tremulous and weak in mind and body; and it was with the eagerness of a child that he pursued his exploration. He climbed down far upon the rocks; on the beaches he pursued the retreating breakers. The merest broken plank or rag or cordage was a treasure in his eyes to be secured at the peril of his life. To see him, with weak and stumbling footsteps, expose himself to the pursuit of the surf, or the snares and pitfalls of the weedy rock, kept me in a perpetual terror. My arm was ready to support him, my hand clutched him by the shirt, I helped him to draw his pitiful discoveries beyond the reach of the returning wave; a nurse accompanying a child of seven would have had no different experience.

Yet, weakened as he was by the reaction from his madness of the night before, the passions that smouldered in his nature were those of a strong man. His terror of the sea, although conquered for the moment, was still undiminished; had the sea been a lake of living flames, he could not have shrunk more panically from its touch; and once, when his foot slipped and he plunged to the mid-leg into a pool of water, the shriek that came up out of his soul was like the cry of death. He sat still for a while, panting like a dog, after that; but his desire for the spoils of shipwreck triumphed once more over his fears; once more he tottered among the curded foam; once more he crawled upon the rocks among the bursting bubbles; once more his whole heart seemed to be set on driftwood, fit, if it was fit for anything, to throw upon the fire. Pleased as he was with what he found, he still incessantly grumbled at his ill-fortune.

"Aros," he said, "is no a place for wrecks ava'—no ava'. A' the years I've dwalt here, this ane maks the second; and the best o' the gear clean tint!"

"Uncle," said I, for we were now on a stretch of open sand, where there was nothing to divert his mind, "I saw you last night as I never thought to see you—you were drunk."

"Na, na," he said, "no as bad as that. I had been drinking, though. And to tell ye the God's truth, it's a thing I cannae mend. There's nae soberer man than me in my ordnar; but when I hear the wind blaw in my lug, it's my belief that I gang gyte."

"You are a religious man," I replied, "and this is sin."

"Ou," he returned, "if it wasnae sin, I dinnae ken that I would care for't. Ye see, man, it's defiance. There's a sair spang o' the auld sin o' the warld in yon sea; it's an unchristian business at the best o't; an' whiles when it gets up, an' the wind skreighs—the wind an' her are a kind of sib, I'm thinkin'—an' thae Merry Men, the daft callants, blawin' and lauchin', and puir souls in the deid thraws warstlin' the leelang nicht wi' their bit ships—weel, it comes ower me like a glamour. I'm a deil, I ken't. But I think naething o' the puir sailor lads; I'm wi' the sea, I'm just like ane o' her ain Merry Men."

I thought I should touch him in a joint of his harness. I turned me towards the sea; the surf was running gaily, wave after wave, with their manes blowing behind them, riding one after another up the beach, towering, curving, falling one upon another on the trampled sand. Without, the salt air, the scared gulls, the widespread army of the sea-chargers, neighing to each other, as they gathered to the assault of Aros; and close before us, that line on the flat sands that, with all their number and their fury, they might never pass.

"Thus far shalt thou go," said I, "and no farther." And then I quoted as solemnly as I was able a verse that I had often before fitted to the chorus of the breakers:

But yet the Lord that is on high
  Is more of might by far,
Than noise of many waters is,
  As great sea billows are.

"Ay," said my kinsman, "at the hinder end, the Lord will triumph; I dinnae misdoobt that. But here on earth, even silly men-folk daur Him to His face. It is nae wise; I am nae sayin' that it's wise; but it's the pride of the eye, and it's the lust o' life, an' it's the wale o' pleesures."

I said no more, for we had now begun to cross a neck of land that lay between us and Sandag; and I withheld my last appeal to the man's better reason till we should stand upon the spot associated with his crime. Nor did he pursue the subject; but he walked beside me with a firmer step. The call that I had made upon his mind acted like a stimulant, and I could see that he had forgotten his search for worthless jetsam, in a profound, gloomy, and yet stirring train of thought. In three or four minutes we had topped the brae and begun to go down upon Sandag. The wreck had been roughly handled by the sea; the stem had been spun round and dragged a little lower down; and perhaps the stern had been forced a little higher, for the two parts now lay entirely separate on the beach. When we came to the grave I stopped, uncovered my head in the thick rain, and, looking my kinsman in the face, addressed him.

"A man," said I, "was in God's providence suffered to escape from mortal dangers; he was poor, he was naked, he was wet, he was weary, he was a stranger; he had every claim upon the bowels of your compassion; it may be that he was the salt of the earth, holy, helpful, and kind; it may be that he was a man laden with iniquities to whom death was the beginning of torment. I ask you in the sight of heaven: Gordon Darnaway, where is the man for whom Christ died?"

He started visibly at the last words; but there came no answer, and his face expressed no feeling but a vague alarm.

"You were my father's brother," I continued; "you have taught me to count your house as if it were my father's house; and we are both sinful men walking before the Lord among the sins and dangers of this life. It is by our evil that God leads us into good; we sin, I dare not say to His temptation, but I must say with His consent; and to any but the brutish man his sins are the beginning of wisdom. God has warned you by this crime; He warns you still by the bloody grave between our feet; and if there shall follow no repentance, no improvement, no return to Him, what can we look for but the following of some memorable judgment?"

Even as I spoke the words, the eyes of my uncle wandered from my face. A change fell upon his looks that cannot be described; his features seemed to dwindle in size, the colour faded from his cheeks, one hand rose waveringly and pointed over my shoulder into the distance, and the oft-repeated name fell once more from his lips: "The *Christ-Anna*!"

I turned, and if I was not appalled to the same degree, as I return thanks to Heaven that I had not the cause, I was still startled by the sight that met my eyes. The form of a man stood upright on the cabin-hutch of the wrecked ship; his back was towards us; he appeared to be scanning the offing with shaded eyes, and his figure was relieved to its full height, which was plainly very great, against the sea and sky. I have said a thousand times that I am not superstitious; but at that moment, with my mind running upon death and sin, the unexplained appearance of a stranger on that sea-girt, solitary island filled me with a surprise that bordered close on terror. It seemed scarce possible that any human soul should have come ashore alive in such a sea as had raged last night along the coasts of Aros; and the only vessel within miles had gone down before our eyes among the Merry Men. I was assailed with doubts that made suspense unbearable, and, to put the matter to the touch at once, stepped forward and hailed the figure like a ship.

He turned about, and I thought he started to behold us. At this my courage instantly revived, and I called and signed to him to draw near, and he, on his part, dropped immediately to the sands, and began slowly to approach, with many stops and hesitations. At each repeated mark of the man's uneasiness I grew the more confident myself, and I advanced another step, encouraging him as I did so with my head and hand. It was plain the castaway had heard indifferent accounts of our island hospitality; and indeed, about this time, the people farther north had a sorry reputation.

"Why," I said, "the man is black!"

And just at that moment, in a voice that I could scarce have recognized, my kinsman began swearing and praying in a mingled stream. I looked at him; he had fallen on his knees, his face was agonized; at each step of the castaway's the pitch of his voice rose, the volubility of his utterance and the fervour of his language redoubled. I call it prayer, for it was addressed to God; but surely no such ranting incongruities were ever before addressed to the Creator by a creature; surely, if prayer can be a sin, this mad harangue was sinful. I ran to my kinsman, I seized him by the shoulders, I dragged him to his feet.

"Silence, man," said I, "respect your God in words, if not in action. Here, on the very scene of your transgressions, He sends you an occasion of atonement. Forward and embrace it; welcome like a father yon creature who comes trembling to your mercy."

With that, I tried to force him towards the black; but he felled me to the ground, burst from my grasp, leaving the shoulder of his jacket, and fled up the hillside towards the top of Aros like a deer. I staggered to my feet again, bruised and somewhat stunned; the negro had paused in surprise, perhaps in terror, some halfway between me and the wreck; my uncle was already far away, bounding from rock to rock; and I thus found myself torn for a time between two duties. But I judged, and I pray Heaven that I judged rightly, in favour of the poor wretch upon the sands; his misfortune was at least not plainly of his own creation; it was one, besides, that I could certainly relieve; and I had begun by that time to regard my uncle as an incurable and dismal lunatic. I advanced accordingly towards the black who now awaited my approach with folded arms, like one prepared for either destiny. As I came nearer, he reached forth his hand with a great gesture, such as I had seen from the pulpit, and spoke to me in something of a pulpit voice, but not a word was comprehensible. I tried him first in English, then in Gaelic, both in vain; so that it was clear we must rely upon the tongue of looks and gestures. Thereupon I signed to him to follow me, which he did readily and with a grave obeisance like a fallen king; all the while there had come no shade of alteration in his face, neither of anxiety while he was still waiting, nor of relief now that he was reassured; if he were a slave, as I supposed, I could not but judge he must have fallen from some high place in his own country, and fallen as he was, I could not but admire his bearing. As we passed the grave, I paused and raised my hands and eyes to heaven in token of respect and sorrow for the dead; and he, as if in answer, bowed low and spread his hands abroad; it was a strange motion, but done like a thing of common custom; and I supposed it was ceremonial in the land from which he came. At the same time he pointed to my uncle, whom we could just see perched upon a knoll, and touched his head to indicate that he was mad.

We took the long way round the shore, for I feared to excite my uncle if we struck across the island; and as we walked, I had time enough to mature the little dramatic exhibition by which I hoped to satisfy my doubts. Accordingly, pausing on a rock, I proceeded to imitate before the negro the action of the man whom I had seen the day before taking bearings with the compass at Sandag. He understood me at once, and, taking the imitation out of my hands, showed me where the boat was, pointed out seaward as if to indicate the position of the schooner, and then down along the edge of the rock with the words *"Espirito Santo,"* strangely pronounced, but clear enough for recognition. I had thus been right in my conjecture; the pretended historical inquiry had been but a cloak for treasure-hunting; the man who had played on Dr. Robertson was the same as the foreigner who visited Grisapol in spring, and now, with many others, lay dead under the Roost of Aros: there had their greed brought them, there should their bones be tossed for evermore. In the meantime the black continued his imitation of the scene, now looking up skyward as though watching the approach of the storm; now, in the character of a seaman, waving the rest to come aboard; now as an officer, running along the rock and entering the boat; and anon bending over imaginary oars with the air of a hurried boatman; but all with the same solemnity of manner, so that I was never even moved to smile. Lastly, he indicated to me, by a pantomime not to be described in words, how he himself had gone up to examine the stranded wreck, and, to his grief and indignation, had been deserted by his comrades; and thereupon folded his arms once more, and stooped his head, like one accepting fate.

The mystery of his presence being thus solved for me, I explained to him by means of a sketch the fate of the vessel and of all aboard her. He showed no surprise nor sorrow, and, with a sudden lifting of his open hand, seemed to dismiss his former friends or masters (whichever they had been) into God's pleasure. Respect came upon me and grew stronger, the more I observed him; I saw he had a powerful mind and a sober and severe character, such as I loved to commune with; and before we reached the house of Aros I had almost forgotten, and wholly forgiven him, his uncanny colour.

To Mary I told all that had passed without suppression, though I own my heart failed me; but I did wrong to doubt her sense of justice.

"You did the right," she said. "God's will be done." And she set out meat for us at once.

As soon as I was satisfied, I bade Rorie keep an eye upon the castaway, who was still eating, and set forth again myself to find my uncle. I had not gone far before I saw him sitting in the same place, upon the very topmost knoll, and seemingly in the same attitude as when I had last observed him. From that point, as I have said, the most of Aros and the neighbouring Ross would be spread below him like a map; and it was plain that he kept a bright look-out in all directions, for my head had scarcely risen above the summit of the first ascent before he had leaped to his feet and turned as if to face me. I hailed him at once, as well as I was able, in the same tones and words as I had often used before, when I had come to summon him to dinner. He made not so much as a movement in reply. I passed on a little farther, and again tried parley, with the same result. But when I began a second time to advance, his insane fears blazed up again, and still in dead silence, but with incredible speed, he began to flee from before me along the rocky summit of the hill. An hour before, he had been dead weary, and I had been comparatively active. But now his strength was recruited by the fervour of insanity, and it would have been vain for me to dream of pursuit. Nay, the very attempt, I thought, might have inflamed his terrors, and thus increased the miseries of our position. And I had nothing left but to turn homeward and make my sad report to Mary.

She heard it, as she had heard the first, with a concerned composure, and, bidding me lie down and take that rest of which I stood so much in need, set forth herself in quest of her misguided father. At that age it would have been a strange thing that put me from either meat or sleep; I slept long and deep; and it was already long past noon before I awoke and came downstairs into the kitchen. Mary, Rorie, and the black castaway were seated about the fire in silence, and I could see that Mary had been weeping. There was cause enough, as I soon learned, for tears. First she, and then Rorie, had been forth to seek my uncle; each in turn had found him perched upon the hill-top, and from each in turn he had silently and swiftly fled. Rorie had tried to chase him, but in vain; madness lent a new vigour to his bounds; he sprang from rock to rock over the wildest gullies; he scoured like the wind along the hill-tops; he doubled and twisted like a hare before the dogs; and Rorie at length gave in; and the last that he saw, my uncle was seated as before upon the crest of Aros. Even during the hottest excitement of the chase, even when the fleet-footed servant had come, for a moment, very near to capture him, the poor lunatic had uttered not a sound. He fled, and he was silent like a beast, and this silence had terrified his pursuer.

There was something heart-breaking in the situation. How to capture the madman, how to feed him in the meanwhile, and what to do with him when he was captured, were the three difficulties that we had to solve.

"The black," said I, "is the cause of this attack. It may even be his presence in the house that keeps my uncle on the hill. We have done the fair thing; he has been fed and warmed under this roof; and now I propose that Rorie put him across the bay in the coble, and take him through the Ross as far as Grisapol."

In this proposal Mary heartily concurred; and bidding the black follow us, we all three descended to the pier. Certainly, Heaven's will was declared against Gordon Darnaway; a thing had happened, never paralleled before in Aros; during the storm the coble had broken loose, and, striking on the rough splinters of the pier, now lay in four feet of water with one side stove in. Three days of work at least would be required to make her float. But I was not to be beaten. I led the whole party round to where the gut was narrowest, swam to the other side, and called to the black to follow me. He signed, with the same clearness and quiet as before, that he knew not the art; and there was truth apparent in his signals, it would have occurred to none of us to doubt his truth; and that hope being over, we must all go back even as we came to the house of Aros, the negro walking in our midst without embarrassment.

All we could do that day was to make one more attempt to communicate with the unhappy madman. Again he was visible on his perch; again he fled in silence. But food and a great cloak were at least left for his comfort; the rain, besides, had cleared away, and the night promised to be even warm. We might compose ourselves, we thought, until the morrow; rest was the chief requisite, that we might be strengthened for unusual exertions, and as none cared to talk, we separated at an early hour.

I lay long awake planning a campaign for the morrow. I was to place the black on the side of Sandag, whence he should head my uncle towards the house; Rorie on the west, I on the east, were to complete the cordon, as best we might. It seemed to me, the more I recalled the configuration of the island, that it should be possible, though hard, to force him down upon the low ground along Aros Bay; and once there, even with the strength of his madness, ultimate escape was hardly to be feared. It was on his terror of the black that I relied; for I made sure, however he might run, it would not be in the direction of the man whom he supposed to have returned from the dead, and thus one point of the compass at least would be secure.

When at length I fell asleep, it was to be awakened shortly after by a dream of wrecks, black men, and submarine adventure; and I found myself so shaken and fevered that I arose, descended the stair, and stepped out before the house. Within, Rorie and the black were asleep together in the kitchen; outside was a wonderful night clear of stars, with here and there a cloud still hanging, last stragglers of the tempest. It was near the top of the flood, and the Merry Men were roaring in the windless quiet of the night. Never, not even in the height of the tempest, had I heard their song with greater awe. Now, when the winds were gathered home, when the deep was dandling itself back into its summer slumber, and when the stars rained their gentle light over land and sea, the voice of these tide-breakers was still raised for havoc. They seemed, indeed, to be a part of the world's evil and the tragic side of life. Nor were their meaningless vociferations the only sounds that broke the silence of the night. For I could hear, now shrill and thrilling and now almost drowned, the note of a human voice that accompanied the uproar of the Roost. I knew it for my kinsman's, and a great fear fell upon me of God's judgments and the evil in the world. I went back again into the darkness of the house as into a place of shelter, and lay long upon my bed pondering these mysteries.

It was late when I again woke, and I leaped into my clothes and hurried to the kitchen. No one was there; Rorie and the black had both stealthily departed long before, and my heart stood still at the discovery. I could rely on Rorie's heart, but I placed no trust in his discretion. If he had thus set out without a word, he was plainly bent upon some service to my uncle. But what service could he hope to render even alone, far less in the company of the man in whom my uncle found his fears incarnated? Even if I were not already too late to prevent some deadly mischief, it was plain I must delay no longer. With the thought I was out of the house, and often as I have run on the rough sides of Aros, I never ran as I did that fatal morning. I do not believe I put twelve minutes to the whole ascent.

My uncle was gone from his perch. The basket had indeed been torn open and the meat scattered on the turf; but, as we found afterwards, no mouthful had been tasted, and there was not another trace of human existence in that wide field of view. Day had already filled the clear heavens; the sun already lighted in a rosy bloom upon the crest of Ben Kyaw; but all below me the rude knolls of Aros and the shield of sea lay steeped in the clear darkling twilight of the dawn.

"Rorie!" I cried; and again "Rorie!" My voice died in the silence, but there came no answer back. If there were indeed an enterprise afoot to catch my uncle, it was plainly not in fleetness of foot, but in dexterity of stalking, that the hunters placed their trust. I ran on farther, keeping the higher spurs, and looking right and left, nor did I pause again till I was on the mount above Sandag. I could see the wreck, the uncovered belt of sand, the waves idly beating the long ledge of rocks, and on either hand the tumbled knolls, boulders, and gullies of the island. But still no human being.

At a stride the sunshine fell on Aros, and the shadows and colours leaped into being. Not half a moment later, below me to the west, sheep began to scatter as in a panic. There came a cry. I saw my uncle running. I saw the black jump up in hot pursuit; and before I had time to understand, Rorie also had appeared, calling directions in Gaelic as to a dog herding sheep.

I took to my heels to interfere, and perhaps I had done better to have waited where I was, for I was the means of cutting off the madman's last escape. There was nothing before him from that moment but the grave, the wreck, and the sea in Sandag Bay. And yet Heaven knows that what I did was for the best.

My uncle Gordon saw in what direction, horrible to him, the chase was driving him. He doubled, darting to the right and left; but high as the fever ran in his veins, the black was still the swifter. Turn where he would, he was still forestalled, still driven toward the scene of his crime. Suddenly he began to shriek aloud, so that the coast re-echoed; and now both I and Rorie were calling on the black to stop. But all was vain, for it was written otherwise. The pursuer still ran, the chase still sped before him screaming; they avoided the grave and skimmed close past the timbers of the wreck; in a breath they had cleared the sand, and still my kinsman did not pause, but dashed straight into the surf; and the black, now almost within reach, still followed swiftly behind him. Rorie and I both stopped, for the thing was now beyond the hands of men, and these were the decrees of God that came to pass before our eyes. There was never a sharper ending. On that steep beach they were beyond their depth at a bound; neither could swim; the black rose once for a moment with a throttling cry; but the current had them, racing seaward, and if ever they came up again, which God alone can tell, it would be ten minutes after, at the far end of Aros Roost, where the seabirds hover fishing.

The Treasure of Franchard

1. By the dying Mountebank

THEY HAD SENT for the doctor from Bourron before six. About eight some villagers came round for the performance, and were told how matters stood. It seemed a liberty for a mountebank to fall ill like real people, and they made off again in dudgeon. By ten Madame Tentaillon was gravely alarmed, and had sent down the street for Doctor Desprez.

The Doctor was at work over his manuscripts in one corner of the little dining-room, and his wife was asleep over the fire in another, when the messenger arrived.

"Sapristi!" said the Doctor, "you should have sent for me before. It was a case for hurry." And he followed the messenger as he was, in his slippers and skull-cap.

The inn was not thirty yards away, but the messenger did not stop there; he went in at one door and out by another into the court, and then led the way by a flight of steps beside the stable to the loft where the mountebank lay sick. If Doctor Desprez were to live a thousand years, he would never forget his arrival in that room; for not only was the scene picturesque, but the moment made a date in his existence. We reckon our lives, I hardly know why, from the date of our first sorry appearance in society, as if from a first humiliation; for no actor can come upon the stage with a worse grace. Not to go farther back, which would be judged too curious, there are subsequently many moving and decisive accidents in the lives of all, which would make as logical a period as this of birth. And here, for instance, Doctor Desprez, a man past forty, who had made what is called a failure in life, and was moreover married, found himself at a new point of departure when he opened the door of the loft above Tentaillon's stable.

It was a large place, lighted only by a single candle set upon the floor. The mounteback lay on his back upon a pallet; a large man, with a Quixotic nose inflamed with drinking. Madame Tentaillon stooped over him, applying a hot water and mustard embrocation to his feet; and on a chair close by sat a little fellow of eleven or twelve, with his feet dangling. These three were the only occupants, except the shadows. But the shadows were a company in themselves; the extent of the room exaggerated them to a gigantic size, and from the low position of the candle the light struck upwards and produced deformed foreshortenings. The mountebank's profile was enlarged upon the wall in caricature, and it was strange to see his nose shorten and lengthen as the flame was blown about by draughts. As for Madame Tentaillon, her shadow was no more than a gross hump of shoulders, with now and again a hemisphere of head. The chair legs were spindled out as long as stilts, and the boy sat perched atop of them, like a cloud, in the corner of the roof.

It was the boy who took the Doctor's fancy. He had a great arched skull, the forehead and the hands of a musician, and a pair of haunting eyes. It was not merely that these eyes were large, or steady, or the softest ruddy brown. There was a look in them, besides, which thrilled the Doctor and made him half uneasy. He was sure he had seen such a look before, and yet he could not remember how or where. It was as if this boy, who was quite a stranger to him, had the eyes of an old friend or an old enemy. And the boy would give him no peace; he seemed profoundly indifferent to what was going on, or rather abstracted from it in a superior contemplation, beating gently with his feet against the bars of the chair, and holding his hands folded on his lap. But, for all that, his eyes kept following the Doctor about the room with a thoughtful fixity of gaze. Desprez could not tell whether he was fascinating the boy, or the boy was fascinating him. He busied himself over the sick man: he put questions, he felt the pulse, he jested, he grew a little hot and swore: and still, whenever he looked round, there were the brown eyes waiting for his with the same inquiring, melancholy gaze.

At last the Doctor hit on the solution at a leap. He remembered the look now. The little fellow, although he was as straight as a dart, had the eyes that go usually with a crooked back; he was not at all deformed, and yet a deformed person seemed to be looking at you from below his brows. The Doctor drew a long breath, he was so much relieved to find a theory (for he loved theories) and to explain away his interest.

For all that, he despatched the invalid with unusual haste, and, still kneeling with one knee on the floor, turned a little round and looked the boy over at his leisure. The boy was not in the least put out, but looked placidly back at the Doctor.

"Is this your father?" asked Desprez.

"Oh, no," returned the boy; "my master."

"Are you fond of him?" continued the Doctor.

"No, sir," said the boy.

Madame Tentaillon and Desprez exchanged expressive glances.

"That is bad, my man," resumed the latter, with a shade of sternness. "Everyone should be fond of the dying, or conceal their sentiments; and your master here is dying. If I have watched a bird a little while stealing my cherries, I have a thought of disappointment when he flies away over my garden wall, and I see him steer for the forest and vanish. How much more a creature such as this, so strong, so astute, so richly endowed with faculties! When I think that, in a few hours, the speech will be silenced, the breath extinct, and even the shadow vanished from the wall, I who never saw him, this lady who knew him only as a guest, are touched with some affection."

The boy was silent for a little, and appeared to be reflecting.

"You did not know him," he replied at last. "He was a bad man."

"He is a little pagan," said the landlady. "For that matter they are all the same, these mountebanks, tumblers, artists, and what not. They have no interior."

But the Doctor was still scrutinising the little pagan, his eyebrows knotted and uplifted.

"What is your name?" he asked.

"Jean-Marie," said the lad.

Desprez leaped upon him with one of his sudden flashes of excitement, and felt his head all over from an ethnological point of view.

"Celtic, Celtic!" he said.

"Celtic!" cried Madame Tentaillon, who had perhaps confounded the word with hydrocephalous. "Poor lad! is it dangerous?"

"That depends," returned the Doctor grimly. And then once more addressing the boy: "And what do you do for your living, Jean-Marie?" he inquired.

"I tumble," was the answer.

"So! Tumble?" repeated Desprez. "Probably healthful. I hazard the guess, Madame Tentaillon, that tumbling is a healthful way of life. And have you never done anything else but tumble?"

"Before I learned that, I used to steal," answered Jean-Marie gravely.

"Upon my word!" cried the Doctor. "You are a nice little man for your age. Madame, when my *confrère* comes from Bourron, you will communicate my unfavourable opinion. I leave the case in his hands; but of course, on any alarming symptom, above all if there should be a sign of rally, do not hesitate to knock me up. I am a doctor no longer, I thank God; but I have been one. Good-night, madame. Good sleep to you, Jean-Marie."

2. Morning Talk

DOCTOR Desprez always rose early. Before the smoke arose, before the first cart rattled over the bridge to the day's labour in the fields, he was to be found wandering in his garden. Now he would pick a bunch of grapes; now he would eat a big pear under the trellis; now he would draw all sorts of fancies on the path with the end of his cane; now he would go down and watch the river running endlessly past the timber landing-place at which he moored his boat. There was no time, he used to say, for making theories like the early morning. "I rise earlier than anyone else in the village," he once boasted. "It is a fair consequence that I know more and wish to do less with my knowledge."

The Doctor was a connoisseur of sunrises, and loved a good theatrical effect to usher in the day. He had a theory of dew, by which he could predict the weather. Indeed, most things served him to that end: the sound of the bells from all the neighbouring villages, the smell of the forest, the visits and the behaviour of both birds and fishes, the look of the plants in his garden, the disposition of cloud, the colour of the light, and last, although not least, the arsenal of meteorological instruments in a louvre-boarded hutch upon the lawn. Ever since he had settled at Gretz, he had been growing more and more into the local meteorologist, the unpaid champion of the local climate. He thought at first there was no place so healthful in the arrondissement. By the end of the second year he protested there was none so wholesome in the whole department. And for some time before he met Jean-Marie he had been prepared to challenge all France and the better part of Europe for a rival to his chosen spot.

"Doctor," he would say—"doctor is a foul word. It should not be used to ladies. It implies disease. I remark it, as a flaw in our civilization, that we have not the proper horror of disease. Now I, for my part, have washed my hands of it; I have renounced my laureation; I am no doctor; I am only a worshipper of the true goddess Hygeia. Ah, believe me, it is she who has the cestus! And here, in this exiguous hamlet, has she placed her shrine: here she dwells and lavishes her gifts; here I walk with her in the early morning, and she shows me how strong she has made the peasants, how fruitful she has made the fields, how the trees grow up tall and comely under her eyes, and the fishes in the river become clean and agile at her presence.—Rheumatism!" he would cry, on some malapert interruption, "oh, yes, I believe we do have a little rheumatism. That could hardly be avoided, you know, on a river. And of course the place stands a little low; and the meadows are marshy, there's no doubt. But, my dear sir, look at Bourron! Bourron stands high. Bourron is close to the forest; plenty of ozone there, you would say. Well, compared with Gretz, Bourron is a perfect shambles."

The morning after he had been summoned to the dying mountebank, the Doctor visited the wharf at the tail of his garden, and had a long look at the running water. This he called prayer; but whether his adorations were addressed to the goddess Hygeia or some more orthodox deity, never plainly appeared. For he had uttered doubtful oracles, sometimes declaring that a river was the type of bodily health, sometimes extolling it as the great moral preacher, continually preaching peace, continuity, and diligence to man's tormented spirits. After he had watched a mile or so of the clear water running by before his eyes, seen a fish or two come to the surface with a gleam of silver, and sufficiently admired the long shadows of the trees falling half across the river from the opposite bank, with patches of moving sunlight in between, he strolled once more up the garden and through his house into the street, feeling cool and renovated.

The sound of his feet upon the causeway began the business of the day; for the village was still sound asleep. The church tower looked very airy in the sunlight; a few birds that turned about it seemed to swim in an atmosphere of more than usual rarity; and the Doctor, walking in long transparent shadows, filled his lungs amply, and proclaimed himself well contented with the morning.

On one of the posts before Tentaillon's carriage entry he espied a little dark figure perched in a meditative attitude, and immediately recognized Jean-Marie.

"Aha!" he said, stopping before him humorously, with a hand on either knee. "So we rise early in the morning, do we? It appears to me that we have all the vices of a philosopher."

The boy got to his feet and made a grave salutation.

"And how is our patient?" asked Desprez.

It appeared the patient was about the same.

"And why do you rise early in the morning?" he pursued.

Jean-Marie, after a long silence, professed that he hardly knew.

"You hardly know?" repeated Desprez. "We hardly know anything, my man, until we try to learn. Interrogate your consciousness. Come, push me this inquiry home. Do you like it?"

"Yes," said the boy slowly; "yes, I like it."

"And why do you like it?" continued the Doctor. "(We are now pursuing the Socratic method.) Why do you like it?"

"It is quiet," answered Jean-Marie; "and I have nothing to do; and then I feel as if I were good."

Doctor Desprez took a seat on the post at the opposite side. He was beginning to take an interest in the talk, for the boy plainly thought before he spoke, and tried to answer truly. "It appears you have a taste for feeling good," said the Doctor. "Now, there you puzzle me extremely; for I thought you said you were a thief; and the two are incompatible."

"It is very bad to steal?" asked Jean-Marie.

"Such is the general opinion, little boy," replied the Doctor.

"No; but I mean as I stole," explained the other. "For I had no choice. I think it is surely right to have bread; it must be right to have bread, there comes so plain a want of it. And then they beat me cruelly if I returned with nothing," he added. "I was not ignorant of right and wrong; for before that I had been well taught by a priest, who was very kind to me." (The Doctor made a horrible grimace at the word "priest.") "But it seemed to me, when one had nothing to eat and was beaten, it was a different affair. I would not have stolen for tartlets, I believe; but anyone would steal for baker's bread."

"And so I suppose," said the Doctor, with a rising sneer, "you prayed God to forgive you, and explained the case to Him at length."

"Why, sir?" asked Jean-Marie. "I do not see."

"Your priest would see, however," retorted Desprez.

"Would he?" asked the boy, troubled for the first time. "I should have thought God would have known."

"Eh?" snarled the Doctor.

"I should have thought God would have understood me," replied the other. "You do not, I see; but then it was God that made me think so, was it not?"

"Little boy, little boy," said Doctor Desprez, "I told you already you had the vices of philosophy; if you display the virtues also, I must go. I am a student of the blessed laws of health, an observer of plain and temperate nature in her common walks; and I cannot preserve my equanimity in presence of a monster. Do you understand?"

"No, sir," said the boy.

"I will make my meaning clear to you," replied the Doctor. "Look there at the sky—behind the belfry first, where it is so light, and then up and up, turning your chin back, right to the top of the dome, where it is already as blue as at noon. Is not that a beautiful colour? Does it not please the heart? We have seen it all our lives, until it has grown in with our familiar thoughts. Now," changing his tone, "suppose that sky to become suddenly of a live and fiery amber, like the colour of clear coals, and growing scarlet towards the top—I do not say it would be any less beautiful; but would you like it as well?"

"I suppose not," answered Jean-Marie.

"Neither do I like you," returned the Doctor roughly. "I hate all odd people, and you are the most curious little boy in all the world."

Jean-Marie seemed to ponder for a while, and then he raised his head again and looked over at the Doctor with an air of candid inquiry. "But are not you a very curious gentleman?" he asked.

The Doctor threw away his stick, bounded on the boy, clasped him to his bosom, and kissed him on both cheeks. "Admirable, admirable imp!" he cried. "What a morning, what an hour for a theorist of forty-two! No," he continued, apostrophizing Heaven. "I did not know such boys existed; I was ignorant they made them so; I had doubted my race; and now! It is like," he added, picking up his stick, "like a lovers' meeting. I have bruised my favourite staff in that moment of enthusiasm. The injury, however, is not grave." He caught the boy looking at him in obvious wonder, embarrassment, and alarm. "Hullo!" said he, "why do you look at me like that? Egad, I believe the boy despises me. Do you despise me, boy?"

"Oh, no," replied Jean-Marie seriously; "only I do not understand."

"You must excuse me, sir," returned the Doctor, with gravity; "I am still so young. Oh, hang him!" he added to himself. And he took his seat again and observed the boy sardonically. "He has spoiled the quiet of my morning," thought he. "I shall be nervous all day, and have a febricule when I digest. Let me compose myself." And so he dismissed his preoccupations by an effort of the will which he had long practised, and let his soul roam abroad in the contemplation of the morning. He inhaled the air, tasting it critically as a connoisseur tastes a vintage, and prolonging the expiration with hygienic gusto. He counted the little flecks of cloud along the sky. He followed the movements of the birds round the church tower—making long sweeps, hanging poised, or turning airy somersaults in fancy, and beating the wind with imaginary pinions. And in this way he regained peace of mind and animal composure, conscious of his limbs, conscious of the sight of his eyes, conscious that the air had a cool taste, like a fruit, at the top of his throat; and at last, in complete abstraction, he began to sing. The Doctor had but one air—"Malbrouck s'en va-t-en guerre"; even with that he was on terms of mere politeness; and his musical exploits were always reserved for moments when he was alone and entirely happy.

He was recalled to earth rudely by a pained expression on the boy's face. "What do you think of my singing?" he inquired, stopping in the middle of a note; and then, after he had waited some little while and received no answer: "What do you think of my singing?" he repeated imperiously.

"I do not like it," faltered Jean-Marie.

"Oh, come!" cried the Doctor. "Possibly you are a performer yourself?"

"I sing better than that," replied the boy.

The Doctor eyed him for some seconds in stupefaction. He was aware that he was angry, and blushed for himself in consequence, which made him angrier. "If this is how you address your master!" he said at last, with a shrug and a flourish of his arms.

"I do not speak to him at all," returned the boy. "I do not like him."

"Then you like me?" snapped Doctor Desprez, with unusual eagerness.

"I do not know," answered Jean-Marie.

The Doctor rose. "I shall wish you a good morning," he said. "You are too much for me. Perhaps you have blood in your veins, perhaps celestial ichor, or perhaps you circulate nothing more gross than respirable air; but of one thing I am inexpugnably assured—that you are no human being. No, boy"—shaking his stick at him—"you are not a human being. Write, write it in your memory—'I am not a human being—I have no pretension to be a human being—I am a dive, a dream, an angel, an acrostic, an illusion—what you please, but not a human being.' And so accept my humble salutations and farewell!"

And with that the Doctor made off along the street in some emotion, and the boy stood, mentally gaping, where he left him.

3. The Adoption

MADAME Desprez, who answered to the Christian name of Anastasie, presented an agreeable type of her sex; exceedingly wholesome to look upon, a stout *brune,* with cool smooth cheeks, steady, dark eyes, and hands that neither art nor nature could improve. She was like the sort of person over whom adversity passes like a summer cloud; she might in the worst of conjunctions knit her brows into one vertical furrow for a moment, but the next it would be gone. She had much of the placidity of a contented nun; with little of her piety, however; for Anastasie was of a very mundane nature, fond of oysters and old wine, and somewhat bold pleasantries, and devoted to her husband for her own sake rather than for his. She was imperturbably good-natured, but had no idea of self-sacrifice. To live in that pleasant old house, with a green garden behind and bright flowers about the window, to eat and drink of the best, to gossip with a neighbour for a quarter of an hour, never to wear stays or a dress except when she went to Fontainebleau shopping, to be kept in a continual supply of racy novels, and to be married to Doctor Desprez and have no ground of jealousy, filled the cup of her nature to the brim. Those who had known the Doctor in bachelor days, when he had aired quite as many theories, but of a different order, attributed his present philosophy to the study of Anastasie. It was her brute enjoyment that he rationalized and perhaps vainly imitated.

Madame Desprez was an artist in the kitchen, and made coffee to a nicety. She had a knack of tidiness, with which she had infected the Doctor; everything was in its place; everything capable of polish shone gloriously; and dust was a thing banished from her empire. Aline, their single servant, had no other business in the world but to scour and burnish. So Doctor Desprez lived in his house like a fatted calf, warmed and cosseted to his heart's content.

The midday meal was excellent. There was a ripe melon, a fish from the river in a memorable Béarnaise sauce, a fat fowl in a fricassee, and a dish of asparagus, followed by some fruit. The Doctor drank half a bottle *plus* one glass, the wife half a bottle *minus* the same quantity, which was a marital privilege, of an excellent Côte-Rôtie, seven years old. Then the coffee was brought, and a flask of Chartreuse for madame, for the Doctor despised and distrusted such decoctions; and then Aline left the wedded pair to the pleasures of memory and digestion.

"It is a very fortunate circumstance, my cherished one," observed the Doctor—"this coffee is adorable—a very fortunate circumstance upon the whole—Anastasie, I beseech you, go without that poison for to-day; only one day, and you will feel the benefit, I pledge my reputation."

"What is this fortunate circumstance, my friend?" inquired Anastasie, not heeding his protest, which was of daily recurrence.

"That we have no children, my beautiful," replied the Doctor. "I think of it more and more as the years go on, and with more and more gratitude towards the Power that dispenses such afflictions. Your health, my darling, my studious quiet, our little kitchen delicacies, how they would all have suffered, how they would all have been sacrificed! And for what? Children are the last word of human imperfection. Health flees before their face. They cry, my dear; they put vexatious questions; they demand to be fed, to be washed, to be educated, to have their noses blown; and then, when the time comes, they break our hearts, as I break this piece of sugar. A pair of professed egoists, like you and me, should avoid offspring, like an infidelity."

"Indeed!" said she; and she laughed. "Now, that is like you—to take credit for the thing you could not help."

"My dear," returned the Doctor solemnly, "we might have adopted."

"Never!" cried madame. "Never, Doctor, with my consent. If the child were my own flesh and blood, I would not say no. But to take another person's indiscretions on my shoulders—my dear friend, I have too much sense."

"Precisely," replied the Doctor. "We both had. And I am all the better pleased with our wisdom, because—because——" He looked at her sharply.

"Because what?" she asked, with a faint premonition of danger.

"Because I have found the right person," said the Doctor firmly, "and shall adopt him this afternoon."

Anastasie looked at him out of a mist. "You have lost your reason," she said; and there was a clang in her voice that seemed to threaten trouble.

17. This and the following four plates are from the first illustrated edition of *Treasure Island*, published in London in 1885. The illustrator, or perhaps illustrators, is unknown. In a letter to his father about this edition, Stevenson wrote: ". . . the French pictures are admirable. The artist has got his types up in Hogarth; he is full of fire and spirit, can draw and can compose, and has understood the book as I meant it . . ." On this page, the passing of the Black Spot: "I saw him pass something from the hollow of the hand that held his stick into the palm of the captain's, which closed upon it instantly."

18. *Treasure Island:* "I said good-bye to mother and the cove where I had lived since I was born, and the dear old 'Admiral Benbow'."

19. *Treasure Island:* "In I got bodily into the apple barrel . . . and, before I had heard a dozen words, I would not have shown myself for all the world."

20. *Treasure Island*, the meeting with Ben Gunn: "Then he hesitated . . . and held out his clasped hands in supplication . . ."

21. *Treasure Island*, the escape from the *Hispaniola*: "The squire raised his gun, the rowing ceased, and we leaned over to the other side to keep the balance . . ."

22. This and the following plate are from *Kidnapped* (London, 1891). The illustrator is William Hole. On this page: "The man . . . leaped up, and caught hold of the brig's bowsprit."

23. *Kidnapped*, William Hole: "Robin . . . struck into the slow measure of a pibroch."

24. "I were liker a man if I struck this creature down": one of William Hole's illustrations to *The Master of Ballantrae* (London, 1891). Hole had been the illustrator for *The Master of Ballantrae* when it was first published as a serial in *Scribner's Magazine*.

"Not so, my dear," he replied; "I retain its complete exercise. To the proof: instead of attempting to cloak my inconsistency, I have, by way of preparing you, thrown it into strong relief. You will there, I think, recognize the philosopher who has the ecstasy to call you wife. The fact is, I have been reckoning all this while without an accident. I never thought to find a son of my own. Now, last night, I found one. Do not unnecessarily alarm yourself, my dear; he is not a drop of blood to me that I know. It is his mind, darling, his mind that calls me father."

"His mind!" she repeated, with a titter between scorn and hysterics. "His mind, indeed! Henri, is this an idiotic pleasantry, or are you mad? His mind! And what of my mind?"

"Truly," replied the Doctor with a shrug, "you have your finger on the hitch. He will be strikingly antipathetic to my ever beautiful Anastasie. She will never understand him; he will never understand her. You married the animal side of my nature, dear; and it is on the spiritual side that I find my affinity for Jean-Marie. So much so, that, to be perfectly frank, I stand in some awe of him myself. You will easily perceive that I am announcing a calamity for you. Do not," he broke out in tones of real solicitude—"do not give way to tears after a meal, Anastasie. You will certainly give yourself a false digestion."

Anastasie controlled herself. "You know how willing I am to humour you," she said, "in all reasonable matters. But on this point—"

"My dear love," interrupted the Doctor, eager to prevent a refusal, "who wished to leave Paris? Who made me give up cards, and the opera, and the boulevard, and my social relations, and all that was my life before I knew you? Have I been faithful? Have I been obedient? Have I not borne my doom with cheerfulness? In all honesty, Anastasie, have I not a right to a stipulation on my side? I have, and you know it. I stipulate my son."

Anastasie was aware of defeat; she struck her colours instantly. "You will break my heart," she sighed.

"Not in the least," said he. "You will feel a trifling inconvenience for a month, just as I did when I was first brought to this vile hamlet; then your admirable sense and temper will prevail, and I see you already as content as ever, and making your husband the happiest of men."

"You know I can refuse you nothing," she said, with a last flicker of resistance; "nothing that will make you truly happier. But will this? Are you sure, my husband? Last night, you say, you found him! He may be the worst of humbugs."

"I think not," replied the Doctor. "But do not suppose me so unwary as to adopt him out of hand. I am, I flatter myself, a finished man of the world; I have had all possibilities in view; my plan is contrived to meet them all. I take the lad as stableboy. If he pilfer, if he grumble, if he desire to change, I shall see I was mistaken; I shall recognise him for no son of mine, and send him tramping."

"You will never do so when the time comes," said his wife; "I know your good heart."

She reached out her hand to him, with a sigh; the Doctor smiled as he took it and carried it to his lips; he had gained his point with greater ease than he had dared to hope; for perhaps the twentieth time he had proved the efficacy of his trusty argument, his Excalibur, the hint of a return to Paris. Six months in the capital, for a man of the Doctor's antecedents and relations, implied no less calamity than total ruin. Anastasie had saved the remainder of his fortune by keeping him strictly in the country. The very name of Paris put her in blue fear; and she would have allowed her husband to keep a menagerie in the back garden, let alone adopting a stable-boy, rather than permit the question of return to be discussed.

About four of the afternoon, the mountebank rendered up his ghost; he had never been conscious since his seizure. Doctor Desprez was present at his last passage, and declared the farce over. Then he took Jean-Marie by the shoulder and led him out into the inn garden where there was a convenient bench beside the river. Here he sat him down and made the boy place himself on his left.

"Jean-Marie," he said very gravely, "this world is exceedingly vast; and even France, which is only a small corner of it, is a great place for a little lad like you. Unfortunately it is full of eager, shouldering people moving on; and there are very few bakers' shops for so many eaters. Your master is dead; you are not fit to gain a living by yourself; you do not wish to steal? No. Your situation then is undesirable; it is for the moment critical. On the other hand, you behold in me a man not old, though elderly, still enjoying the youth of the heart and the intelligence; a man of instruction; easily situated in this world's affairs; keeping a good table—a man, neither as friend nor host, to be despised.

I offer you your food and clothes, and to teach you lessons in the evening, which will be infinitely more to the purpose for a lad of your stamp than those of all the priests in Europe. I propose no wages, but if ever you take a thought to leave me, the door shall be open, and I will give you a hundred francs to start the world upon. In return, I have an old horse and chaise, which you would very speedily learn to clean and keep in order. Do not hurry yourself to answer, and take it or leave it as you judge aright. Only remember this, that I am no sentimentalist or charitable person, but a man who lives rigorously to himself; and that if I make the proposal, it is for my own ends—it is because I perceive clearly an advantage to myself. And now, reflect."

"I shall be very glad. I do not see what else I can do. I thank you, sir, most kindly, and I will try to be useful," said the boy.

"Thank you," said the Doctor warmly, rising at the same time and wiping his brow, for he had suffered agonies while the thing hung in the wind. A refusal, after the scene at noon, would have placed him in a ridiculous light before Anastasie. "How hot and heavy is the evening, to be sure! I have always had a fancy to be a fish in summer, Jean-Marie, here in the Loing beside Gretz. I should lie under a water-lily and listen to the bells, which must sound most delicately down below. That would be a life—do you not think so too?"

"Yes," said Jean-Marie.

"Thank God you have imagination!" cried the Doctor, embracing the boy with his usual effusive warmth, though it was a proceeding that seemed to disconcert the sufferer almost as much as if he had been an English schoolboy of the same age. "And now," he added, "I will take you to my wife."

Madame Desprez sat in the dining-room in a cool wrapper. All the blinds were down, and the tile floor had been recently sprinkled with water; her eyes were half shut, but she affected to be reading a novel as they entered. Though she was a bustling woman, she enjoyed repose between whiles and had a remarkable appetite for sleep.

The Doctor went through a solemn form of introduction, adding, for the benefit of both parties, "You must try to like each other for my sake."

"He is very pretty," said Anastasie. "Will you kiss me, my pretty little fellow?"

The Doctor was furious, and dragged her into the passage. "Are you a fool, Anastasie?" he said. "What is all this I hear about the tact of women? Heaven knows, I have not met with it in my experience. You address my little philosopher as if he were an infant. He must be spoken to with more respect, I tell you; he must not be kissed and Georgy-porgy'd like an ordinary child."

"I only did it to please you, I am sure," replied Anastasie; "but I will try to do better."

The Doctor apologized for his warmth. "But I do wish him," he continued, "to feel at home among us. And really your conduct was so idiotic, my cherished one, and so utterly and distantly out of place, that a saint might have been pardoned a little vehemence in disapproval. Do, do try—if it is possible for a woman to understand young people—but of course it is not, and I waste my breath. Hold your tongue as much as possible at least, and observe my conduct narrowly; it will serve you for a model."

Anastasie did as she was bidden, and considered the Doctor's behaviour. She observed that he embraced the boy three times in the course of the evening, and managed generally to confound and abash the little fellow out of speech and appetite. But she had the true womanly heroism in little affairs. Not only did she refrain from the cheap revenge of exposing the Doctor's errors to himself, but she did her best to remove their ill-effect on Jean-Marie. When Desprez went out for his last breath of air before retiring for the night, she came over to the boy's side and took his hand.

"You must not be surprised nor frightened by my husband's manners," she said. "He is the kindest of men, but so clever that he is sometimes difficult to understand. You will soon grow used to him, and then you will love him, for that nobody can help. As for me, you may be sure, I shall try to make you happy, and will not bother you at all. I think we should be excellent friends, you and I. I am not clever, but I am very good-natured. Will you give me a kiss?"

He held up his face, and she took him in her arms and then began to cry. The woman had spoken in complaisance; but she had warmed to her own words, and tenderness followed. The Doctor, entering, found them enlaced: he concluded that his wife was in fault; and he was just beginning, in an awful voice, "Anastasie—," when she looked up at him, smiling, with an upraised finger, and he held his peace, wondering, while she led the boy to his attic.

4. The Education of a Philosopher

THE installation of the adopted stable-boy was thus happily effected, and the wheels of life continued to run smoothly in the Doctor's house. Jean-Marie did his horse and carriage duty in the morning; sometimes helped with the housework; sometimes walked abroad with the Doctor, to drink wisdom from the fountain-head; and was introduced at night to the sciences and the dead tongues. He retained his singular placidity of mind and manner; he was rarely in fault; but he made only a very partial progress in his studies, and remained much of a stranger in the family.

The Doctor was a pattern of regularity. All forenoon he worked on his great book, the "Comparative Pharmacopœia, or Historical Dictionary of all Medicines," which as yet consisted principally of slips of paper and pins. When finished, it was to fill many personable volumes, and to combine antiquarian interest with professional utility. But the Doctor was studious of literary graces and the picturesque; an anecdote, a touch of manners, a moral qualification, or a sounding epithet was sure to be preferred before a piece of science; a little more, and he would have written the "Comparative Pharmacopœia" in verse! The article "Mummia", for instance, was already complete, though the remainder of the work had not progressed beyond the letter A. It was exceedingly copious and entertaining, written with quaintness and colour, exact, erudite, a literary article; but it would hardly have afforded guidance to a practising physician of to-day. The feminine good sense of his wife had led her to point this out with uncompromising sincerity; for the Dictionary was duly read aloud to her, betwixt sleep and waking, as it proceeded towards an infinitely distant completion; and the Doctor was a little sore on the subject of mummies, and sometimes resented an allusion with asperity.

After the midday meal and a proper period of digestion, he walked, sometimes alone, sometimes accompanied by Jean-Marie; for madame would have preferred any hardship rather than walk.

She was, as I have said, a very busy person, continually occupied about material comforts, and ready to drop asleep over a novel the instant she was disengaged. This was the less objectionable as she never snored or grew distempered in complexion when she slept. On the contrary, she looked the very picture of luxurious and appetising ease, and woke without a start to the perfect possession of her faculties. I am afraid she was greatly an animal, but she was a very nice animal to have about. In this way she had little to do with Jean-Marie; but the sympathy which had been established between them on the first night remained unbroken; they held occasional conversations, mostly on household matters; to the extreme disappointment of the Doctor, they occasionally sallied off together to that temple of debasing superstition, the village church; madame and he, both in their Sunday best, drove twice a month to Fontainbleau and returned laden with purchases; and in short, although the Doctor still continued to regard them as irreconcilably antipathetic, their relation was as intimate, friendly, and confidential as their natures suffered.

I fear, however, that in her heart of hearts madame kindly despised and pitied the boy. She had no admiration for his class of virtues; she liked a smart, polite, forward, roguish sort of boy, cap in hand, light of foot, meeting the eye; she liked volubility, charm, a little vice—the promise of a second Doctor Desprez. And it was her indefeasible belief that Jean-Marie was dull. "Poor dear boy," she had said once, "how sad it is that he should be so stupid!" She had never repeated that remark, for the Doctor had raged like a wild bull, denouncing the brutal bluntness of her mind, bemoaning his own fate to be so unequally mated with an ass, and, what touched Anastasie more nearly, menacing the table china by the fury of his gesticulations. But she adhered silently to her opinion; and when Jean-Marie was sitting, stolid, blank, but not unhappy, over his unfinished tasks, she would snatch her opportunity in the Doctor's absence, go over to him, put her arms about his neck, lay her cheek to his, and communicate her sympathy with his distress. "Do not mind," she would say; "I, too, am not all clever, and I can assure you that it makes no difference in life."

The Doctor's view was naturally different. That gentleman never wearied of the sound of his own voice, which was, to say the truth, agreeable enough to hear. He now had a listener, who was not cynically indifferent as Anastasie, and who sometimes put him on his mettle by the most relevant objection. Besides, was he not educating the boy?

And education, philosophers are agreed, is the most philosophical of duties. What can be more heavenly to poor mankind than to have one's own hobby grow into a duty to the State? Then, indeed, do the ways of life become ways of pleasantness. Never had the Doctor seen reason to be more content with his endowments. Philosophy flowed smoothly from his lips. He was so agile a dialectician that he could trace his nonsense, when challenged, back to some root in sense, and prove it to be a sort of flower upon his system. He slipped out of antinomies like a fish, and left his disciple marvelling at the rabbi's depth.

Moreover, deep down in his heart the Doctor was disappointed with the ill-success of his more formal education. A boy, chosen by so acute an observer for his aptitude, and guided along the path of learning by so philosophic an instructor, was bound, by the nature of the universe, to make a more obvious and lasting advance. Now Jean-Marie was slow in all things, impenetrable in others; and his power of forgetting was fully on a level with his power to learn. Therefore the Doctor cherished his peripatetic lectures, to which the boy attended, and which he generally appeared to enjoy, and by which he often profited.

Many and many were the talks they had together; and health and moderation proved the subject of the Doctor's divagations. To these he lovingly returned.

"I lead you," he would say, "by the green pastures. My system, my beliefs, my medicines, are resumed in one phrase—to avoid excess. Blessed nature, healthy, temperate nature, abhors and exterminates excess. Human law, in this matter, imitates at a great distance her provisions; and we must strive to supplement the efforts of the law. Yes, boy, we must be a law to ourselves and for our neighbours—*lex armata*—armed, emphatic, tyrannous law. If you see a crapulous human ruin snuffing, dash from him his box! The judge, though in a way an admission of disease, is less offensive to me than either the doctor or the priest. Above all the doctor—the doctor and the purulent trash and garbage of his pharmacopœia! Pure air—from the neighbourhood of a pinetum for the sake of the turpentine—unadulterated wine, and the reflections of an unsophisticated spirit in the presence of the works of nature—these, my boy, are the best medical appliances and the best religious comforts. Devote yourself to these.

Hark! there are the bells of Bourron (the wind is in the north, it will be fair). How clear and airy is the sound! The nerves are harmonised and quieted; the mind attuned to silence; and observe how easily and regularly beats the heart! Your enlightened doctor would see nothing in these sensations; and yet you yourself perceive they are a part of health.—Did you remember your cinchona this morning? Good. Cinchona also is a work of nature; it is, after all, only the bark of a tree which we might gather for ourselves if we lived in the locality.—What a world is this! Though a professed atheist, I delight to bear my testimony to the world. Look at the gratuitous remedies and pleasures that surround our path! The river runs by the garden end, our bath, our fishpond, our natural system of drainage. There is a well in the court which sends up sparkling water from the earth's very heart, clean, cool, and, with a little wine, most wholesome. The district is notorious for its salubrity; rheumatism is the only prevalent complaint, and I myself have never had a touch of it. I tell you—and my opinion is based upon the coldest, clearest processes of reason—if I, if you, desired to leave this home of pleasures, it would be the duty, it would be the privilege, of our best friend to prevent us with a pistol bullet."

One beautiful June day they sat upon the hill outside the village. The river, as blue as heaven, shone here and there among the foliage. The indefatigable birds turned and flickered about Gretz church tower. A healthy wind blew from over the forest, and the sound of innumerable thousands of tree-tops and innumerable millions on millions of green leaves was abroad in the air, and filled the ear with something between whispered speech and singing. It seemed as if every blade of grass must hide a cigale; and the fields rang merrily with their music, jingling far and near as with the sleigh-bells of the fairy queen. From their station on the slope the eye embraced a large space of poplar'd plain upon the one hand, the waving hill-tops of the forest on the other, and Gretz itself in the middle, a handful of roofs. Under the bestriding arch of the blue heavens, the place seemed dwindled to a toy. It seemed incredible that people dwelt, and could find room to turn or air to breathe, in such a corner of the world. The thought came home to the boy, perhaps for the first time, and he gave it words.

"How small it looks!" he sighed.

"Ay," replied the Doctor, "small enough now. Yet it was once a walled city; thriving, full of furred burgesses and men in armour, humming with affairs—with tall spires, for aught that I know, and portly towers along the battlements. A thousand chimneys ceased smoking at the curfew bell. There were gibbets at the gate as thick as scarecrows. In time of war, the assault swarmed against it with ladders, the arrows fell like leaves, the defenders sallied hotly over the drawbridge, each side uttered its cry as they plied their weapons. Do you know that the walls extended as far as the Commanderie? Tradition so reports. Alas, what a long way off is all this confusion—nothing left of it but my quiet words spoken in your ear—and the town itself shrunk to the hamlet underneath us! By-and-by came the English wars—you shall hear more of the English, a stupid people, who sometimes blundered into good—and Gretz was taken, sacked, and burned. It is the history of many towns; but Gretz never rose again; it was never rebuilt; its ruins were a quarry to serve the growth of rivals; and the stones of Gretz are now erect along the streets of Nemours. It gratifies me that our old house was the first to rise after the calamity; when the town had come to an end, it inaugurated the hamlet."

"I too, am glad of that," said Jean-Marie.

"It should be the temple of the humbler virtues," responded the Doctor with a savoury gusto. "Perhaps one of the reasons why I love my little hamlet as I do, is that we have a similar history, she and I. Have I told you that I was once rich?"

"I do not think so," answered Jean-Marie. "I do not think I should have forgotten. I am sorry you should have lost your fortune."

"Sorry?" cried the Doctor. "Why, I find I have scarce begun your education after all. Listen to me! Would you rather live in the old Gretz or in the new, free from the alarms of war, with the green country at the door, without noise, passports, the exactions of the soldiery, or the jangle of the curfew-bell to send us off to bed by sundown?"

"I suppose I should prefer the new," replied the boy.

"Precisely," returned the Doctor; "so do I. And in the same way, I prefer my present moderate fortune to my former wealth. Golden mediocrity! cried the adorable ancients; and I subscribe to their enthusiasm. Have I not got good wine, good food, good air, the fields and the forests for my walk, a house, an admirable wife, a boy whom I protest I cherish like a son? Now, if I were still rich, I should indubitably make my residence in Paris—you know Paris—Paris and Paradise are not convertible terms. This pleasant noise of the wind streaming among leaves changed into the grinding Babel of the street, the stupid glare of plaster substituted for this quiet pattern of greens and greys, the nerves shattered, the digestion falsified—picture the fall! Already you perceive the consequences; the mind is stimulated, the heart steps to a different measure, and the man is himself no longer. I have passionately studied myself—the true business of philosophy. I know my character as the musician knows the ventages of his flute. Should I return to Paris, I should ruin myself gambling; nay, I go further—I should break the heart of my Anastasie with infidelities."

This was too much for Jean-Marie. That a place should so transform the most excellent of men transcended his belief. Paris, he protested, was even an agreeable place of residence. "Nor when I lived in that city did I feel much difference," he pleaded.

"What!" cried the Doctor. "Did you not steal when you were there?"

But the boy could never be brought to see that he had done anything wrong when he stole. Nor, indeed, did the Doctor think he had; but that gentleman was never very scrupulous when in want of a retort.

"And now," he concluded, "do you begin to understand? My only friends were those who ruined me. Gretz has been my academy, my sanatorium, my heaven of innocent pleasures. If millions are offered me, I wave them back: *Retro, Sathanas!*—Evil one, begone! Fix your mind on my example; despise riches, avoid the debasing influence of cities. Hygiene—hygiene and mediocrity of fortune—these be your watchwords during life!"

The Doctor's system of hygiene strikingly coincided with his tastes; and his picture of the perfect life was a faithful description of the one he was leading at the time. But it is easy to convince a boy, whom you supply with all the facts for the discussion. And besides, there was one thing admirable in the philosophy, and that was the enthusiasm of the philosopher. There was never any one more vigorously determined to be pleased; and if he was not a great logician, and so had no right to convince the intellect, he was certainly something of a poet, and had a fascination to seduce that heart. What he could not achieve in his customary humour of a radiant admiration of himself and his circumstances, he sometimes effected in his fits of gloom.

"Boy," he would say, "avoid me to-day. If I were superstitious, I should even beg for an interest in your prayers. I am in the black fit; the evil spirit of King Saul, the hag of the merchant Abudah, the personal devil of the mediæval monk, is with me—is in me," tapping on his breast. "The vices of my nature are now uppermost; innocent pleasures woo me in vain; I long for Paris, for my wallowings in the mire. See," he would continue, producing a handful of silver, "I denude myself, I am not to be trusted with the price of a fare. Take it, keep it for me, squander it on deleterious candy, throw it in the deepest of the river—I will homologate your action. Save me from that part of myself which I disown. If you see me falter, do not hesitate; if necessary, wreck the train! I speak, of course, by a parable. Any extremity were better than for me to reach Paris alive."

Doubtless the Doctor enjoyed these little scenes, as a variation in his part; they represented the Byronic element in the somewhat artificial poetry of his existence; but to the boy, though he was dimly aware of their theatricality, they represented more. The Doctor made perhaps too little, the boy possibly too much, of the reality and gravity of these temptations.

One day a great light shone for Jean-Marie. "Could not riches be used well?" he asked.

"In theory, yes," replied the Doctor. "But it is found in experience that no one does so. All the world imagine they will be exceptional when they grow wealthy; but possession is debasing, new desires spring up; and the silly taste for ostentation eats out the heart of pleasure."

"Then you might be better if you had less," said the boy.

"Certainly not," replied the Doctor; but his voice quavered as he spoke.

"Why?" demanded pitiless innocence.

Doctor Desprez saw all the colours of the rainbow in a moment; the stable universe appeared to be about capsizing with him. "Because," said he—affecting deliberation after an obvious pause—"because I have formed my life for my present income. It is not good for men of my years to be violently dissevered from their habits."

That was a sharp brush. The Doctor breathed hard, and fell into taciturnity for the afternoon. As for the boy, he was delighted with the resolution of his doubts; even wondered that he had not forseen the obvious and conclusive answer. His faith in the Doctor was a stout piece of goods. Desprez was inclined to be a sheet in the wind's eye after dinner, especially after Rhône wine, his favourite weakness. He would then remark on the warmth of his feeling for Anastasie, and with inflamed cheeks and a loose, flustered smile, debate upon all sorts of topics and be feebly and indiscreetly witty. But the adopted stable-boy would not permit himself to entertain a doubt that savoured of ingratitude. It is quite true that a man may be a second father to you, and yet take too much drink; but the best natures are ever slow to accept such truths.

The Doctor thoroughly possessed his heart, but perhaps he exaggerated his influence over his mind. Certainly Jean-Marie adopted some of his master's opinions, but I have yet to learn that he ever surrendered one of his own. Convictions existed in him by divine right; they were virgin, unwrought, the brute metal of decision. He could add others indeed, but he could not put away; neither did he care if they were perfectly agreed among themselves; and his spiritual pleasures had nothing to do with turning them over or justifying them in words. Words were with him a mere accomplishment, like dancing. When he was by himself, his pleasures were almost vegetable. He would slip into the woods towards Achères, and sit in the mouth of a cave among grey birches. His soul stared straight out of his eyes; he did not move or think; sunlight, thin shadows moving in the wind, the edge of firs against the sky, occupied and bound his faculties. He was pure unity, a spirit wholly abstracted. A single mood filled him, to which all the objects of sense contributed, as the colours of the spectrum merge and disappear in white light.

So while the Doctor made himself drunk with words, the adopted stable-boy bemused himself with silence.

5. Treasure Trove

THE Doctor's carriage was a two-wheeled gig with a hood; a kind of vehicle in much favour among country doctors. On how many roads has one not seen it, a great way off between the poplars!—in how many village streets, tied to a gate-post! This sort of chariot is affected—particularly at the trot—by a kind of pitching movement to and fro across the axle, which well entitles it to the style of a noddy. The hood describes a considerable arc against the landscape, with a solemnly absurd effect on the contemplative pedestrian. To ride in such a carriage cannot be numbered among the things that appertain to glory; but I have no doubt it may be useful in liver complaints. Thence, perhaps, its wide popularity among physicians.

One morning early, Jean-Marie led forth the Doctor's noddy, opened the gate, and mounted to the driving-seat. The Doctor followed, arrayed from top to toe in spotless linen, armed with an immense flesh-coloured umbrella, and girt with a botanical case on a baldric; and the equipage drove off smartly in a breeze of its own provocation. They were bound for Franchard, to collect plants, with an eye to the "Comparative Pharmacopœia".

A little rattling on the open roads, and they came to the borders of the forest and struck into an unfrequented track; the noddy yawed softly over the sand, with an accompaniment of snapping twigs. There was a great, green, softly murmuring cloud of congregated foliage overhead. In the arcades of the forest the air retained the freshness of the night. The athletic bearing of the trees, each carrying its leafy mountain, pleased the mind like so many statues; and the lines of the trunk led the eye admiringly upward to where the extreme leaves sparkled in a patch of azure. Squirrels leaped in mid-air. It was a proper spot for a devotee of the goddess Hygeia.

"Have you not been to Franchard, Jean-Marie?" inquired the Doctor. "I fancy not."

"Never," replied the boy.

"It is a ruin in a gorge," continued Desprez, adopting his expository voice; "the ruin of a hermitage and chapel. History tells us much of

Franchard; how the recluse was often slain by robbers; how he lived on a most insufficient diet; how he was expected to pass his days in prayer. A letter is preserved, addressed to one of these solitaries by the superior of his order, full of admirable hygienic advice; bidding him go from his book to praying, and so back again, for variety's sake, and when he was weary of both, to stroll about his garden and observe the honey-bees. It is to this day my own system. You must often have remarked me leaving the 'Pharmacopœia'—often even in the middle of a phrase—to come forth into the sun and air. I admire the writer of that letter from my heart; he was a man of thought on the most important subjects. But, indeed, had I lived in the Middle Ages (I am heartily glad that I did not) I should have been an eremite myself—if I had not been a professed buffoon, that is. These were the only philosophical lives yet open: laughter or prayer; sneers, we might say, and tears. Until the sun of the Positive arose, the wise man had to make his choice between these two."

"I have been a buffoon, of course," observed Jean-Marie.

"I cannot imagine you to have excelled in your profession," said the Doctor, admiring the boy's gravity. "Do you ever laugh?"

"Oh, yes," replied the other. "I laugh often. I am very fond of jokes."

"Singular being!" said Desprez. "But I divagate (I perceive in a thousand ways that I grow old). Franchard was at length destroyed in the English wars, the same that levelled Gretz. But—here is the point—the hermits (for there were already more than one) had forseen the danger and carefully concealed the sacrificial vessels. These vessels were of monstrous value, Jean-Marie—monstrous value—priceless, we may say, exquisitely worked, of exquisite material. And now, mark me, they have never been found. In the reign of Louis Quatorze some fellows were digging hard by the ruins. Suddenly—tock!—the spade hit upon an obstacle. Imagine the men looking one to another; imagine how their hearts bounded, how their colour came and went. It was a coffer, and in Franchard, the place of buried treasure! They tore it open like famished beasts. Alas! it was not the treasure; only some priestly robes, which, at the touch of the eating air, fell upon themselves and instantly wasted into dust. The perspiration of these good fellows turned cold upon them, Jean-Marie. I will pledge my reputation, if there was anything like a cutting wind, one or other had a pneumonia for his trouble."

"I should like to have seen them turning into dust," said Jean-Marie. "Otherwise, I should not have cared so greatly."

"You have no imagination," cried the Doctor. "Picture to yourself the scene. Dwell on the idea—a great treasure lying in the earth for centuries: the material for a giddy, copious, opulent existence not employed; dresses and exquisite pictures unseen; the swiftest galloping horses not stirring a hoof, arrested by a spell; women with the beautiful faculty of smiles, not smiling; cards, dice, opera, singing, orchestras, castles, beautiful parks and gardens, big ships with a tower of sailcloth, all lying unborn in a coffin—and the stupid trees growing overhead in the sunlight, year after year. The thought drives one frantic."

"It is only money," replied Jean-Marie. "It would do harm."

"Oh, come!" cried Desprez, "that is philosophy; it is all very fine, but not to the point just now. And besides, it is not 'only money', as you call it; there are works of art in the question; the vessels were carved. You speak like a child. You weary me exceedingly, quoting my words out of all logical connection, like a parroquet."

"And at any rate, we have nothing to do with it," returned the boy submissively.

They struck the Route Ronde at that moment; and the sudden change to the rattling causeway combined, with the Doctor's irritation, to keep him silent. The noddy jigged along; the trees went by, looking on silently, as if they had something on their minds. The Quadrilateral was passed; then came Franchard. They put up the horse at the little solitary inn, and went forth strolling. The gorge was dyed deeply with heather; the rocks and birches standing luminous in the sun. A great humming of bees about the flowers disposed Jean-Marie to sleep, and he sat down against a clump of heather, while the Doctor went briskly to and fro, with quick turns, culling his simples.

The boy's head had fallen a little forward, his eyes were closed, his fingers had fallen lax about his knees, when a sudden cry called him to his feet. It was a strange sound, thin and brief; it fell dead, and silence returned as though it had never been interrupted. He had not recognized the Doctor's voice; but, as there was no one else in all the valley, it was plainly the Doctor who had given utterance to the sound. He looked right and left, and there was Desprez, standing in a niche between two boulders, and looking round on his adopted son with a countenance as white as paper.

"A viper!" cried Jean-Marie, running towards him. "A viper! You are bitten!"

The Doctor came down heavily out of the cleft, and advanced in silence to meet the boy, whom he took roughly by the shoulder.

"I have found it," he said, with a gasp.

"A plant?" asked Jean-Marie.

Desprez had a fit of unnatural gaiety, which the rocks took up and mimicked. "A plant!" he repeated scornfully. "Well—yes—a plant. And here," he added suddenly, showing his right hand, which he had hitherto concealed behind his back—"here is one of the bulbs,"

Jean-Marie saw a dirty platter, coated with earth.

"That?" said he. "It is a plate!"

"It is a coach and horses," cried the Doctor. "Boy," he continued, growing warmer, "I plucked away a great pad of moss from between these boulders, and disclosed a crevice; and when I looked in, what do you suppose I saw? I saw a house in Paris with a court and garden, I saw my wife shining with diamonds, I saw myself a deputy, I saw you —well, I—I saw your future," he concluded, rather feebly. "I have just discovered America," he added.

"But what is it?" asked the boy.

"The Treasure of Franchard," cried the Doctor; and, throwing his brown straw hat upon the ground, he whooped like an Indian and sprang upon Jean-Marie, whom he suffocated with embraces and bedewed with tears. Then he flung himself down among the heather and once more laughed until the valley rang.

But the boy had now an interest of his own, a boy's interest. No sooner was he released from the Doctor's accolade than he ran to the boulders, sprang into the niche, and thrusting his hand into the crevice, drew forth one after another, encrusted with the earth of ages, the flagons, candlesticks, and patens of the hermitage of Franchard. A casket came last, tightly shut and very heavy.

"Oh, what fun!" he cried.

But when he looked back at the Doctor, who had followed close behind and was silently observing, the words died from his lips. Desprez was once more the colour of ashes; his lip worked and trembled; a sort of bestial greed possessed him.

"This is childish," he said. "We lose precious time. Back to the inn, harness the trap, and bring it to yon bank. Run for your life, and remember—not one whisper. I stay here to watch."

Jean-Marie did as he was bid, though not without surprise. The noddy was brought round to the spot indicated; and the two gradually transported the treasure from its place of concealment to the boot below the driving-seat. Once it was all stored the Doctor recovered his gaiety.

"I pay my grateful duties to the genius of this dell," he said. "Oh, for a live coal, a heifer, and a jar of country wine! I am in the vein for sacrifice, for a superb libation. Well, and why not? We are at Franchard. English pale ale is to be had—not classical, indeed, but excellent. Boy, we shall drink ale."

"But I thought it was so unwholesome," said Jean-Marie, "and very dear besides."

"Fiddle-de-dee!" exclaimed the Doctor gaily. "To the inn!"

And he stepped into the noddy, tossing his head, with an elastic, youthful air. The horse was turned, and in a few seconds they drew up beside the palings of the inn garden.

"Here," said Desprez—"here, near the table, so that we may keep an eye upon things."

They tied the horse and entered the garden, the Doctor singing, now in fantastic high notes, now producing deep reverberations from his chest. He took a seat, rapped loudly on the table, assailed the waiter with witticisms; and when the bottle of Bass was at length produced, far more charged with gas than the most delirious champagne, he filled out a long glassful of froth and pushed it over to Jean-Marie. "Drink," he said; "drink deep."

"I would rather not," faltered the boy, true to his training.

"What?" thundered Desprez.

"I am afraid of it," said Jean-Marie: "my stomach—"

"Take it or leave it," interrupted Desprez fiercely; "but understand it once for all—there is nothing so contemptible as a precisian."

Here was a new lesson! The boy sat bemused, looking at the glass but not tasting it, while the Doctor emptied and refilled his own, at first with clouded brow, but gradually yielding to the sun, the heady, prickling beverage, and his own predisposition to be happy.

"Once in a way," he said at last, by way of a concession to the boy's more rigorous attitude, "once in a way, and at so critical a moment, this ale is nectar for the gods. The habit, indeed, is debasing; wine, the juice of the grape, is the true drink of the Frenchman, as I have often had occasion to point out; and I do not know that I can blame you for refusing this outlandish stimulant. You can have some wine and cakes. Is the bottle empty? Well, we will not be proud; we will have pity on your glass."

The beer being done, the Doctor chafed bitterly while Jean-Marie finished his cakes. "I burn to be gone," he said, looking at his watch. "Good God, how slow you eat!" And yet to eat slowly was his own particular prescription, the main secret of longevity!

His martyrdom, however, reached an end at last; the pair resumed their places in the buggy, and Desprez, leaning luxuriously back, announced his intention of proceeding to Fontainebleau.

"To Fontainebleau?" repeated Jean-Marie.

"My words are always measured," said the Doctor. "On!"

The Doctor was driven through the glades of Paradise; the air, the light, the shining leaves, the very movements of the vehicle, seemed to fall in tune with his golden meditations; with his head thrown back, he dreamed a series of sunny visions, ale and pleasure dancing in his veins. At last he spoke.

"I shall telegraph for Casimir," he said. "Good Casimir! a fellow of the lower order of intelligence, Jean-Marie, distinctly not creative, not poetic; and yet he will repay your study; his fortune is vast, and is entirely due to his own exertions. He is the very fellow to help us to dispose of our trinkets, find us a suitable house in Paris, and manage the details of our installation. Admirable Casimir, one of my oldest comrades! It was on his advice, I may add, that I invested my little fortune in Turkish bonds; when we have added these spoils of the Mediæval Church to our stake in the Mohametan empire, little boy, we shall positively roll among doubloons, positively roll! Beautiful forest," he cried, "farewell! Though called to other scenes, I will not forget thee. Thy name is graven in my heart. Under the influence of prosperity I become dithyrambic, Jean-Marie. Such is the impulse of the natural soul; such was the constitution of primæval man. And I—well, I will not refuse the credit—I have preserved my youth like a virginity; another, who should have led the same snoozing, countrified existence for these years, another had become rusted, become stereotyped; but I, I praise my happy constitution, retain the spring unbroken. Fresh opulence and a new sphere of duties find me unabated in ardour and only more mature by knowledge. For this prospective change, Jean-Marie—it may probably have shocked you. Tell me now, did it not strike you as an inconsistency? Confess—it is useless to dissemble—it pained you?"

"Yes," said the boy.

"You see," returned the Doctor, with sublime fatuity, "I read your thoughts! Nor am I surprised—your education is not yet complete; the higher duties of men have not been yet presented to you fully. A hint—till we have leisure—must suffice. Now that I am once more in possession of a modest competence; now that I have so long prepared myself in silent meditation, it becomes my superior duty to proceed to Paris. My scientific training, my undoubted command of language, mark me out for the service of my country. Modesty in such a case would be a snare. If sin were a philosophical expression, I should call it sinful. A man must not deny his manifest abilities, for that is to evade his obligations. I must be up and doing; I must be no skulker in life's battle."

So he rattled on, copiously greasing the joint of his inconsistency with words; while the boy listened silently, his eyes fixed on the horse, his mind seething. It was all lost eloquence; no array of words could unsettle a belief of Jean-Marie's; and he drove into Fontainebleau filled with pity, horror, indignation, and despair.

In the town Jean-Marie was kept a fixture on the driving-seat, to guard the treasure; while the Doctor, with a singular, slightly tipsy airiness of manner, fluttered in and out of cafés, where he shook hands with garrison officers, and mixed an absinthe with the nicety of old experience; in and out of shops, from which he returned laden with costly fruits, real turtle, a magnificent piece of silk for his wife, a preposterous cane for himself, and a képi of the newest fashion for the boy; in and out of the telegraph office, whence he despatched his telegram, and where three hours later he received an answer promising a visit on the morrow; and generally pervaded Fontainebleau with the first fine aroma of his divine good humour.

The sun was very low when they set forth again; the shadows of the forest trees extended across the broad white road that led them home; the penetrating odour of the evening wood had already arisen, like a cloud of incense, from that broad field of tree-tops; and even in the streets of the town, where the air had been baked all day between white walls, it came in whiffs and pulses, like a distant music. Half-way home, the last gold flicker vanished from a great oak upon the left; and when they came forth beyond the borders of the wood, the plain was already sunken in pearly greyness, and a great, pale moon came swinging skyward through the filmy poplars.

The Doctor sang, the Doctor whistled, the Doctor talked. He spoke of the woods, and the wars, and the deposition of dew; he brightened and babbled of Paris; he soared into cloudy bombast on the glories of the political arena. All was to be changed; as the day departed, it took with it the vestiges of an outworn existence, and to-morrow's sun was to inaugurate the new. "Enough," he cried, "of this life of maceration!" His wife (still beautiful, or he was sadly partial) was to be no longer buried; she should now shine before society. Jean-Marie would find the world at his feet; the roads open to success, wealth, honour, and posthumous renown. "And oh, by the way," said he, "for God's sake keep your tongue quiet! You are, of course, a very silent fellow; it is a quality I gladly recognize in you—silence, golden silence! But this is a matter of gravity. No word must get abroad; none but the good Casimir is to be trusted; we shall probably dispose of the vessels in England."

"But they are not even ours?" the boy said, almost with a sob—it was the only time he had spoken.

"Ours in this sense, that they are nobody else's," replied the Doctor. "But the State would have some claim. If they were stolen, for instance, we should be unable to demand their restitution; we should have no title; we should be unable even to communicate with the police. Such is the monstrous condition of the law. It is a mere instance of what remains to be done, of the injustices that may yet be righted by an ardent, active, and philosophical deputy."

Jean-Marie put his faith in Madame Desprez; and as they drove forward down the road from Bourron, between the rustling poplars, he prayed in his teeth, and whipped up the horse to an unusual speed. Surely, as soon as they arrived, madame would assert her character, and bring this waking nightmare to an end.

Their entrance into Gretz was heralded and accompanied by a most furious barking; all the dogs in the village seemed to smell the treasure in the noddy. But there was no one in the street, save three lounging landscape painters at Tentaillon's door. Jean-Marie opened the green gate and led in the horse and carriage; and almost at the same moment Madame Desprez came to the kitchen threshold with a lighted lantern; for the moon was not yet high enough to clear the garden walls.

"Close the gates, Jean-Marie!" cried the Doctor, somewhat unsteadily alighting. "Anastasie, where is Aline?"

"She has gone to Montereau to see her parents," said madame.

"All is for the best!" exclaimed the Doctor fervently. "Here, quick, come near to me; I do not wish to speak too loud," he continued. "Darling, we are wealthy!"

"Wealthy!" repeated the wife.

"I have found the Treasure of Franchard," replied her husband. "See, here are the first fruits; a pineapple, a dress for my ever-beautiful—it will suit her—trust a husband's, trust a lover's taste! Embrace me, darling! This grimy episode is over; the butterfly unfolds its painted wings. To-morrow Casimir will come; in a week we may be in Paris—happy at last! You shall have diamonds. Jean-Marie, take it out of the boot, with religious care, and bring it piece by piece into the dining-room. We shall have plate at table! Darling, hasten and prepare this turtle; it will be a whet—it will be an addition to our meagre ordinary. I myself will proceed to the cellar. We shall have a bottle of that little Beaujolais you like, and finish with the Hermitage; there are still three bottles left. Worthy wine for a worthy occasion."

"But, my husband; you put me in a whirl," she cried. "I do not comprehend."

"The turtle, my adored, the turtle!" cried the Doctor; and he pushed her towards the kitchen, lantern and all.

Jean-Marie stood dumbfounded. He had pictured to himself a different scene—a more immediate protest, and his hope began to dwindle on the spot.

The Doctor was everywhere, a little doubtful on his legs, perhaps, and now and then taking the wall with his shoulder; for it was long since he had tasted absinthe, and he was even then reflecting that the absinthe had been a misconception. Not that he regretted excess on such a glorious day, but he made a mental memorandum to beware; he must not, a second time, become the victim of a deleterious habit. He had his wine out of the cellar in a twinkling; he arranged the sacrificial vessels, some on the white table-cloth, some on the sideboard, still crusted with historic earth. He was in and out of the kitchen, plying Anastasie with vermouth, heating her with glimpses of the future, estimating their new wealth at ever larger figures; and before they sat down to supper, the lady's virtue had melted in the fire of his enthusiasm, her timidity had disappeared; she, too, had begun to speak disparagingly of the life at Gretz; and as she took her place and helped the soup, her eyes shone with the glitter of prospective diamonds.

All through the meal, she and the Doctor made and unmade fairy plans. They bobbed and bowed and pledged each other. Their faces ran over with smiles; their eyes scattered sparkles, as they projected the Doctor's political honours and the lady's drawing-room ovations.

"But you will not be a Red!" cried Anastasie.

"I am Left Centre to the core," replied the Doctor.

"Madame Gastein will present us—we shall find ourselves forgotten," said the lady.

"Never," protested the Doctor. "Beauty and talent leave a mark."

"I have positively forgotten how to dress," she sighed.

"Darling, you make me blush," cried he. "Yours has been a tragic marriage!"

"But your success—to see you appreciated, honoured, your name in all the papers, that will be more than pleasure—it will be heaven!" she cried.

"And once a week," said the Doctor, archly scanning the syllables, "once a week—one good little game of baccarat?"

"Only once a week?" she questioned, threatening him with a finger.

"I swear it by my political honour," cried he.

"I spoil you," she said, and gave him her hand.

He covered it with kisses.

Jean-Marie escaped into the night. The moon swung high over Gretz. He went down to the garden end and sat on the jetty. The river ran by with eddies of oily silver, and a low, monotonous song. Faint veils of mist moved among the poplars on the farther side. The reeds were quietly nodding. A hundred times already had the boy sat, on such a night, and watched the streaming river with untroubled fancy. And this perhaps was to be the last. He was to leave this familiar hamlet, this green, rustling country, this bright and quiet stream; he was to pass into the great city; his dear lady mistress was to move bedizened in saloons; his good, garrulous, kind-hearted master to become a brawling deputy; and both be lost for ever to Jean-Marie and their better selves. He knew his own defects; he knew he must sink into less and less consideration in the turmoil of a city life, sink more and more from the child into the servant. And he began dimly to believe the Doctor's prophecies of evil. He could see a change in both. His generous incredulity failed him for this once; a child must have perceived that the Hermitage had completed what the absinthe had begun. If this were the first day, what would be the last? "If necessary, wreck the train," thought he, remembering the Doctor's parable. He looked round on the delightful scene; he drank deep of the charmed night air, laden with the scent of hay. "If necessary, wreck the train," he repeated. And he rose and returned to the house.

6. A Criminal Investigation, in Two Parts

THE next morning there was a most unusual outcry in the Doctor's house. The last thing before going to bed, the Doctor had locked up some valuables in the dining-room cupboard; and behold, when he rose again, as he did about four o'clock, the cupboard had been broken open, and the valuables in question had disappeared. Madame and Jean-Marie were summoned from their rooms, and appeared in hasty toilets; they found the Doctor raving, calling the heavens to witness and avenge his injury, pacing the room barefooted, with the tails of his nightshirt flirting as he turned.

"Gone!" he said; "the things are gone, the fortune gone! We are paupers once more. Boy! what do you know of this? Speak up, sir, speak up. Do you know of it? Where are they?" He had him by the arm, shaking him like a bag, and the boy's words, if he had any, were jolted forth in inarticulate murmurs. The Doctor, with a revulsion from his own violence, set him down again. He observed Anastasie in tears. "Anastasie," he said, in quite an altered voice, "compose yourself, command your feelings. I would not have you give way to passion like the vulgar. This—this trifling accident must be lived down. Jean-Marie, bring me my smaller medicine-chest. A gentle laxative is indicated."

And he dosed the family all round, leading the way himself with a double quantity. The wretched Anastasie, who had never been ill in the whole course of her existence, and whose soul recoiled from remedies, wept floods of tears as she sipped, and shuddered, and protested, and then was bullied and shouted at until she sipped again. As for Jean-Marie, he took his portion down with stoicism.

"I have given him a less amount," observed the Doctor, "his youth protecting him against emotion. And now that we have thus parried any morbid consequences, let us reason."

"I am so cold," wailed Anastasie.

"Cold!" cried the Doctor. "I give thanks to God that I am made of fierier material. Why, madame, a blow like this would set a frog into a transpiration. If you are cold, you can retire; and, by the way, you might throw me down my trousers. It is chilly for the legs."

"Oh, no!" protested Anastasie; "I will stay with you."

"Nay, madam, you shall not suffer for your devotion," said the Doctor. "I will myself fetch you a shawl." And he went upstairs and returned more fully clad and with an armful of wraps for the shivering Anastasie. "And now," he resumed, "to investigate this crime. Let us proceed by induction. Anastasie, do you know anything that can help us?" Anastasie knew nothing. "Or you, Jean-Marie?"

"Not I," replied the boy steadily.

"Good," returned the Doctor. "We shall now turn our attention to the material evidences. (I was born to be a detective; I have the eye and the systematic spirit.) First, violence has been employed. The door was broken open; and it may be observed, in passing, that the lock was dear indeed at what I paid for it: a crow to pluck with Master Goguelat. Second, here is the instrument employed, one of our own table-knives, one of our best, my dear; which seems to indicate no preparation on the part of the gang—if gang it was. Thirdly, I observe that nothing has been removed except the Franchard dishes and the casket; our own silver has been minutely respected. This is wily; it shows intelligence, a knowledge of the code, a desire to avoid legal consequences. I argue from this fact that the gang numbers persons of respectability—outward, of course, and merely outward, as the robbery proves. But I argue, second, that we must have been observed at Franchard itself by some occult observer, and dogged throughout the day with a skill and patience that I venture to qualify as consummate. No ordinary man, no occasional criminal, would have shown himself capable of this combination. We have in our neighbourhood, it is far from improbable, a retired bandit of the highest order of intelligence."

"Good heaven!" cried the horrified Anastasie. "Henri, how can you?"

"My cherished one, this is a process of induction," said the Doctor. "If any of my steps are unsound, correct me. You are silent? Then do not, I beseech you, be so vulgarly illogical as to revolt from my conclusion. We have now arrived," he resumed, "at some idea of the composition of the gang—for I incline to the hypothesis of more than one—and we now leave this room, which can disclose no more, and turn our attention to the court and garden. (Jean-Marie, I trust you are observantly following my various steps; this is an excellent piece of education for you.) Come with me to the door. No steps on the court; it is unfortunate our court should be paved. On what small matters hang the destiny of these delicate investigations! Hey! What have we here? I have led you to the very spot," he said, standing grandly backward and indicating the green gate. "An escalade, as you can now see for yourselves, has taken place."

Sure enough, the green paint was in several places scratched and broken; and one of the panels preserved the print of a nailed shoe. The foot had slipped, however, and it was difficult to estimate the size of the shoe, and impossible to distinguish the pattern of the nails.

"The whole robbery," concluded the Doctor, "step by step, has been reconstituted. Inductive science can no further go."

"It is wonderful," said his wife. "You should indeed have been a detective, Henri. I had no idea of your talents."

"My dear," replied Desprez condescendingly, "a man of scientific imagination combines the lesser faculties; he is a detective just as he is a publicist or a general; there are but local applications of his special talents. But now," he continued, "would you have me go further? Would you have me lay my finger on the culprits—or rather, for I cannot promise quite so much, point out to you the very house where they consort? It may be a satisfaction, at least it is all we are likely to get, since we are denied the remedy of law. I reach the further stage in this way. In order to fill my outline of the robbery, I require a man likely to be in the forest idling, I require a man of education, I require a man superior to considerations of morality. The three requisites all centre in Tentaillon's boarders. They are painters, therefore they are continually lounging in the forest. They are painters, therefore they are not unlikely to have some smattering of education. Lastly, because they are painters, they are probably immoral. And this I prove in two ways. First, painting is an art which merely addresses the eye; it does not in any particular exercise the moral sense. And second, painting, in common with all the other arts, implies the dangerous quality of imagination. A man of imagination is never moral; he outsoars literal demarcations and reviews life under too many shifting lights to rest content with the invidious distinctions of the law!"

"But you always say—at least, so I understood you"—said madame, "that these lads display no imagination whatever."

"My dear, they displayed imagination, and of a very fantastic order, too," returned the Doctor, "when they embraced their beggarly profession. Besides—and this is an argument exactly suited to your intellectual level—many of them are English and American. Where else should we expect to find a thief?—And now you had better get your coffee. Because we have lost a treasure, there is no reason for starving. For my part, I shall break my fast with white wine. I feel unaccountably heated and thirsty to-day. I can only attribute it to the shock of the discovery. And yet, you will bear me out, I supported the emotion nobly."

The Doctor had now talked himself back into an admirable humour; and as he sat in the arbour and slowly imbibed a large allowance of white wine and picked a little bread and cheese with no very impetuous appetite, if a third of his meditations ran upon the missing treasure, the other two-thirds were more pleasingly busied in the retrospect of his detective skill.

About eleven Casimir arrived; he had caught an early train to Fontainebleau, and driven over to save time; and now his cab was stabled in Tentaillon's, and he remarked, studying his watch, that he could spare an hour and a half. He was much the man of business, decisively spoken, given to frowning in an intellectual manner. Anastasie's born brother, he did not waste much sentiment on the lady, gave her an English family kiss, and demanded a meal without delay.

"You can tell me your story while we eat," he observed. "Anything good to-day, Stasie?"

He was promised something good. The trio sat down to table in the arbour, Jean-Marie waiting as well as eating, and the Doctor recounted what had happened in his richest narrative manner. Casimir heard it with explosions of laughter.

"What a streak of luck for you, my good brother," he observed, when the tale was over. "If you had gone to Paris, you would have played dick-duck-drake with the whole consignment in three months. Your own would have followed; and you would have come to me in a procession like the last time. But I give you warning—Stasie may weep and Henri ratiocinate—it will not serve you twice. Your next collapse will be fatal. I thought I had told you so, Stasie? Hey? No sense?"

The Doctor winced and looked furtively at Jean-Marie; but the boy seemed apathetic.

"And then again," broke out Casimir, "what children you are—vicious children, my faith! How could you tell the value of this trash? It might have been worth nothing, or next door."

"Pardon me," said the Doctor. "You have your usual flow of spirits, I perceive, but even less than your usual deliberation. I am not entirely ignorant of these matters."

"Not entirely ignorant of anything ever I heard of," interrupted Casimir, bowing, and raising his glass with a sort of pert politeness.

"At least," resumed the Doctor, "I gave my mind to the subject—that you may be willing to believe—and I estimate that our capital would be doubled." And he described the nature of the find.

"My word of honour!" said Casimir, "I half believe you! But much would depend on the quality of the gold."

"The quality, my dear Casimir, was—" And the Doctor, in default of language, kissed his finger-tips.

"I would not take your word for it, my good friend," retorted the man of business. "You are a man of very rosy views. But this robbery," he continued—"this robbery is an odd thing. Of course I pass over your nonsense about gangs and landscape painters. For me, that is a dream. Who was in the house last night?"

"None but ourselves," replied the Doctor.

"And this young gentleman?" asked Casimir, jerking a nod in the direction of Jean-Marie.

"He too"—the Doctor bowed.

"Well; and, if it is a fair question, who is he?" pursued the brother-in-law.

"Jean-Marie," answered the Doctor, "combines the functions of a son and stable-boy. He began as the latter, but he rose rapidly to the more honourable rank in our affections. He is, I may say, the greatest comfort in our lives."

"Ha!" said Casimir. "And previous to becoming one of you?"

"Jean-Marie has lived a remarkable existence; his experience has been eminently formative," replied Desprez. "If I had had to choose an education for my son, I should have chosen such another. Beginning life with mountebanks and thieves, passing onward to the society and friendship of philosophers, he may be said to have skimmed the volume of human life."

"Thieves?" repeated the brother-in-law, with a meditative air.

The Doctor could have bitten his tongue out. He foresaw what was coming, and prepared his mind for a vigorous defence.

"Did you ever steal yourself?" asked Casimir, turning suddenly on Jean-Marie, and for the first time employing a single eyeglass which hung round his neck.

"Yes, sir," replied the boy, with a deep blush.

Casimir turned to the others with pursed lips, and nodded to them meaningly. "Hey?" said he; "how is that?"

"Jean-Marie is a teller of the truth," returned the Doctor, throwing out his bust.

"He has never told a lie," added madame. "He is the best of boys."

"Never told a lie, has he not?" reflected Casimir. "Strange, very strange. Give me your attention, my young friend," he continued. "You knew about this treasure?"

"He helped to bring it home," interposed the Doctor.

"Desprez, I ask you nothing but to hold your tongue," returned Casimir. "I mean to question this stable-boy of yours; and if you are so certain of his innocence, you can afford to let him answer for himself. Now, sir," he resumed, pointing his eyeglass straight at Jean-Marie. "You knew it could be stolen with impunity? You knew you could not be prosecuted? Come! Did you, or did you not?"

"I did," answered Jean-Marie, in a miserable whisper. He sat there changing colour like a revolving pharos, twisting his fingers hysterically, swallowing air, the picture of guilt.

"You knew where it was put?" resumed the inquisitor.

"Yes," from Jean-Marie.

"You say you have been a thief before," continued Casimir. "Now how am I to know that you are not one still? I suppose you could climb the green gate?"

"Yes," still lower, from the culprit.

"Well, then, it was you who stole these things. You know it, and you dare not deny it. Look me in the face! Raise your sneak's eyes, and answer!"

But in place of anything of that sort Jean-Marie broke into a dismal howl and fled from the arbour. Anastasie, as she pursued to capture and reassure the victim, found time to send one Parthian arrow—"Casimir, you are a brute!"

"My brother," said Desprez, with the greatest dignity, "you take upon yourself a licence—"

"Desprez," interrupted Casimir, "for Heaven's sake be a man of the world. You telegraph me to leave my business and come down here on yours. I come, I ask the business, you say 'Find me this thief!' Well, I find him; I say 'There he is!' You need not like it, but you have no manner of right to take offence."

"Well," returned the Doctor, "I grant that; I will even thank you for your mistaken zeal. But your hypothesis was so extravagantly monstrous—"

"Look here," interrupted Casimir; "was it you or Stasie?"

"Certainly not," answered the Doctor.

"Very well; then it was the boy. Say no more about it," said the brother-in-law, and he produced a cigar-case.

"I will say this much more," returned Desprez: "if that boy came and told me so himself, I should not believe him; and if I did believe him, so implicit is my trust, I should conclude that he had acted for the best."

"Well, well," said Casimir indulgently. "Have you a light? I must be going. And by the way, I wish you would let me sell your Turks for you. I always told you it meant smash. I tell you so again. Indeed, it was partly that that brought me down. You never acknowledge my letters—a most unpardonable habit."

"My good brother," replied the Doctor blandly, "I have never denied your ability in business; but I can perceive your limitations."

"Egad, my friend, I can return the compliment," observed the man of business. "Your limitation is to be downright irrational."

"Observe the relative position," returned the Doctor with a smile. "It is your attitude to believe through thick and thin in one man's judgment—your own. I follow the same opinion, but critically and with open eyes. Which is the more irrational?—I leave it to yourself."

"Oh, my dear fellow!" cried Casimir, "stick to your Turks, stick to your stable-boy, go to the devil in general in your own way and be done with it. But don't ratiocinate with me—I cannot bear it. And so, ta-ta. I might as well have stayed away for any good I've done. Say good-bye from me to Stasie, and to the sullen hang-dog of a stable-boy, if you insist on it; I'm off."

And Casimir departed. The Doctor that night dissected his character before Anastasie. "One thing, my beautiful," he said, "he has learned one thing from his lifelong acquaintance with your husband: the word *ratiocinate*. It shines in his vocabulary, like a jewel in a muck-heap. And, even so, he continually misapplies it. For you must have observed he uses it as a sort of taunt, in the sense of *to ergotize*, implying, as it were—the poor, dear fellow!—a vein of sophistry. As for his cruelty to Jean-Marie, it must be forgiven him—it is not his nature, it is the nature of his life. A man who deals with money, my dear, is a man lost."

With Jean-Marie the process of reconciliation had been somewhat slow. At first he was inconsolable, insisted on leaving the family, went from paroxysm to paroxysm of tears; and it was only after Anastasie had been closeted for an hour with him, alone, that she came forth, sought out the Doctor, and, with tears in her eyes, acquainted that gentleman with what had passed.

"At first, my husband, he would hear of nothing," she said. "Imagine! if he had left us! what would the treasure be to that! Horrible treasure, it has brought all this about! At last, after he had sobbed his very heart out, he agrees to stay on a condition—we are not to mention this matter, this infamous suspicion, not even to mention the robbery. On that agreement only, the poor, cruel boy will consent to remain among his friends."

"But this inhibition," said the Doctor, "this embargo—it cannot possibly apply to me?"

"To all of us," Anastasie assured him.

"My cherished one," Desprez protested, "you must have misunderstood. It cannot apply to me. He would naturally come to me."

"Henri," she said, "it does; I swear to you it does."

"This is a painful, a very painful circumstance," the Doctor said, looking a little black. "I cannot affect, Anastasie, to be anything but justly wounded. I feel this, I feel it, my wife, acutely."

"I knew you would," she said. "But if you had seen his distress! We must make allowances, we must sacrifice our feelings."

"I trust, my dear, you have never found me averse to sacrifices," returned the Doctor very stiffly.

"And you will let me go and tell him that you have agreed? It will be like your noble nature," she cried.

So it would, he perceived—it would be like his noble nature! Up jumped his spirits, triumphant at the thought. "Go, darling," he said nobly, "reassure him. The subject is buried; more—I make an effort, I have accustomed my will to these exertions—and it is forgotten."

A little after, but still with swollen eyes and looking mortally sheepish, Jean-Marie reappeared and went ostentatiously about his business. He was the only unhappy member of the party that sat down that night to supper. As for the Doctor, he was radiant. He thus sang the requiem of the treasure:

"This has been, on the whole, a most amusing episode," he said. "We are not a penny the worse—nay, we are immensely gainers. Our philosophy has been exercised; some of the turtle is still left—the most wholesome of delicacies; I have my staff, Anastasie has her new dress, Jean-Marie is the proud possessor of a fashionable képi. Besides, we had a glass of Hermitage last night; the glow still suffuses my memory. I was growing positively niggardly with that Hermitage, positively niggardly. Let me take the hint: we had one bottle to celebrate the appearance of our visionary fortune; let us have a second to console us for its occultation. The third I hereby dedicate to Jean-Marie's wedding breakfast."

7. The Fall of the House of Desprez

THE Doctor's house has not yet received the compliment of a description, and it is now high time that the omission were supplied, for the house is itself an actor in the story, and one whose part is nearly at an end. Two storeys in height, walls of a warm yellow, tiles of an ancient ruddy brown diversified with moss and lichen, it stood with one wall to the street in the angle of the Doctor's property. It was roomy, draughty, and inconvenient. The large rafters were here and there engraven with rude marks and patterns; the hand-rail of the stair was carved in countrified arabesques; a stout timber pillar, which did duty to support the dining-room roof, bore mysterious characters on its darker sides, runes, according to the Doctor; nor did he fail, when he ran over the legendary history of the house and its possessors, to dwell upon the Scandinavian scholar who had left them. Floors, doors, and rafters made a great variety of angles; every room had a particular inclination; the gable had tilted towards the garden, after the manner of a leaning tower, and one of the former proprietors had buttressed the building from that side with a great strut of wood, like the derrick of a crane. Altogether, it had many marks of ruin; it was a house for the rats to desert; and nothing but its excellent brightness—the window-glass polished and shining, the paint well scoured, the brasses radiant, the very prop all wreathed about with climbing flowers—nothing but its air of a well-tended, smiling veteran, sitting, crutch and all, in the sunny corner of a garden, marked it as a house for comfortable people to inhabit. In poor or idle management it would soon have hurried into the blackguard stages of decay. As it was, the whole family loved it, and the Doctor was never better inspired than when he narrated its imaginary story and drew the character of its successive masters, from the Hebrew merchant who had re-edified its walls after the sack of the town, and past the mysterious engraver of the runes, down to the long-headed, dirty-handed boor from whom he had himself acquired it at a ruinous expense. As for any alarm about its security, the idea had never presented itself. What had stood four centuries might well endure a little longer.

Indeed, in this particular winter, after the finding and losing of the treasure, the Desprez had an anxiety of a very different order, and one which lay nearer their hearts. Jean-Marie was plainly not himself. He had fits of hectic activity, when he made unusual exertions to please, spoke more and faster, and redoubled in attention to his lessons. But these were interrupted by spells of melancholia and brooding silence, when the boy was little better than unbearable.

"Silence," the Doctor moralized—"you see, Anastasie, what comes of silence. Had the boy properly unbosomed himself, the little disappointment about the treasure, the little annoyance about Casimir's incivility would long ago have been forgotten. As it is, they prey upon him like a disease. He loses flesh, his appetite is variable and, on the whole, impaired. I keep him on the strictest regimen, I exhibit the most powerful tonics; both in vain."

"Don't you think you drug him too much?" asked madame, with an irrepressible shudder.

"Drug?" cried the Doctor; "I drug? Anastasie, you are mad!"

Time went on, and the boy's health still slowly declined. The Doctor blamed the weather, which was cold and boisterous. He called in his *confrère* from Bourron, took a fancy for him, magnified his capacity, and was pretty soon under treatment himself—it scarcely appeared for what complaint. He and Jean-Marie had each medicine to take at different periods of the day. The Doctor used to lie in wait for the exact moment, watch in hand. "There is nothing like regularity," he would say, fill out the doses, and dilate on the virtues of the draught; and if the boy seemed none the better, the Doctor was not at all the worse.

Gunpowder Day, the boy was particularly low. It was scowling, squally weather. Huge broken companies of cloud sailed swiftly overhead; raking gleams of sunlight swept the village, and were followed by intervals of darkness and white, flying rain. At times the wind lifted up its voice and bellowed. The trees were all scourging themselves along the meadows, the last leaves flying like dust.

The Doctor, between the boy and the weather, was in his element; he had a theory to prove. He sat with his watch out and a barometer in front of him, waiting for the squalls and noting their effect upon the human pulse. "For the true philosopher," he remarked delightedly, "every fact in nature is a toy." A letter came to him; but, as its arrival coincided with the approach of another gust, he merely crammed it into his pocket, gave the time to Jean-Marie, and the next moment they were both counting their pulses as if for a wager.

At nightfall the wind rose into a tempest. It besieged the hamlet, apparently from every side, as if with batteries of cannon; the houses shook and groaned; live coals were blown upon the floor. The uproar and terror of the night kept people long awake, sitting with pallid faces giving ear.

It was twelve before the Desprez family retired. By half-past one, when the storm was already somewhat past its height, the Doctor was awakened from a troubled slumber, and sat up. A noise still rang in his ears, but whether of this world or of the world of dreams he was not certain. Another clap of wind followed. It was accompanied by a sickening movement of the whole house, and in the subsequent lull Desprez could hear the tiles pouring like a cataract into the loft above his head. He plucked Anastasie bodily out of bed.

"Run!" he cried, thrusting some wearing apparel into her hands; "the house is falling! To the garden!"

She did not pause to be twice bidden; she was down the stair in an instant. She had never before suspected herself of such activity. The Doctor meanwhile, with the speed of a piece of pantomime business, and undeterred by broken shins, proceeded to rout out Jean-Marie, tore Aline from her virgin slumbers, seized her by the hand, and tumbled downstairs and into the garden, with the girl tumbling behind him, still not half awake.

The fugitives rendezvoused in the arbour by some common instinct. Then came a bull's-eye flash of straggling moonshine, which disclosed their four figures standing huddled from the wind in a raffle of flying drapery, and not without a considerable need for more. At the humiliating spectacle Anastasie clutched her night-dress desperately about her and burst loudly into tears. The Doctor flew to console her; but she elbowed him away. She suspected everybody of being the general public, and thought the darkness was alive with eyes.

Another gleam and another violent gust arrived together; the house was seen to rock on its foundation, and, just as the light was once more eclipsed, a crash which triumphed over the shouting of the wind announced its fall, and for a moment the whole garden was alive with skipping tiles and brickbats. One such missile grazed the Doctor's ear; another descended on the bare foot of Aline, who instantly made the night hideous with her shrieks.

By this time the hamlet was alarmed, lights flashed from the windows, hails reached the party, and the Doctor answered, nobly contending against Aline and the tempest. But this prospect of help only awakened Anastasie to a more active stage of terror.

"Henri, people will be coming," she screamed in her husband's ear.

"I trust so," he replied.

"They cannot. I would rather die," she wailed.

"My dear," said the Doctor reprovingly, "you are excited. I gave you some clothes. What have you done with them?"

"Oh, I don't know—I must have thrown them away! Where are they?" she sobbed.

Desprez groped about in the darkness. "Admirable!" he remarked; "my green velveteen trousers! This will exactly meet your necessities."

"Give them to me!" she cried fiercely; but as soon as she had them in her hands her mood appeared to alter—she stood silent for a moment, and then pressed the garment back upon the Doctor. "Give it to Aline," she said—"poor girl."

"Nonsense!" said the Doctor. "Aline does not know what she is about. Aline is beside herself with terror; and at any rate, she is a peasant. Now I am really concerned at this exposure for a person of your house-keeping habits; my solicitude and your fantastic modesty both point to the same remedy—the pantaloons." He held them ready.

"It is impossible. You do not understand," she said with dignity.

By this time rescue was at hand. It had been found impracticable to enter by the street, for the gate was blocked with masonry, and the nodding ruin still threatened further avalanches. But between the Doctor's garden and the one on the right hand there was that very picturesque contrivance—a common well; the door on the Desprez' side had chanced to be unbolted, and now, through the arched aperture a man's bearded face and an arm supporting a lantern were introduced into the world of windy darkness where Anastasie concealed her woes. The light struck here and there among the tossing apple boughs, it glinted on the grass; but the lantern and the glowing face became the centre of the world. Anastasie crouched back from the intrusion.

"This way!" shouted the man. "Are you all safe?"

Aline, still screaming, ran to the new-comer, and was presently hauled head-foremost through the wall.

"Now, Anastasie, come on; it is your turn," said the husband.

"I cannot," she replied.

"Are we all to die of exposure, madame?" thundered Doctor Desprez.

"You can go!" she cried. "Oh, go, go away! I can stay here: I am quite warm."

The Doctor took her by the shoulders with an oath.

"Stop!" she screamed. "I will put them on."

She took the detested lendings in her hand once more; but her repulsion was stronger than shame. "Never!" she cried, shuddering, and flung them far away into the night.

Next moment the Doctor had whirled her to the well. The man was there and the lantern; Anastasie closed her eyes and appeared to herself to be about to die. How she was transported through the arch she knew not; but once on the other side she was received by the neighbour's wife, and enveloped in a friendly blanket.

Beds were made ready for the two women, clothes of very various sizes for the Doctor and Jean-Marie; and for the remainder of the night, while madame dozed in and out on the borderland of hysterics, her husband sat beside the fire and held forth to the admiring neighbours. He showed them, at length, the causes of the accident: for years, he explained, the fall had been impending; one sign had followed another, the joints had opened, the plaster had cracked, the old walls bowed inward; last, not three weeks ago, the cellar door had begun to work with difficulty in its grooves. "The cellar!" he said, gravely shaking his head over a glass of mulled wine. "That reminds me of my poor vintages. By a manifest providence the Hermitage was nearly at an end. One bottle—I lose but one bottle of that incomparable wine. It had been set apart against Jean-Marie's wedding. Well, I must lay down some more; it will be an interest in life. I am, however, a man somewhat advanced in years. My great work is now buried in the fall of my humble roof; it will never be completed—my name will have been writ in water. And yet you find me calm—I would say cheerful. Can your priest do more?"

By the first glimpse of day the party sallied forth from the fireside into the street. The wind had fallen, but still charioted a world of troubled clouds; the air bit like a frost; and the party, as they stood about the ruins in the rainy twilight of the morning, beat upon their breasts and blew into their hands for warmth. The house had entirely fallen, the walls outward, the roof in; it was a mere heap of rubbish, with here and there a forlorn spear of broken rafter. A sentinel was placed over the ruins to protect the property, and the party adjourned to Tentaillon's to break their fast at the Doctor's expense. The bottle circulated somewhat freely; and before they left the table it had begun to snow.

For three days the snow continued to fall, and the ruins, covered with tarpaulin and watched by sentries, were left undisturbed. The Desprez meanwhile had taken up their abode at Tentaillon's. Madame spent her time in the kitchen, concocting little delicacies, with the admiring aid of Madame Tentaillon, or sitting by the fire in thoughtful abstraction. The fall of the house affected her wonderfully little; the blow had been parried by another; and in her mind she was continually fighting over again the battle of the trousers. Had she done right? Had she done wrong? And now she would applaud her determination; and anon, with a horrid flush of unavailing penitence, she would regret the trousers. No juncture in her life had so much exercised her judgment. In the meantime the Doctor had become vastly pleased with his situation. Two of the summer boarders still lingered behind the rest, prisoners for lack of a remittance; they were both English, but one of them spoke French pretty fluently, and was, besides, a humorous, agile-minded fellow, with whom the Doctor could reason by the hour, secure of comprehension. Many were the glasses they emptied, many the topics they discussed.

"Anastasie," the Doctor said on the third morning, "take an example from your husband, from Jean-Marie! The excitement has done more for the boy than all my tonics, he takes his turn as sentry with positive gusto. As for me, you behold me. I have made friends with the Egyptians; and my Pharaoh is, I swear it, a most agreeable companion. You alone are hipped. About a house—a few dresses? What are they in comparison to the 'Pharmacopœia'—the labour of years lying buried below stones and sticks in this depressing hamlet? The snow falls; I shake it from my cloak! Imitate me. Our income will be impaired, I grant it, since we must rebuild; but moderation, patience, and philosophy will gather about the hearth. In the meanwhile, the Tentaillons are obliging; the table, with your additions, will pass; only the wine is execrable—well, I shall send for some to-day. My Pharaoh will be gratified to drink a decent glass; aha! and I shall see if he possesses that acme of organisation—a palate. If he has a palate, he is perfect."

"Henri," she said, shaking her head; "you are a man; you cannot understand my feelings; no woman could shake off the memory of so public a humiliation."

The Doctor could not restrain a titter. "Pardon me, darling," he said; "but really, to the philosophical intelligence, the incident appears so small a trifle. You looked extremely well—"

"Henri!" she cried.

"Well, well, I will say no more," he replied. "Though, to be sure, if you had consented to indue—*A propos*," he broke off, "and my trousers! They are lying in the snow—my favourite trousers!" And he dashed in quest of Jean-Marie.

Two hours afterwards the boy returned to the inn with a spade under one arm and a curious sop of clothing under the other.

The Doctor ruefully took it in his hands. "They have been!" he said. "Their tense is past. Excellent pantaloons, you are no more! Stay, something in the pocket," and he produced a piece of paper. "A letter! ay, now I mind me; it was received on the morning of the gale, when I was absorbed in delicate investigations. It is still legible. From poor, dear Casimir! It is as well," he chuckled, "that I have educated him to patience. Poor Casimir and his correspondence—his infinitesimal, timorous, idiotic correspondence!"

He had by this time cautiously unfolded the wet letter; but, as he bent himself to decipher the writing, a cloud descended on his brow.

"*Bigre*!" he cried, with a galvanic start.

And then the letter was whipped into the fire, and the Doctor's cap was on his head in the turn of a hand.

"Ten minutes! I can catch it, if I run," he cried. "It is always late. I go to Paris. I shall telegraph."

"Henri! what is wrong?" cried his wife.

"Ottoman Bonds!" came from the disappearing Doctor; and Anastasie and Jean-Marie were left face to face with the wet trousers. Desprez had gone to Paris for the second time in seven years; he had gone to Paris with a pair of wooden shoes, a knitted spencer, a black blouse, a country night-cap, and twenty francs in his pocket. The fall of the house was but a secondary marvel; the whole world might have fallen and scarce left his family more petrified.

8. The Wages of Philosophy

ON THE morning of the next day, the Doctor, a mere spectre of himself, was brought back in the custody of Casimir. They found Anastasie and the boy sitting together by the fire; and Desprez, who had exchanged his toilette for a ready-made rig-out of poor materials, waved his hand as he entered, and sank speechless on the nearest chair. Madame turned direct to Casimir.

"What is wrong?" she cried.

"Well," replied Casimir, "what have I told you all along? It has come. It is a clean shave, this time; so you may as well bear up and make the best of it. House down, too, eh? Bad luck, upon my soul."

"Are we—are we—ruined?" she gasped.

The Doctor stretched out his arms to her. "Ruined," he replied, "you are ruined by your sinister husband."

Casimir observed the consequent embrace through his eyeglass; then he turned to Jean-Marie. "You hear?" he said. "They are ruined; no more pickings, no more house, no more fat cutlets. It strikes me, my friend, that you had best be packing; the present speculation is about worked out." And he nodded to him meaningly.

"Never!" cried Desprez, springing up. "Jean-Marie, if you prefer to leave me, now that I am poor, you can go; you shall receive your hundred francs, if so much remains to me. But if you will consent to stay"—the Doctor wept a little—"Casimir offers me a place—as clerk," he resumed. "The emoluments are slender, but they will be enough for three. It is too much already to have lost my fortune; must I lose my son?"

Jean-Marie sobbed bitterly, but without a word.

"I don't like boys who cry," observed Casimir. "This one is always crying. Here! you clear out of this for a little; I have business with your master and mistress, and these domestic feelings may be settled after I am gone. March!" and he held the door open.

Jean-Marie slunk out like a detected thief.

By twelve they were all at table but Jean-Marie.

"Hey?" said Casimir. "Gone, you see. Took the hint at once."

"I do not, I confess," said Desprez—"I do not seek to excuse his absence. It speaks of a want of heart that disappoints me sorely."

"Want of manners," corrected Casimir. "Heart, he never had. Why, Desprez, for a clever fellow, you are the most gullible mortal in creation. Your ignorance of human nature and human business is beyond belief. You are swindled by heathen Turks, swindled by vagabond children, swindled right and left, upstairs and downstairs. I think it must be your imagination. I thank my stars I have none."

"Pardon me," replied Desprez, still humbly, but with a return of spirit at sight of a distinction to be drawn; "pardon me, Casimir. You possess, even to an eminent degree, the commercial imagination. It was the lack of that in me—it appears it is my weak point—that has led to these repeated shocks. By the commercial imagination the financier forecasts the destiny of his investments, marks the falling house—"

"Egad," interrupted Casimir: "our friend the stable-boy appears to have his share of it."

The Doctor was silenced; and the meal was continued and finished principally to the tune of the brother-in-law's not very consolatory conversation. He entirely ignored the two young English painters, turning a blind eyeglass to their salutations, and continuing his remarks as if he were alone in the bosom of his family; and with every second word he ripped another stitch out of the air balloon of Desprez's vanity. By the time coffee was over the poor Doctor was as limp as a napkin.

"Let us go and see the ruins," said Casimir.

They strolled forth into the street. The fall of the house, like the loss of a front tooth, had quite transformed the village. Through the gap the eye commanded a great stretch of open snowy country, and the place shrank in comparison. It was like a room with an open door. The sentinel stood by the green gate, looking very red and cold, but he had a pleasant word for the Doctor and his wealthy kinsman.

Casimir looked at the mound of ruins, he tried the quality of the tarpaulin. "H'm," he said, "I hope the cellar arch has stood. If it has, my good brother, I will give you a good price for the wines."

"We shall start digging to-morrow," said the sentry. "There is no more fear of snow."

"My friend," returned Casimir sententiously, "you had better wait till you get paid."

The Doctor winced, and began dragging his offensive brother-in-law towards Tentaillon's. In the house there would be fewer auditors and these already in the secret of his fall.

"Hullo!" cried Casimir, "there goes the stable-boy with his luggage; no, egad, he is taking it into the inn."

And sure enough, Jean-Marie was seen to cross the snowy street and enter Tentaillon's, staggering under a large hamper.

The Doctor stopped with a sudden, wild hope.

"What can he have?" he said. "Let us go and see." And he hurried on.

"His luggage, to be sure," answered Casimir. "He is on the move—thanks to the commercial imagination."

"I have not seen that hamper for—for ever so long," remarked the Doctor.

"Nor will you see it much longer," chuckled Casimir; "unless, indeed, we interfere. And by the way, I insist on an examination."

"You will not require," said Desprez, positively with a sob; and, casting a moist, triumphant glance at Casimir, he began to run.

"What the devil is up with him, I wonder?" Casimir reflected; and then, curiosity taking the upper hand, he followed the Doctor's example and took to his heels.

The hamper was so heavy and large, and Jean-Marie himself so little and so weary, that it had taken him a great while to bundle it upstairs to the Desprez' private room; and he had just set it down on the floor in front of Anastasie, when the Doctor arrived, and was closely followed by the man of business. Boy and hamper were both in a most sorry plight; for the one had passed four months underground in a certain cave on the way to Achères, and the other had run about five miles as hard as his legs would carry him, half that distance under a staggering weight.

"Jean-Marie," cried the Doctor, in a voice that was only too seraphic to be called hysterical, "is it—? It is!" he cried. "Oh, my son, my son!" And he sat down upon the hamper and sobbed like a little child.

"You will not go to Paris now," said Jean-Marie sheepishly.

"Casimir," said Desprez, raising his wet face, "do you see that boy, that angel boy? He is the thief; he took the treasure from a man unfit to be entrusted with its use; he brings it back to me when I am sobered and humbled. These, Casimir, are the Fruits of my Teaching, and this moment is the Reward of my Life."

"*Tiens*," said Casimir.

Story of the Young Man with the Cream Tarts

FROM

The Suicide Club

DURING HIS residence in London, the accomplished Prince Florizel of Bohemia gained the affection of all classes by the seduction of his manner and by a well-considered generosity. He was a remarkable man even by what was known of him; and that was but a small part of what he actually did. Although of a placid temper in ordinary circumstances, and accustomed to take the world with as much philosophy as any ploughman, the Prince of Bohemia was not without a taste for ways of life more adventurous and eccentric than that to which he was destined by his birth. Now and then, when he fell into a low humour, when there was no laughable play to witness in any of the London theatres, and when the season of the year was unsuitable to those field sports in which he excelled all competitors, he would summon his confidant and Master of the Horse, Colonel Geraldine, and bid him prepare himself against an evening ramble. The Master of the Horse was a young officer of a brave and even temerarious disposition. He greeted the news with delight, and hastened to make ready. Long practice and a varied acquaintance of life had given him a singular facility in disguise; he could adapt not only his face and bearing, but his voice and almost his thoughts, to those of any rank, character, or nation; and in this way he diverted attention from the Prince, and sometimes gained admission for the pair into strange societies. The civil authorities were never taken into the secret of these adventures;

the imperturbable courage of the one and the ready invention and chivalrous devotion of the other had brought them through a score of dangerous passes; and they grew in confidence as time went on.

One evening in March they were driven by a sharp fall of sleet into an Oyster Bar in the immediate neighbourhood of Leicester Square. Colonel Geraldine was dressed and painted to represent a person connected with the Press in reduced circumstances; while the Prince had, as usual, travestied his appearance by the addition of false whiskers and a pair of large adhesive eyebrows. These lent him a shaggy and weather-beaten air, which, for one of his urbanity, formed the most impenetrable disguise. Thus equipped, the commander and his satellite sipped their brandy and soda in security.

The bar was full of guests, male and female; but though more than one of these offered to fall into talk with our adventurers, none of them promised to grow interesting upon a nearer acquaintance. There was nothing present but the lees of London and the commonplace of disrespectability; and the Prince had already fallen to yawning, and was beginning to grow weary of the whole excursion, when the swing doors were pushed violently open, and a young man, followed by a couple of commissionaires, entered the bar. Each of the commissionaires carried a large dish of cream tarts under a cover, which they at once removed; and the young man made the round of the company, and pressed these confections upon every one's acceptance with an exaggerated courtesy. Sometimes his offer was laughingly accepted; sometimes it was firmly, or even harshly, rejected. In these latter cases the newcomer always ate the tart himself, with some more or less humorous commentary.

At last he accosted Prince Florizel.

"Sir," said he, with a profound obeisance, proffering the tart at the same time between his thumb and forefinger, "will you so far honour an entire stranger? I can answer for the quality of the pastry, having eaten two dozen and three of them myself since five o'clock."

"I am in the habit," replied the Prince, "of looking not so much to the nature of a gift as to the spirit in which it is offered."

"The spirit, sir," returned the young man, with another bow, "is one of mockery."

"Mockery?" repeated Florizel. "And whom do you propose to mock?"

"I am not here to expound my philosophy," replied the other, "but to distribute these cream tarts. If I mention that I heartily include myself in the ridicule of the transaction, I hope you will consider honour satisfied and condescend. If not, you will constrain me to eat my twenty-eighth, and I own to being weary of the exercise."

"You touch me," said the Prince, "and I have all the will in the world to rescue you from this dilemma, but upon one condition. If my friend and I eat your cakes—for which we have neither of us any natural inclination—we shall expect you to join us at supper by way of recompense."

The young man seemed to reflect.

"I have still several dozen upon hand," he said at last; "and that will make it necessary for me to visit several more bars before my great affair is concluded. This will take some time; and if you are hungry—"

The Prince interrupted him with a polite gesture.

"My friend and I will accompany you," he said; "for we have already a deep interest in your very agreeable mode of passing an evening. And now that the preliminaries of peace are settled, allow me to sign the treaty for both."

And the Prince swallowed the tart with the best grace imaginable.

"It is delicious," said he.

"I perceive you are a connoisseur," replied the young man.

Colonel Geraldine likewise did honour to the pastry; and every one in that bar having now either accepted or refused his delicacies, the young man with the cream tarts led the way to another and similar establishment. The two commissionaires, who seemed to have grown accustomed to their absurd employment, followed immediately after; and the Prince and the Colonel brought up the rear, arm in arm, and smiling to each other as they went. In this order the company visited two other taverns, where scenes were enacted of a like nature to that already described—some refusing, some accepting, the favours of this vagabond hospitality, and the young man himself eating each rejected tart.

On leaving the third saloon the young man counted his store. There were but nine remaining, three in one tray and six in the other.

"Gentlemen," said he, addressing himself to his two new followers, "I am unwilling to delay your supper. I am positively sure you must be hungry. I feel that I owe you a special consideration. And on this great day for me, when I am closing a career of folly by my most conspicuously silly action, I wish to behave handsomely to all who give me countenance. Gentlemen, you shall wait no longer. Although my constitution is shattered by previous excesses, at the risk of my life I liquidate the suspensory condition."

With these words he crushed the nine remaining tarts into his mouth, and swallowed them at a single movement each. Then, turning to the commissionaires, he gave them a couple of sovereigns.

"I have to thank you," said he, "for your extraordinary patience."

And he dismissed them with a bow apiece. For some seconds he stood looking at the purse from which he had just paid his assistants, then, with a laugh, he tossed it into the middle of the street, and signified his readiness for supper.

In a small French restaurant in Soho, which had enjoyed an exaggerated reputation for some little while, but had already begun to be forgotten, and in a private room up two pair of stairs, the three companions made a very elegant supper, and drank three or four bottles of champagne, talking the while upon indifferent subjects. The young man was fluent and gay, but he laughed louder than was natural in a person of polite breeding; his hands trembled violently, and his voice took sudden and surprising inflections, which seemed to be independent of his will. The dessert had been cleared away, and all three had lighted their cigars, when the Prince addressed him in these words:

"You will, I am sure, pardon my curiosity. What I have seen of you has greatly pleased but even more puzzled me. And though I should be loth to seem indiscreet, I must tell you that my friend and I are persons very well worthy to be entrusted with a secret. We have many of our own, which we are continually revealing to improper ears. And if, as I suppose, your story is a silly one, you need have no delicacy with us, who are two of the silliest men in England. My name is Godall, Theophilus Godall; my friend is Major Alfred Hammersmith—or at least, such is the name by which he chooses to be known. We pass our lives entirely in the search for extravagant adventures; and there is no extravagance with which we are not capable of sympathy."

"I like you, Mr. Godall," returned the young man; "you inspire me with a natural confidence; and I have not the slightest objection to your friend the Major, whom I take to be a nobleman in masquerade. At least, I am sure he is no soldier."

25. An illustration by the well-known artist and typographer W. A. Dwiggins for *The Strange Case of Dr. Jekyll and Mr. Hyde* (New York, 1929).

26. This and the following plate are from the first illustrated edition of *The Black Arrow*, with illustrations by H. M. Paget, published in London in 1891. On this page: "The Lancastrians had already resumed their archery, and the shafts fell thick in the mouth of the street; but the duke, minding them not at all, deliberately drew his sword and dubbed Richard a knight upon the spot."

27. *The Black Arrow*, H. M. Paget: " 'Richard,' he said, very gravely. 'I heard you. Ye took the better part and pardoned; I took the worse, and there lays the clay of mine enemy. Pray for me!' And he wrung him by the hand."

28. This and the following plate are from the first edition of *The Wrecker* (London, 1892), which was written by Stevenson in collaboration with his stepson, Lloyd Osbourne. The illustrations were by William Hole (this plate) and W. L. Metcalf (Plate 29). On this page: "She lay head to the reef, where the huge blue wall of the rollers was for ever raging up and crumbling down; and to gain her starboard side, we must pass below the stern."

29. *The Wrecker*, W. L. Metcalf: "I threw myself beside him, as he replaced the box on its bottom and removed the lid. I cannot tell what I expected; a million's worth of diamonds might perhaps have pleased me; my cheeks burned, my heart throbbed to bursting; and lo! there was disclosed but a trayful of papers, neatly taped, and a cheque-book of the customary pattern."

30. An early example of trick photography used for publicity; a double exposure of Richard Mansfield as Dr. Jekyll and as Mr. Hyde in *Dr. Jekyll and Mr. Hyde*, a stage adaptation of Stevenson's story, dramatized by T. Russell Sullivan, which opened at the Lyceum Theatre, London, on 4 August 1888.

31. Drawing of a scene from *Treasure Island* on stage at the Strand Theatre, London, in 1922.

32. Frontispiece by Joseph Strong, the husband of Stevenson's step-daughter, Isobel, for the first edition of *The Silverado Squatters* (London, 1883): Stevenson and Fanny in the wood cabin in which they spent their honeymoon.

The Colonel smiled at this compliment to the perfection of his art; and the young man went on in a more animated manner.

"There is every reason why I should not tell you my story. Perhaps that is just the reason why I am going to do so. At least, you seem so well prepared to hear a tale of silliness that I cannot find it in my heart to disappoint you. My name, in spite of your example, I shall keep to myself. My age is not essential to the narrative. I am descended from my ancestors by ordinary generation, and from them I inherited the very eligible human tenement which I still occupy, and a fortune of three hundred pounds a year. I suppose they also handed on to me a hare-brain humour, which it has been my chief delight to indulge. I received a good education. I can play the violin nearly well enough to earn money in the orchestra of a penny gaff, but not quite. The same remark applies to the flute and the French horn. I learned enough of whist to lose about a hundred a year at that scientific game. My acquaintance with French was sufficient to enable me to squander money in Paris with almost the same facility as in London. In short, I am a person full of manly accomplishments. I have had every sort of adventure, including a duel about nothing. Only two months ago I met a young lady exactly suited to my taste in mind and body; I found my heart melt; I saw that I had come upon my fate at last, and was in the way to fall in love. But when I came to reckon up what remained to me of my capital, I found it amounted to something less than four hundred pounds! I ask you fairly—can a man who respects himself fall in love on four hundred pounds? I concluded, certainly not; left the presence of my charmer, and slightly accelerating my usual rate of expenditure, came this morning to my last eighty pounds. This I divided into two equal parts; forty I reserved for a particular purpose; the remaining forty I was to dissipate before the night. I have passed a very entertaining day, and played many farces besides that of the cream tarts which procured me the advantage of your acquaintance; for I was determined, as I told you, to bring a foolish career to a still more foolish conclusion; and when you saw me throw my purse into the street, the forty pounds were at an end. Now you know me as well as I know myself: a fool, but consistent in his folly; and, as I will ask you to believe, neither a whimperer nor a coward."

From the whole tone of the young man's statement it was plain that he harboured very bitter and contemptuous thoughts about himself.

His auditors were led to imagine that his love affair was nearer his heart than he admitted, and that he had a design on his own life. The farce of the cream tarts began to have very much the air of a tragedy in disguise.

"Why, is this not odd," broke out Geraldine, giving a look to Prince Florizel, "that we three fellows should have met by the merest accident in so large a wilderness as London, and should be so nearly in the same condition?"

"How?" cried the young man. "Are you, too, ruined? Is this supper a folly like my cream tarts? Has the devil brought three of his own together for a last carouse?"

"The devil, depend upon it, can sometimes do a very gentlemanly thing," returned Prince Florizel; "and I am so much touched by this coincidence, that, although we are not entirely in the same case, I am going to put an end to the disparity. Let your heroic treatment of the last cream tarts be my example."

So saying, the Prince drew out his purse and took from it a small bundle of bank-notes.

"You see, I was a week or so behind you, but I mean to catch you up and come neck and neck into the winning-post," he continued. "This," laying one of the notes upon the table, "will suffice for the bill. As for the rest——"

He tossed them into the fire, and they went up the chimney in a single blaze.

The young man tried to catch his arm, but as the table was between them his interference came too late.

"Unhappy man," he cried, "you should not have burned them all! You should have kept forty pounds."

"Forty pounds!" repeated the Prince. "Why, in Heaven's name, forty pounds?"

"Why not eighty?" cried the Colonel; "for to my certain knowledge there must have been a hundred in the bundle."

"It was only forty pounds he needed," said the young man gloomily. "But without them there is no admission. The rule is strict. Forty pounds for each. Accursed life, where a man cannot even die without money!"

The Prince and the Colonel exchanged glances.

"Explain yourself," said the latter. "I have still a pocket-book tolerably well lined, and I need not say how readily I should share my wealth with Godall. But I must know to what end: you must certainly tell us what you mean."

The young man seemed to awaken; he looked uneasily from one to the other, and his face flushed deeply.

"You are not fooling me?" he asked. "You are indeed ruined men like me?"

"Indeed, I am for my part," replied the Colonel.

"And for mine," said the Prince, "I have given you proof. Who but a ruined man would throw his notes into the fire? The action speaks for itself."

"A ruined man—yes," returned the other suspiciously, "or else a millionaire."

"Enough, sir," said the Prince; "I have said so, and I am not accustomed to have my word remain in doubt."

"Ruined?" said the young man. "Are you ruined, like me? Are you, after a life of indulgence, come to such a pass that you can only indulge yourself in one thing more? Are you"—he kept lowering his voice as he went on—"are you going to give yourselves that last indulgence? Are you going to avoid the consequences of your folly by the one infallible and easy path? Are you going to give the slip to the sheriff's officers of conscience by the one open door?"

Suddenly he broke off and attempted to laugh.

"Here is your health!" he cried, emptying his glass, "and good night to you, my merry ruined men."

Colonel Geraldine caught him by the arm as he was about to rise.

"You lack confidence in us", he said, "and you are wrong. To all your questions I make answer in the affirmative. But I am not so timid, and can speak the Queen's English plainly. We, too, like yourself, have had enough of life, and are determined to die. Sooner or later, alone or together, we meant to seek out Death and beard him where he lies ready. Since we have met you, and your case is more pressing, let it be tonight—and at once—and, if you will, all three together. Such a penniless trio," he cried, "should go arm in arm into the halls of Pluto, and give each other some countenance among the shades!"

Geraldine had hit exactly on the manners and intonations that became the part he was playing. The Prince himself was disturbed, and looked over at his confidant with a shade of doubt. As for the young man, the flush came back darkly into his cheek, and his eyes threw out a spark of light.

"You are the men for me!" he cried, with an almost terrible gaiety. "Shake hands upon the bargain!" (His hand was cold and wet.) "You little know in what a company you will begin the march! You little know in what a happy moment for yourselves you partook of my—cream tarts! I am only a unit, but I am a unit in an army. I know Death's private door. I am one of his familiars, and can show you into eternity without ceremony and yet without scandal."

They called upon him eagerly to explain his meaning.

"Can you muster eighty pounds between you?" he demanded.

Geraldine ostentatiously consulted his pocket-book, and replied in the affirmative.

"Fortunate beings!" cried the young man. "Forty pounds is the entry money of the Suicide Club."

"The Suicide Club," said the Prince, "why, what the devil is that?"

"Listen," said the young man; "this is the age of conveniences, and I have to tell you of the last perfection of the sort. We have affairs in different places; and hence railways were invented. Railways separated us infallibly from our friends; and so telegraphs were made that we might communicate speedily at great distances. Even in hotels we have lifts to spare us a climb of some hundred steps. Now, we know that life is only a stage to play the fool upon as long as the part amuses us. There was one more convenience lacking to modern comfort; a decent easy way to quit that stage; the back stairs to liberty; or, as I said this moment, Death's private door. This, my two fellow-rebels, is supplied by the Suicide Club. Do not suppose that you and I are alone, or even exceptional, in the highly reasonable desire that we profess. A large number of our fellow-men, who have grown heartily sick of the performance in which they are expected to join daily and all their lives long, are only kept from flight by one or two considerations. Some have families who would be shocked, or even blamed, if the matter became public; others have a weakness at heart and recoil from the circumstances of death. That is, to some extent, my own experience. I cannot put a pistol to my head and draw the trigger; for something stronger than myself withholds the act; and although I loathe life, I have not strength enough in my body to take hold of death and be done with it. For such as I and for all who desire to be out of the coil without posthumous scandal, the Suicide Club has been inaugurated. How this has been managed, what is its history, or what may be its ramifications in other lands, I am myself uninformed; and what I know of its constitution, I am not at liberty to communicate to you. To this extent, however, I am at your service. If you are truly tired of life, I will introduce you tonight to a meeting; and if not tonight, at least some time within the week, you will be easily relieved of your existences. It is now (consulting his watch) eleven; by half-past, at latest, we must leave this place; so that you have half an hour before you to consider my proposal. It is more serious than a cream tart," he added, with a smile; "and I suspect more palatable."

"More serious, certainly," returned Colonel Geraldine; "and as it is so much more so, will you allow me five minutes' speech in private with my friend, Mr. Godall?"

"It is only fair," answered the young man. "If you will permit, I will retire."

"You will be very obliging," said the Colonel.

As soon as the two were alone—"What," said Prince Florizel, "is the use of this confabulation, Geraldine? I see you are flurried, whereas my mind is very tranquilly made up. I will see the end of this."

"Your Highness," said the Colonel, turning pale; "let me ask you to consider the importance of your life, not only to your friends, but to the public interest. 'If not tonight,' said this madman; but supposing that tonight some irreparable disaster were to overtake your Highness's person, what, let me ask you, what would be my despair, and what the concern and disaster of a great nation?"

"I will see the end of this," repeated the Prince in his most deliberate tones; "and have the kindness, Colonel Geraldine, to remember and respect your word of honour as a gentleman. Under no circumstances, recollect, nor without my special authority, are you to betray the incognito under which I choose to go abroad. These were my commands, which I now reiterate. And now," he added, "let me ask you to call for the bill."

Colonel Geraldine bowed in submission; but he had a very white face as he summoned the young man of the cream tarts, and issued his directions to the waiter. The Prince preserved his undisturbed demeanour, and described a Palais Royal farce to the young suicide with great humour and gusto. He avoided the Colonel's appealing looks without ostentation, and selected another cheroot with more than usual care. Indeed, he was now the only man of the party who kept any command over his nerves.

The bill was discharged, the Prince giving the whole change of the note to the astonished waiter; and the three drove off in a four-wheeler. They were not long upon the way before the cab stopped at the entrance to a rather dark court. Here all descended.

After Geraldine had paid the fare, the young man turned, and addressed Prince Florizel as follows:

"It is still time, Mr. Godall, to make good your escape into thraldom. And for you, too, Major Hammersmith. Reflect well before you take another step; and if your hearts say no—here are the cross-roads."

"Lead on, sir," said the Prince. "I am not the man to go back from a thing once said."

"Your coolness does me good," replied their guide. "I have never seen anyone so unmoved at this conjuncture; and yet you are not the first whom I have escorted to this door. More than one of my friends has preceded me, where I knew I must shortly follow. But this is of no interest to you. Wait for me here for only a few moments; I shall return as soon as I have arranged the preliminaries of your introduction."

And with that the young man, waving his hand to his companions, turned into the court, entered a doorway and disappeared.

"Of all our follies," said Colonel Geraldine in a low voice, "this is the wildest and most dangerous."

"I perfectly believe so," returned the Prince.

"We have still," pursued the Colonel, "a moment to ourselves. Let me beseech your Highness to profit by the opportunity and retire. The consequences of this step are so dark, and may be so grave, that I feel myself justified in pushing a little further than usual the liberty which your Highness is so condescending as to allow me in private."

"Am I to understand that Colonel Geraldine is afraid?" asked his Highness, taking his cheroot from his lips, and looking keenly into the other's face.

"My fear is certainly not personal," replied the other proudly; "of that your Highness may rest well assured."

"I had supposed as much," returned the Prince, with undisturbed good humour; "but I was unwilling to remind you of the difference in our stations. No more—no more," he added, seeing Geraldine about to apologise, "you stand excused."

And he smoked placidly, leaning against a railing, until the young man returned.

"Well," he asked, "has our reception been arranged?"

"Follow me," was the reply. "The President will see you in the cabinet. And let me warn you to be frank in your answers. I have stood your guarantee; but the Club requires a searching inquiry before admission; for the indiscretion of a single member would lead to the dispersion of the whole society for ever."

The Prince and Geraldine put their heads together for a moment. "Bear me out in this," said the one; and "bear me out in that," said the other; and by boldly taking up the characters of men with whom both were acquainted, they had come to an agreement in a twinkling, and were ready to follow their guide into the President's cabinet.

There were no formidable obstacles to pass. The outer door stood open; the door of the cabinet was ajar; and there, in a small but very high apartment, the young man left them once more.

"He will be here immediately." he said, with a nod, as he disappeared.

Voices were audible in the cabinet through the folding doors which formed one end; and now and then the noise of a champagne cork, followed by a burst of laughter, intervened among the sounds of conversation. A single tall window looked out upon the river and the Embankment; and by the disposition of the lights they judged themselves not far from Charing Cross station. The furniture was scanty, and the coverings worn to the thread; and there was nothing movable except a hand-bell in the centre of a round table, and the hats and coats of a considerable party hung round the wall on pegs.

"What sort of a den is this?" said Geraldine.

"That is what I have come to see," replied the Prince. "If they keep live devils on the premises, the thing may grow amusing."

Just then the folding door was opened no more than was necessary for the passage of a human body; and there entered at the same moment a louder buzz of talk, and the redoubtable President of the Suicide Club. The President was a man of fifty or upwards; large and rambling in his gait, with shaggy side whiskers, a bald top to his head, and a veiled grey eye, which now and then emitted a twinkle. His mouth, which embraced a large cigar, he kept continually screwing round and round and from side to side, as he looked sagaciously and coldly at the strangers. He was dressed in light tweeds, with his neck very open in a striped shirt collar; and carried a minute-book under one arm.

"Good evening," said he, after he had closed the door behind him. "I am told you wish to speak with me."

"We have a desire, sir, to join the Suicide Club," replied the Colonel.

The President rolled his cigar about in his mouth.

"What is that?" he said abruptly.

"Pardon me," returned the Colonel, "but I believe you are the person best qualified to give us information on that point."

"I?" cried the President. "A Suicide Club? Come, come! this is a frolic for All Fools' Day. I can make allowances for gentlemen who get merry in their liquor; but let there be an end to this."

"Call your Club what you will," said the Colonel, "you have some company behind these doors, and we insist on joining it."

"Sir," returned the President curtly, "you have made a mistake. This is a private house, and you must leave instantly."

The Prince had remained quietly in his seat throughout this little colloquy; but now, when the Colonel looked over to him as much as to say, "Take your answer and come away, for God's sake!" he drew his cheroot from his mouth, and spoke:

"I have come here," said he, "upon the invitation of a friend of yours. He has doubtless informed you of my intention in thus intruding on your party. Let me remind you that a person in my circumstances has exceedingly little to bind him, and is not at all likely to tolerate much rudeness. I am a very quiet man, as a usual thing; but, my dear sir, you are either going to oblige me in the little matter of which you are aware, or you shall very bitterly repent that you ever admitted me to your ante-chamber."

The President laughed aloud.

"That is the way to speak," said he. "You are a man who is a man. You know the way to my heart, and can do what you like with me. Will you," he continued, addressing Geraldine, "will you step aside for a few minutes? I shall finish first with your companion, and some of the Club's formalities require to be fulfilled in private."

With these words he opened the door of a small closet, into which he shut the Colonel.

"I believe in you," he said to Florizel, as soon as they were alone; "but are you sure of your friend?"

"Not so sure as I am of myself, though he has more cogent reasons," answered Florizel, "but sure enough to bring him here without alarm. He has had enough to cure the most tenacious man of life. He was cashiered the other day for cheating at cards."

"A good reason, I dare say," replied the President; "at least, we have another in the same case, and I feel sure of him. Have you also been in the Service, may I ask?"

"I have," was the reply; "but I was too lazy—I left it early."

"What is your reason for being tired of life?" pursued the President.

"The same, as near as I can make out," answered the Prince; "unadulterated laziness."

The President started. "D—n it," said he, "you must have something better than that."

"I have no more money," added Florizel. "That is also a vexation, without doubt. It brings my sense of idleness to an acute point."

The President rolled his cigar round in his mouth for some seconds, directing his gaze straight into the eyes of this unusual neophyte; but the Prince supported his scrutiny with unabashed good temper.

"If I had not a deal of experience," said the President at last, "I should turn you off. But I know the world; and this much anyway, that the most frivolous excuses for a suicide are often the toughest to stand by. And when I downright like a man, as I do you, sir, I would rather strain the regulation than deny him."

The Prince and the Colonel, one after the other, were subjected to a long and particular interrogatory: the Prince alone; but Geraldine in the presence of the Prince, so that the President might observe the countenance of the one while the other was being warmly cross-examined. The result was satisfactory; and the President, after having booked a few details of each case, produced a form of oath to be accepted. Nothing could be conceived more passive than the obedience promised, or more stringent than the terms by which the juror bound himself. The man who forfeited a pledge so awful could scarcely have a rag of honour or any of the consolations of religion left to him. Florizel signed the document, but not without a shudder;

the Colonel followed his example with an air of great depression. Then the President received the entry money; and without more ado, introduced the two friends into the smoking-room of the Suicide Club.

The smoking-room of the Suicide Club was the same height as the cabinet into which it opened, but much larger, and papered from top to bottom with an imitation of oak wainscot. A large and cheerful fire and a number of gas-jets illuminated the company. The Prince and his follower made the number up to eighteen. Most of the party were smoking and drinking champagne; a feverish hilarity reigned, with sudden and rather ghastly pauses.

"Is this a full meeting?" asked the Prince.

"Middling," said the President. "By the way," he added, "if you have any money, it is usual to offer some champagne. It keeps up a good spirit, and is one of my own little perquisites."

"Hammersmith," said Florizel, "I may leave the champagne to you."

And with that he turned away and began to go round among the guests. Accustomed to play the host in the highest circles, he charmed and dominated all whom he approached; there was something at once winning and authoritative in his address; and his extraordinary coolness gave him yet another distinction in this half-maniacal society. As he went from one to another he kept both his eyes and ears open, and soon began to gain a general idea of the people among whom he found himself. As in all other places of resort, one type predominated: people in the prime of youth, with every show of intelligence and sensibility in their appearance, but with little promise of strength or the quality that makes success. Few were much above thirty and not a few were still in their teens. They stood, leaning on tables and shifting their feet; sometimes they smoked extraordinarily fast, and sometimes they let their cigars go out; some talked well, but the conversation of others was plainly the result of nervous tension, and was equally without wit or purport. As each new bottle of champagne was opened, there was a manifest improvement in gaiety. Only two were seated—one in a chair in the recess of the window with his head hanging and his hands plunged deep into his trouser pockets, pale, visibly moist with perspiration, saying never a word, a very wreck of soul and body; the other sat on the divan close by the chimney, and attracted notice by a trenchant dissimilarity from all the rest. He was probably upwards of forty, but he looked fully ten years older; and Florizel thought he had never seen a man more naturally hideous, nor one more ravaged by disease and ruinous excitements. He was no more than skin and bone, was partly paralysed, and wore spectacles of such unusual power that his eyes appeared through the glasses greatly magnified and distorted in shape. Except the Prince and the President, he was the only person in the room who preserved the composure of ordinary life.

There was little decency among the members of the Club. Some boasted of the disgraceful actions, the consequences of which had reduced them to seek refuge in death; and the others listened without disapproval. There was a tacit understanding against moral judgments; and whoever passed the Club doors enjoyed already some of the immunities of the tomb. They drank to each other's memories, and to those of notable suicides in the past. They compared and developed their different views of death—some declaring that it was no more than blackness and cessation; others full of a hope that that very night they should be scaling the stars and commercing with the mighty dead.

"To the eternal memory of Baron Trenck, the type of suicides!" cried one. "He went out of a small cell into a smaller, that he might come forth again to freedom."

"For my part," said a second, "I wish no more than a bandage for my eyes and cotton for my ears. Only they have no cotton thick enough in this world."

A third was for reading the mysteries of life in a future state; and a fourth professed that he would never have joined the Club if he had not been induced to believe in Mr. Darwin.

"I could not bear," said this remarkable suicide, "to be descended from an ape."

Altogether the Prince was disappointed by the bearing and conversation of the members.

"It does not seem to me," he thought, "a matter for so much disturbance. If a man has made up his mind to kill himself, let him do it, in God's name, like a gentleman. This flutter and big talk is out of place."

In the meanwhile Colonel Geraldine was a prey to the blackest apprehensions; the Club and its rules were still a mystery, and he looked round the room for someone who should be able to set his mind at rest. In his survey his eye lighted on the paralytic person with the strong spectacles; and seeing him so exceedingly tranquil, he besought the President, who was going in and out of the room under a pressure of business, to present him to the gentleman on the divan.

The functionary explained the needlessness of all such formalities within the Club, but nevertheless presented Mr. Hammersmith to Mr. Malthus.

Mr. Malthus looked at the Colonel curiously, and then requested him to take a seat upon his right.

"You are a newcomer," he said, "and wish information? You have come to the proper source. It is two years since I first visited this charming Club."

The Colonel breathed again. If Mr. Malthus had frequented the place for two years there could be little danger for the Prince in a single evening. But Geraldine was none the less astonished, and began to suspect a mystification.

"What!" cried he, "two years! I thought—but indeed I see I have been made the subject of a pleasantry."

"By no means," replied Mr. Malthus mildly. "My case is peculiar. I am not, properly speaking, a suicide at all; but, as it were, an honorary member. I rarely visit the Club twice in two months. My infirmity and the kindness of the President have procured me these little immunities, for which besides I pay at an advanced rate. Even as it is my luck has been extraordinary."

"I am afraid," said the Colonel, "that I must ask you to be more explicit. You must remember that I am still most imperfectly acquainted with the rules of the Club."

"An ordinary member who comes here in search of death like yourself," replied the paralytic, "returns every evening until fortune favours him. He can even, if he is penniless, get board and lodging from the President: very fair, I believe, and clean, although, of course, not luxurious; that could hardly be, considering the exiguity (if I may so express myself) of the subscription. And then the President's company is a delicacy in itself."

"Indeed!" cried Geraldine, "he had not greatly prepossessed me."

"Ah!" said Mr. Malthus, "you do not know the man: the drollest fellow! What stories! What cynicism! He knows life to admiration, and between ourselves, is probably the most corrupt rogue in Christendom."

"And he also," asked the Colonel, "is a permanency—like yourself, if I may say so without offence?"

"Indeed, he is a permanency in a very different sense from me," replied Mr. Malthus. "I have been graciously spared, but I must go at last. Now he never plays. He shuffles and deals for the Club, and makes the necessary arrangements. That man, my dear Mr. Hammersmith, is the very soul of ingenuity. For three years he has pursued in London his useful, and, I think I may add, his artistic calling; and not so much as a whisper of suspicion has been once aroused. I believe him myself to be inspired. You doubtless remember the celebrated case, six months ago, of the gentleman who was accidentally poisoned in a chemist's shop? That was one of the least rich, one of the least racy, of his notions; but then, how simple! and how safe!"

"You astound me," said the Colonel. "Was that unfortunate gentlemen one of the——" He was about to say "victims"; but bethinking himself in time, he substituted—"members of the Club?"

In the same flash of thought it occurred to him that Mr. Malthus himself had not at all spoken in the tone of one who is in love with death; and he added hurriedly:

"But I perceive I am still in the dark. You speak of shuffling and dealing; pray for what end? And since you seem rather unwilling to die than otherwise, I must own that I cannot conceive what brings you here at all."

"You say truly that you are in the dark," replied Mr. Malthus with more animation. "Why, my dear sir, this Club is the temple of intoxication. If my enfeebled health could support the excitement more often, you may depend upon it I should be more often here. It requires all the sense of duty engendered by a long habit of ill-health and careful regimen, to keep me from excess in this, which is, I may say, my last dissipation. I have tried them all, sir," he went on, laying his hand on Geraldine's arm, "all without exception, and I declare to you, upon my honour, there is not one of them that has not been grossly and untruthfully overrated. People trifle with love. Now, I deny that love is a strong passion. Fear is the strong passion; it is with fear that you must trifle, if you wish to taste the intensest joys of living. Envy me—envy me, sir," he added with a chuckle, "I am a coward!"

Geraldine could scarcely repress a movement of repulsion for this deplorable wretch; but he commanded himself with an effort and continued his inquiries.

"How, sir," he asked, "is the excitement so artfully prolonged? And where is there any element of uncertainty?"

"I must tell you how the victim for every evening is selected," returned Mr. Malthus; "and not only the victim, but another member, who is to be the instrument in the Club's hands, and death's high priest for that occasion."

"Good God!" said the Colonel, "do they then kill each other?"

"The trouble of suicide is removed in that way," returned Malthus with a nod.

"Merciful Heavens!" ejaculated the Colonel, "and may you—may I—may the—my friend I mean—may any of us be pitched upon this evening as the slayer of another man's body and immortal spirit? Can such things be possible among men born of women? Oh! infamy of infamies!"

He was about to rise in his horror, when he caught the Prince's eye. It was fixed upon him from across the room with a frowning and angry stare. And in a moment Geraldine recovered his composure.

"After all," he added, "why not? And since you say the game is interesting, *vogue la galère*—I follow the Club!"

Mr. Malthus had keenly enjoyed the Colonel's amazement and disgust. He had the vanity of wickedness; and it pleased him to see another man give way to a generous movement, while he felt himself, in his entire corruption, superior to such emotions.

"You now, after your first moment of surprise," said he, "are in a position to appreciate the delights of our society. You can see how it combines the excitement of a gaming-table, a duel, and a Roman amphitheatre. The Pagans did well enough; I cordially admire the refinement of their minds; but it has been reserved for a Christian country to attain this extreme, this quintessence, this absolute poignancy. You will understand how vapid are all amusements to a man who has acquired a taste for this one. The game we play," he continued, "is one of extreme simplicity. A full pack—but I perceive you are about to see the thing in progress. Will you lend me the help of your arm? I am unfortunately paralysed."

Indeed, just as Mr. Malthus was beginning his description, another pair of folding-doors was thrown open, and the whole Club began to pass, not without some hurry, into the adjoining room. It was similar in every respect to the one from which it was entered, but somewhat differently furnished. The centre was occupied by a long green table, at which the President sat shuffling a pack of cards with great particularity. Even with the stick and the Colonel's arm, Mr. Malthus walked with so much difficulty that everyone was seated before this pair and the Prince, who had waited for them, entered the apartment; and in consequence, the three took seats close together at the lower end of the board.

"It is a pack of fifty-two," whispered Mr. Malthus. "Watch for the ace of spades, which is the sign of death, and the ace of clubs, which designates the official of the night. Happy, happy young men!" he added. "You have good eyes, and can follow the game. Alas! I cannot tell an ace from a deuce across the table."

And he proceeded to equip himself with a second pair of spectacles.

"I must at least watch the faces," he explained.

The Colonel rapidly informed his friend of all that he had learned from the honorary member, and of the horrible alternative that lay before them. The Prince was conscious of a deadly chill and a contraction about his heart; he swallowed with difficulty, and looked from side to side like a man in a maze.

"One bold stroke," whispered the Colonel, "and we may still escape."

But the suggestion recalled the Prince's spirits.

"Silence!" said he. "Let me see that you can play like a gentleman for any stake, however serious."

And he looked about him, once more to all appearance at his ease, although his heart beat quickly, and he was conscious of an unpleasant heat in his bosom. The members were all very quiet and intent; everyone was pale, but none so pale as Mr. Malthus. His eyes protruded; his head kept nodding involuntarily upon his spine; his hands found their way, one after the other, to his mouth, where they made clutches at his tremulous and ashen lips. It was plain that the honorary member enjoyed his membership on very startling terms.

"Attention, gentlemen!" said the President.

And he began slowly dealing the cards about the table in the reverse direction, pausing until each man had shown his card. Nearly everyone hesitated; and sometimes you would see a player's fingers stumble more than once before he could turn over the momentous slip of pasteboard. As the Prince's turn drew nearer, he was conscious of a growing and almost suffocating excitement; but he had somewhat of the gambler's nature, and recognized almost with astonishment that there was a degree of pleasure in his sensations. The nine of clubs fell to his lot; the three of spades was dealt to Geraldine; and the queen of hearts to Mr. Malthus, who was unable to suppress a sob of relief. The young man of the cream tarts almost immediately afterwards turned over the ace of clubs, and remained frozen with horror, the card still resting on his finger; he had not come there to kill, but to be killed; and the Prince in his generous sympathy with his position almost forgot the peril that still hung over himself and his friend.

The deal was coming round again, and still Death's card had not come out. The players held their respiration, and only breathed by gasps. The Prince received another club; Geraldine had a diamond; but when Mr. Malthus turned up his card a horrible noise, like that of something breaking, issued from his mouth; and he rose from his seat and sat down again, with no sign of his paralysis. It was the ace of spades. The honorary member had trifled once too often with his terrors.

Conversation broke out again almost at once. The players relaxed their rigid attitudes, and began to rise from the table and stroll back by twos and threes into the smoking-room. The President stretched his arms and yawned, like a man who has finished his day's work. But Mr. Malthus sat in his place, with his head in his hands, and his hands upon the table, drunk and motionless—a thing stricken down.

The Prince and Geraldine made their escape at once. In the cold night air their horror of what they had witnessed was redoubled.

"Alas!" cried the Prince, "to be bound by an oath in such a matter! To allow this wholesale trade in murder to be continued with profit and impunity! If I but dared to forfeit my pledge!"

"That is impossible for your Highness," replied the Colonel, "whose honour is the honour of Bohemia. But I dare, and may with propriety, forfeit mine."

"Geraldine," said the Prince, "if your honour suffers in any of the adventures into which you follow me, not only will I never pardon you, but—what I believe will much more sensibly affect you—I should never forgive myself."

"I receive your Highness's commands," replied the Colonel. "Shall we go from this accursed spot?"

"Yes," said the Prince. "Call a cab in Heaven's name, and let me try to forget in slumber the memory of this night's disgrace."

But it was notable that he carefully read the name of the court before he left it.

The next morning, as soon as the Prince was stirring, Colonel Geraldine brought him a daily newspaper, with the following paragraph marked:

> MELANCHOLY ACCIDENT.—This morning, about two o'clock, Mr. Bartholomew Malthus, of 16 Chepstow Place, Westbourne Grove, on his way home from a party at a friend's house, fell over the upper parapet in Trafalgar Square, fracturing his skull and breaking a leg and an arm. Death was instantaneous. Mr. Malthus, accompanied by a friend, was engaged in looking for a cab at the time of the unfortunate occurrence. As Mr. Malthus was paralytic, it is thought that his fall may have been occasioned by another seizure. The unhappy gentleman was well known in the most respectable circles, and his loss will be widely and deeply deplored.

"If ever a soul went straight to hell," said Geraldine solemnly, "it was that paralytic man's."

The Prince buried his face in his hands and remained silent.

"I am almost rejoiced," continued the Colonel, "to know that he is dead. But for our young man of the cream tarts I confess my heart bleeds."

"Geraldine," said the Prince, raising his face, "that unhappy lad was last night as innocent as you and I, and this morning the guilt of blood is on his soul. When I think of the President, my heart grows sick within me. I do not know how it shall be done, but I shall have that scoundrel at my mercy as there is a God in Heaven. What an experience, what a lesson, was that game of cards!"

"One," said the Colonel, "never to be repeated."

The Prince remained so long without replying that Geraldine grew alarmed.

"You cannot mean to return," he said. "You have suffered too much and seen too much horror already. The duties of your high position forbid the repetition of the hazard."

"There is much in what you say," replied Prince Florizel, "and I am not altogether pleased with my own determination. Alas! in the clothes of the greatest potentate, what is there but a man? I never felt my weakness more acutely than now, Geraldine, but it is stronger than I. Can I cease to interest myself in the fortunes of the unhappy young man who supped with us some hours ago? Can I leave the President to follow his nefarious career unwatched? Can I begin an adventure so entrancing, and not follow it to an end? No, Geraldine: you ask of the Prince more than the man is able to perform. Tonight, once more, we take our places at the table of the Suicide Club."

Colonel Geraldine fell upon his knees.

"Will your Highness take my life?" he cried. "It is his—his freely; but do not, oh do not! let him ask me to countenance so terrible a risk."

"Colonel Geraldine," replied the Prince, with some haughtiness of manner, "your life is absolutely your own. I only looked for obedience; and when that is unwillingly rendered, I shall look for that no longer. I add one word: your importunity in this affair has been sufficient."

The Master of the Horse regained his feet at once.

"Your Highness," he said, "may I be excused in my attendance this afternoon? I dare not, as an honourable man, venture a second time into that fatal house until I have perfectly ordered my affairs. Your Highness shall meet, I promise him, with no more opposition from the most devoted and grateful of his servants."

"My dear Geraldine," returned Prince Florizel, "I always regret when you oblige me to remember my rank. Dispose of your day as you think fit, but be here before eleven in the same disguise."

The Club, on this second evening, was not so fully attended; and when Geraldine and the Prince arrived, there were not above half a dozen persons in the smoking-room. His Highness took the President aside and congratulated him warmly on the demise of Mr. Malthus.

"I like," he said, "to meet with capacity, and certainly find much of it in you. Your profession is of a very delicate nature, but I see you are well qualified to conduct it with success and secrecy."

The President was somewhat affected by these compliments from one of his Highness's superior bearing. He acknowledged them almost with humility.

"Poor Malthy!" he added, "I shall hardly know the Club without him. The most of my patrons are boys, sir, and poetical boys, who are not much company for me. Not but what Malthy had some poetry, too; but it was of a kind that I could understand."

"I can readily imagine you should find yourself in sympathy with Mr. Malthus," returned the Prince. "He struck me as a man of a very original disposition."

The young man of the cream tarts was in the room, but painfully depressed and silent. His late companions sought in vain to lead him into conversation.

"How bitterly I wish," he cried, "that I had never brought you to this infamous abode! Begone, while you are clean-handed. If you could have heard the old man scream as he fell, and the noise of his bones upon the pavement! Wish me, if you have any kindness to so fallen a being—wish the ace of spades for me tonight!"

A few more members dropped in as the evening went on, but the Club did not muster more than the devil's dozen when they took their places at the table. The Prince was again conscious of a certain joy in his alarms; but he was astonished to see Geraldine so much more self-possessed than on the night before.

"It is extraordinary," thought the Prince, "that a will, made or unmade, should so greatly influence a young man's spirit."

"Attention, gentlemen!" said the President, and he began to deal.

Three times the cards went all round the table, and neither of the marked cards had yet fallen from his hand. The excitement as he began the fourth distribution was overwhelming. There were just cards enough to go once more entirely round. The Prince, who sat second from the dealer's left, would receive, in the reverse mode of dealing practised at the Club, the second last card. The third player turned up a black ace—it was the ace of clubs. The next received a diamond, the next a heart, and so on; but the ace of spades was still undelivered. At last, Geraldine, who sat upon the Prince's left, turned his card; it was an ace, but the ace of hearts.

When Prince Florizel saw his fate upon the table in front of him, his heart stood still. He was a brave man, but the sweat poured off his face. There were exactly fifty chances out of a hundred that he was doomed. He reversed the card; it was the ace of spades. A loud roaring filled his brain, and the table swam before his eyes. He heard the player on his right break into a fit of laughter that sounded between mirth and disappointment; he saw the company rapidly dispersing, but his mind was full of other thoughts. He recognized how foolish, how criminal, had been his conduct. In perfect health, in the prime of his years, the heir to a throne, he had gambled away his future and that of a brave and loyal country. "God," he cried, "God forgive me!" And with that, the confusion of his senses passed away, and he regained his self-possession in a moment.

To his surprise Geraldine had disappeared. There was no one in the card-room but his destined butcher consulting with the President, and the young man of the cream tarts, who slipped up to the Prince and whispered in his ear:

"I would give a million, if I had it, for your luck."

His Highness could not help reflecting, as the young man departed, that he would have sold his opportunity for a much more moderate sum.

The whispered conference now came to an end. The holder of the ace of clubs left the room with a look of intelligence, and the President, approaching the unfortunate Prince, proffered him his hand.

"I am pleased to have met you, sir," said he, "and pleased to have been in a position to do you this trifling service. At least, you cannot complain of delay. On the second evening—what a stroke of luck!"

The Prince endeavoured in vain to articulate something in response, but his mouth was dry and his tongue seemed paralysed.

"You feel a little sickish?" asked the President, with some show of solicitude. "Most gentlemen do. Will you take a little brandy?"

The Prince signified in the affirmative, and the other immediately filled some of the spirit into a tumbler.

"Poor old Malthy!" ejaculated the President, as the Prince drained the glass. "He drank near upon a pint, and little enough good it seemed to do him!"

"I am more amenable to treatment," said the Prince, a good deal revived. "I am my own man again at once, as you perceive. And so, let me ask you, what are my directions?"

"You will proceed along the Strand in the direction of the City, and on the left-hand pavement, until you meet the gentleman who has just left the room. He will continue your instructions, and him you will have the kindness to obey; the authority of the Club is vested in his person for the night. And now," added the President, "I wish you a pleasant walk."

Florizel acknowledged the salutation rather awkwardly, and took his leave. He passed through the smoking-room, where the bulk of the players were still consuming champagne, some of which he had himself ordered and paid for; and he was surprised to find himself cursing them in his heart. He put on his hat and great-coat in the cabinet, and selected his umbrella from a corner. The familiarity of these acts, and the thought that he was about them for the last time, betrayed him into a fit of laughter which sounded unpleasantly in his own ears. He conceived a reluctance to leave the cabinet, and turned instead to the window. The sight of the lamps and the darkness recalled him to himself.

"Come, come, I must be a man," he thought, "and tear myself away."

At the corner of Box Court three men fell upon Prince Florizel, and he was unceremoniously thrust into a carriage, which at once drove rapidly away. There was already an occupant.

"Will your Highness pardon my zeal?" said a well-known voice.

The Prince threw himself upon the Colonel's neck in a passion of relief.

"How can I ever thank you?" he cried. "And how was this effected?"

Although he had been willing to march upon his doom, he was overjoyed to yield to friendly violence, and return once more to life and hope.

"You can thank me effectually enough," replied the Colonel, "by avoiding all such dangers in the future. And as for your second question, all has been managed by the simplest means. I arranged this afternoon with a celebrated detective. Secrecy has been promised and paid for. Your own servants have been principally engaged in the affair. The house in Box Court has been surrounded since nightfall, and this, which is one of your own carriages, has been awaiting you for nearly an hour."

"And the miserable creature who was to have slain me—what of him?" inquired the Prince.

"He was pinioned as he left the Club," replied the Colonel, "and now awaits your sentence at the Palace, where he will soon be joined by his accomplices."

"Geraldine," said the Prince, "you have saved me against my explicit orders, and you have done well. I owe you not only my life, but a lesson; and I should be unworthy of my rank if I did not show myself grateful to my teacher. Let it be yours to choose the manner."

There was a pause, during which the carriage continued to speed through the streets, and the two men were each buried in his own reflections. The silence was broken by Colonel Geraldine.

"Your Highness," said he, "has by this time a considerable body of prisoners. There is at least one criminal among the number to whom justice should be dealt. Our oath forbids us all recourse to law; and discretion would forbid it equally if the oath were loosened. May I inquire your Highness's intention?"

"It is decided," answered Florizel; "the President must fall in a duel. It only remains to choose his adversary."

"Your Highness has permitted me to name my own recompense," said the Colonel. "Will he permit me to ask the appointment of my brother? It is an honourable post, but I dare assure your Highness that the lad will acquit himself with credit."

"You ask me an ungracious favour," said the Prince, "but I must refuse you nothing."

The Colonel kissed the hand with the greatest affection; and at that moment the carriage rolled under the archway of the Prince's splendid residence.

An hour after, Florizel in his official robes, and covered with all the orders of Bohemia, received the members of the Suicide Club.

"Foolish and wicked men," said he, "as many of you as have been driven into this strait by the lack of fortune shall receive employment and remuneration from my officers. Those who suffer under a sense of guilt must have recourse to a higher and more generous Potentate than I. I feel pity for all of you, deeper than you can imagine; tomorrow you shall tell me your stories; and as you answer more frankly, I shall be the more able to remedy your misfortunes. As for you," he added, turning to the President, "I should only offend a person of your parts by any offer of assistance; but I have instead a piece of diversion to propose to you. Here," laying his hand on the shoulder of Colonel Geraldine's young brother, "is an officer of mine who desires to make a little tour upon the Continent: and I ask you, as a favour, to accompany him on this excursion. Do you," he went on, changing his tone, "do you shoot well with the pistol? Because you may have need of that accomplishment. When two men go travelling together, it is best to be prepared for all. Let me add that, if by any chance you should lose young Mr. Geraldine upon the way, I shall always have another member of my household to place at your disposal; and I am known, Mr. President, to have long eyesight and as long an arm."

With these words, said with much sternness, the Prince concluded his address. Next morning the members of the Club were suitably provided for by his munificence, and the President set forth upon his travels, under the supervision of Mr. Geraldine, and a pair of faithful and adroit lackeys, well trained in the Prince's household. Not content with this, discreet agents were put in possession of the house in Box Court, and all letters or visitors for the Suicide Club or its officials were to be examined by Prince Florizel in person.

The Donkey, the Pack, and the Pack-saddle

FROM

Travels with a Donkey in the Cévennes

IN A LITTLE place called Le Monastier, in a pleasant highland valley fifteen miles from Le Puy, I spent about a month of fine days. Monastier is notable for the making of lace, for drunkenness, for freedom of language, and for unparalleled political dissension. There are adherents of each of the four French parties—Legitimists, Orleanists, Imperialists, and Republicans—in this little mountain-town; and they all hate, loathe, decry, and calumniate each other. Except for business purposes, or to give each other the lie in a tavern brawl, they have laid aside even the civility of speech. 'Tis a mere mountain Poland. In the midst of this Babylon I found myself a rallying point; everyone was anxious to be kind and helpful to the stranger. This was not merely from the natural hospitality of mountain people, nor even from the surprise with which I was regarded as a man living of his own free will in Le Monastier, when he might just as well have lived anywhere else in this big world; it arose a good deal from my projected excursion southward through the Cévennes. A traveller of my sort was a thing hitherto unheard of in that district. I was looked upon with contempt, like a man who should project a journey to the moon, but yet with a respectful interest, like one setting forth for the inclement Pole. All were ready to help in my preparations; a crowd of sympathizers supported me at the critical moment of a bargain; not a step was taken but was heralded by glasses round and celebrated by a dinner or a breakfast.

It was already hard upon October before I was ready to set forth, and at the high altitudes over which my road lay there was no Indian summer to be looked for. I was determined, if not to camp out, at least to have the means of camping out in my possession; for there is nothing more harassing to an easy mind than the necessity of reaching shelter by dusk, and the hospitality of a village inn is not always to be reckoned sure by those who trudge on foot. A tent, above all for a solitary traveller, is troublesome to pitch, and troublesome to strike again; and even on the march it forms a conspicuous feature in your baggage. A sleeping-sack, on the other hand, is always ready—you have only to get into it; it serves a double purpose—a bed by night, a portmanteau by day; and it does not advertise your intention of camping out to every curious passer-by. This is a huge point. If the camp is not secret, it is but a troubled resting-place; you become a public character; the convivial rustic visits your bedside after an early supper; and you must sleep with one eye open, and be up before the day. I decided on a sleeping-sack; and after repeated visits to Le Puy, and a deal of high living for myself and my advisers, a sleeping-sack was designed, constructed, and triumphantly brought home.

This child of my invention was nearly six feet square, exclusive of two triangular flaps to serve as a pillow by night and as the top and bottom of the sack by day. I call it "the sack", but it was never a sack by more than courtesy; only a sort of long roll or sausage, a green waterproof cart-cloth without and blue sheep's fur within. It was commodious as a valise, warm and dry for a bed. There was luxurious turning room for one; and at a pinch the thing might serve for two. I could bury myself in it up to the neck; for my head I trusted to a fur cap, with a hood to fold down over my ears and a band to pass under my nose like a respirator; and in case of heavy rain I proposed to make myself a little tent, or tentlet, with my waterproof coat, three stones and a bent branch.

It will readily be conceived that I could not carry this huge package on my own, merely human, shoulders. It remained to choose a beast of burden. Now, a horse is a fine lady among animals, flighty, timid, delicate in eating, of tender health; he is too valuable and too restive to be left alone, so that you are chained to your brute as to a fellow galley-slave; a dangerous road puts him out of his wits; in short, he's an uncertain and exacting ally, and adds thirty-fold to the troubles of the voyager. What I required was something cheap and small and hardy, and of a stolid and peaceful temper; and all these requisites pointed to a donkey.

There dwelt an old man in Monastier, of rather unsound intellect according to some, much followed by street-boys, and known to fame as Father Adam. Father Adam had a cart, and to draw the cart a diminutive she-ass, not much bigger than a dog, the colour of a mouse, with a kindly eye and a determined under-jaw. There was something neat and high-bred, a quakerish elegance, about the rogue that hit my fancy on the spot. Our first interview was in Monastier market-place. To prove her good temper, one child after another was set upon her back to ride, and one after another went head over heels into the air; until a want of confidence began to reign in youthful bosoms, and the experiment was discontinued from a dearth of subjects. I was already backed by a deputation of my friends; but as if this were not enough, all the buyers and sellers came round and helped me in the bargain; and the ass and I and Father Adam were the centre of a hubbub for near half an hour. At length she passed into my service for the consideration of sixty-five francs and a glass of brandy. The sack had already cost eighty francs and two glasses of beer; so that Modestine, as I instantly baptized her, was upon all accounts the cheaper article. Indeed, that was as it should be; for she was only an appurtenance of my mattress, or self-acting bedstead on four castors.

I had a last interview with Father Adam in a billiard-room at the witching hour of dawn, when I administered the brandy. He professed himself greatly touched by the separation, and declared he had often bought white bread for the donkey when he had been content with black bread for himself; but this, according to the best authorities, must have been a flight of fancy. He had a name in the village for brutally misusing the ass; yet it is certain that he shed a tear, and the tear made a clean mark down one cheek.

By the advice of a fallacious local saddler, a leather pad was made for me with rings to fasten on my bundle; and I thoughtfully completed my kit and arranged my toilette. By way of armoury and utensils, I took a revolver, a little spirit-lamp and pan, a lantern and some halfpenny candles, a jack-knife, and a large leather flask. The main cargo consisted of two entire changes of warm clothing—besides my travelling wear of country velveteen, pilot-coat, and knitted spencer—

some books, and my railway-rug, which, being also in the form of a bag, made me a double castle for cold nights. The permanent larder was represented by cakes of chocolate and tins of Bologna sausage. All this, except what I carried about my person, was easily stowed into the sheepskin bag; and by good fortune I threw in my empty knapsack, rather for convenience of carriage than from any thought that I should want it on my journey. For more immediate needs I took a leg of cold mutton, a bottle of Beaujolais, an empty bottle to carry milk, an egg-beater, and a considerable quantity of black bread and white, like Father Adam, for myself and donkey, only in my scheme of things the destinations were reversed.

Monastrians, of all shades of thought in politics, had agreed in threatening me with many ludicrous misadventures, and with sudden death in many surprising forms. Cold, wolves, robbers, above all the nocturnal practical joker, were daily and eloquently forced on my attention. Yet in these vaticinations, the true, patent danger was left out. Like Christian, it was from my pack I suffered by the way. Before telling my own mishaps, let me in two words relate the lesson of my experience. If the pack is well strapped at the ends, and hung at full length—not doubled, for your life—across the pack-saddle, the traveller is safe. The saddle will certainly not fit, such is the imperfection of our transitory life; it will assuredly topple and tend to overset; but there are stones on every roadside, and a man soon learns the art of correcting any tendency to overbalance with a well-adjusted stone.

On the day of my departure I was up a little after five; by six, we began to load the donkey; and ten minutes after, my hopes were in the dust. The pad would not stay on Modestine's back for half a moment. I returned it to its maker, with whom I had so contumelious a passage that the street outside was crowded from wall to wall with gossips looking on and listening. The pad changed hands with much vivacity; perhaps it would be more descriptive to say that we threw it at each other's heads; and, at any rate, we were very warm and unfriendly, and spoke with a deal of freedom.

I had a common donkey pack-saddle—a *barde*, as they call it—fitted upon Modestine; and once more loaded her with my effects. The doubled sack, my pilot-coat (for it was warm, and I was to walk in my waistcoat), a great bar of black bread, and an open basket containing the white bread, the mutton, and the bottles, were all corded together in a very elaborate system of knots, and I looked on the result with fatuous content. In such a monstrous deck-cargo, all poised above the donkey's shoulders, with nothing below to balance, on a brand-new pack-saddle that had not yet been worn to fit the animal, and fastened with brand-new girths that might be expected to stretch and slacken by the way, even a very careless traveller should have seen disaster brewing. That elaborate system of knots, again, was the work of too many sympathizers to be very artfully designed. It is true they tightened the cords with a will; as many as three at a time would have a foot against Modestine's quarters, and be hauling with clenched teeth; but I learned afterwards that one thoughtful person, without any exercise of force, can make a more solid job than half-dozen heated and enthusiastic grooms. I was then but a novice; even after the misadventure of the pad nothing could disturb my security, and I went forth from the stable-door as an ox goeth to the slaughter.

The Green Donkey-driver

FROM

Travels with a Donkey in the Cévennes

THE BELL OF Monastier was just striking nine as I got quit of these preliminary troubles and descended the hill through the common. As long as I was within sight of the windows, a secret shame and the fear of some laughable defeat withheld me from tampering with Modestine. She tripped along upon her four small hoofs with a sober daintiness of gait; from time to time she shook her ears or her tail; and she looked so small under the bundle that my mind misgave me. We got across the ford without difficulty—there was no doubt about the matter, she was docility itself—and once on the other bank, where the road begins to mount through pine-woods, I took in my right hand the unhallowed staff, and with a quaking spirit applied it to the donkey. Modestine brisked up her pace for perhaps three steps, and then relapsed into her former minuet. Another application had the same effect, and so with the third. I am worthy of the name of an Englishman, and it goes against my conscience to lay my hand rudely on a female. I desisted, and looked her all over from head to foot; the poor brute's knees were trembling and her breathing was distressed; it was plain that she could go no faster on a hill. God forbid, thought I, that I should brutalize this innocent creature; let her go at her own pace, and let me patiently follow.

What that pace was, there is no word mean enough to describe; it was something as much slower than a walk as a walk is slower than a run; it kept me hanging on each foot for an incredible length of time; in five minutes it exhausted the spirit and set up a fever in all the muscles of the leg. And yet I had to keep close at hand and measure my advance exactly upon hers; for if I dropped a few yards into the rear, or went on a few yards ahead, Modestine came instantly to a halt and began to browse. The thought that this was to last from here to Alais nearly broke my heart. Of all conceivable journeys, this promised to be the most tedious. I tried to tell myself it was a lovely day; I tried to charm my foreboding spirit with tobacco; but I had a vision ever present to me of the long, long roads, up hill and down dale, and a pair of figures ever infinitesimally moving, foot by foot, a yard to the minute, and, like things enchanted in a nightmare, approaching no nearer to the goal.

In the meantime there came up behind us a tall peasant, perhaps forty years of age, of an ironical snuffy countenance, and arrayed in the green tail-coat of the country. He overtook us hand over hand, and stopped to consider our pitiful advance.

"Your donkey," says he, "is very old?"

I told him, I believed not.

Then, he supposed, we had come far.

I told him, we had but newly left Monastier.

"*Et vous marchez comme ça*!" cried he; and, throwing back his head, he laughed long and heartily. I watched him, half prepared to feel offended, until he had satisfied his mirth; and then, "You must have no pity on these animals," said he; and, plucking a switch out of a thicket, he began to lace Modestine about the stern-works, uttering a cry. The rogue pricked up her ears and broke into a good round pace, which she kept up without flagging, and without exhibiting the least symptom of distress, as long as the peasant kept beside us. Her former panting and shaking had been, I regret to say, a piece of comedy.

My *deus ex machina,* before he left me, supplied some excellent, if inhumane, advice; presented me with the switch, which he declared she would feel more tenderly than my cane; and finally taught me the true cry or masonic word of donkey-drivers, "Proot!" All the time, he regarded me with a comical, incredulous air, which was embarrassing to confront; and smiled over my donkey-driving, as I might have smiled over his orthography, or his green tail-coat. But it was not my turn for the moment.

I was proud of my new lore, and thought I had learned the art to perfection. And certainly Modestine did wonders for the rest of the forenoon, and I had a breathing space to look about me. It was

Sabbath; the mountain-fields were all vacant in the sunshine; and as we came down through St. Martin de Frugères, the church was crowded to the door, there were people kneeling without upon the steps, and the sound of the priest's chanting came forth out of the dim interior. It gave me a home feeling on the spot; for I am a countryman of the Sabbath, so to speak, and all Sabbath observances, like a Scottish accent, strike in me mixed feelings, grateful and the reverse. It is only a traveller, hurrying by like a person from another planet, who can rightly enjoy the peace and beauty of the great ascetic feast. The sight of the resting country does his spirit good. There is something better than music in the wide unusual silence; and it disposes him to amiable thoughts, like the sound of a little river or the warmth of sunlight.

In this pleasant humour I came down the hill to where Goudet stands in a green end of a valley, with Château Beaufort opposite upon a rocky steep, and the stream, as clear as crystal, lying in a deep pool between them. Above and below, you may hear it wimpling over the stones, an amiable stripling of a river, which it seems absurd to call the Loire. On all sides, Goudet is shut in by mountains; rocky footpaths, practicable at best for donkeys, join it to the outer world of France; and the men and women drink and swear, in their green corner, or look up at the snow-clad peaks in winter from the threshold of their homes, in an isolation, you would think, like that of Homer's Cyclops. But it is not so; the postman reaches Goudet with the letter-bag; the aspiring youth of Goudet are within a day's walk of the railway at Le Puy; and here in the inn you may find an engraved portrait of the hosts' nephew, Régis Senac, "Professor of Fencing and Champion of the two Americas", a distinction gained by him, along with the sum of five hundred dollars, at Tammany Hall, New York, on the 10th April, 1876.

I hurried over my mid-day meal, and was early forth again. But, alas, as we climbed the interminable hill upon the other side, "Proot!" seemed to have lost its virtue. I prooted like a lion, I prooted mellifluously like a sucking-dove; but Modestine would be neither softened nor intimidated. She held doggedly to her pace; nothing but a blow would move her, and that only for a second. I must follow at her heels, incessantly belabouring. A moment's pause in this ignoble toil, and she relapsed into her own private gait. I think I never heard of anyone in as mean a situation. I must reach the lake of Bouchet, where I meant to camp, before sun-down, and, to have even a hope of this, I must instantly maltreat this uncomplaining animal. The sound of my blows sickened me. Once, when I looked at her, she had a faint resemblance to a lady of my acquaintance who formerly loaded me with kindness; and this increased my horror of my cruelty.

To make matters worse, we encountered another donkey, ranging at will upon the roadside; and this other donkey chanced to be a gentleman. He and Modestine met nickering for joy, and I had to separate the pair and beat down their young romance with a renewed and feverish bastinado. If the other donkey had had the heart of a male under his hide, he would have fallen upon me tooth and hoof; and this was a kind of consolation—he was plainly unworthy of Modestine's affection. But the incident saddened me, as did everything that spoke of my donkey's sex.

It was blazing hot up the valley, windless, with vehement sun upon my shoulders; and I had to labour so consistently with my stick that the sweat ran into my eyes. Every five minutes, too, the pack, the basket, and the pilot-coat would take an ugly slew to one side or the other; and I had to stop Modestine, just when I had got her to a tolerable pace of about two miles an hour, to tug, push, shoulder, and readjust the load. And at last, in the village of Ussel, saddle and all, the whole hypothec turned round and grovelled in the dust below the donkey's belly. She, none better pleased, incontinently drew up and seemed to smile; and a party of one man, two women, and two children came up, and, standing round me in a half-circle, encouraged her by their example.

I had the devil's own trouble to get the thing righted; and the instant I had done so, without hesitation, it toppled and fell down upon the other side. Judge if I was hot! And yet not a hand was offered to assist me. The man, indeed, told me I ought to have a package of a different shape. I suggested, if he knew nothing better to the point in my predicament, he might hold his tongue. And the good-natured dog agreed with me smilingly. It was the most despicable fix. I must plainly content myself with the pack for Modestine, and take the following items for my own share of the portage: a cane, a quart flask, a pilot-jacket heavily weighted in the pockets, two pounds of black bread, and an open basket full of meats and bottles. I believe I may say I am not devoid of greatness of soul; for I did not recoil from this infamous burden. I disposed it, Heavens knows how, so as to be mildly portable, and then proceeded to steer Modestine through the village. She tried, as was indeed her invariable habit, to enter every house and every courtyard in the whole length; and, encumbered as I was, without a hand to help myself, no words can render an idea of my difficulties. A priest, with six or seven others, was examining a church in process of repair, and he and his acolytes laughed loudly as they saw my plight. I remembered having laughed myself when I had seen good men struggling with adversity in the person of a jackass, and the recollection filled me with penitence. That was in my old light days, before this trouble came upon me. God knows at least that I shall never laugh again, thought I. But oh, what a cruel thing is a farce to those engaged in it!

A little out of the village, Modestine, filled with the demon, set her heart upon a by-road, and positively refused to leave it. I dropped all my bundles, and, I am ashamed to say, struck the poor sinner twice across the face. It was pitiful to see her lift up her head with shut eyes, as if waiting for another blow. I came very near crying; but I did a wiser thing than that, and sat squarely down by the roadside to consider my situation under the cheerful influence of tobacco and a nip of brandy. Modestine, in the meanwhile, munched some black bread with a contrite hypocritical air. It was plain that I must make a sacrifice to the gods of shipwreck. I threw away the empty bottle destined to carry milk; I threw away my own white bread, and, disdaining to act by general average, kept the black bread for Modestine; lastly, I threw away the cold leg of mutton and the egg-whisk, although this last was dear to my heart. Thus I found room for everything in the basket, and even stowed the boating-coat on the top. By means of an end of cord I slung it under one arm; and although the cord cut my shoulder, and the jacket hung almost to the ground, it was with a heart greatly lightened that I set forth again.

I had now an arm free to thrash Modestine, and cruelly I chastised her. If I were to reach the lakeside before dark, she must bestir her little shanks to some tune. Already the sun had gone down into a windy-looking mist; and although there were still a few streaks of gold far off to the east on the hills and the black fir-woods, all was cold and grey about our onward path. An infinity of little country by-roads led hither and thither among the fields. It was the most pointless labyrinth. I could see my destination overhead, or rather the peak that dominates it; but choose as I pleased, the roads always ended by turning away from it, and sneaking back towards the valley, or northward along the margin of the hills. The failing light, the waning colour, the naked, unhomely, stony country through which I was travelling, threw me into some despondency. I promise you, the stick was not idle; I think every decent step that Modestine took must have cost me at least two emphatic blows. There was not another sound in the neighbourhood but that of my unwearying bastinado.

Suddenly, in the midst of my toils, the load once more bit the dust, and, as by enchantment, all the cords were simultaneously loosened, and the road scattered with my dear possessions. The packing was to begin again from the beginning; and as I had to invent a new and better system, I do not doubt but I lost half an hour. It began to be dusk in earnest as I reached a wilderness of turf and stones. It had the air of being a road which should lead everywhere at the same time; and I was falling into something not unlike despair when I saw two figures stalking towards me over the stones. They walked one behind the other like tramps, but their pace was remarkable. The son led the way, a tall, ill-made, sombre, Scottish-looking man; the mother followed, all in her Sunday's best, with an elegantly embroidered ribbon to her cap, and a new felt hat atop, and proffering, as she strode along with kilted petticoats, a string of obscene and blasphemous oaths.

I hailed the son, and asked him my direction. He pointed loosely west and north-west, muttered an inaudible comment, and, without slackening his pace for an instant, stalked on, as he was going, right athwart my path. The mother followed without so much as raising her head. I shouted and shouted after them, but they continued to scale the hillside, and turned a deaf ear to my outcries. At last, leaving Modestine by herself, I was constrained to run after them, hailing the while. They stopped as I drew near, the mother still cursing; and I could see she was a handsome, motherly, respectable-looking woman. The son once more answered me roughly and inaudibly, and was for setting out again. But this time I simply collared the mother, who was nearest me, and, apologising for my violence, declared that I could not let them go until they had put me on my road. They were neither of them offended—rather mollified than otherwise; told me I had only to follow them; and then the mother asked me what I wanted by the lake at such an hour. I replied, in the Scottish manner, by inquiring if she had far to go herself. She told me, with another oath, that she had an hour and a half's road before her. And then, without salutation, the pair strode forward again up the hillside in the gathering dusk.

I returned for Modestine, pushed her briskly forward, and, after a sharp ascent of twenty minutes, reached the edge of a plateau. The view, looking back on my day's journey, was both wild and sad. Mount Mézenc and the peaks beyond St. Julien stood out in trenchant gloom against a cold glitter in the east; and the intervening field of hills had fallen together into one broad wash of shadow, except here and there the outline of a wooded sugar-loaf in black, here and there a white irregular patch to represent a cultivated farm; and here and there a blot where the Loire, the Gazeille, or the Laussonne wandered in a gorge.

Soon we were on a high-road, and surprise seized on my mind as I beheld a village of some magnitude close at hand; for I had been told that the neighbourhood of the lake was uninhabited except by trout. The road smoked in the twilight with children driving home cattle from the fields; and a pair of mounted stride-legged women, hat and cap and all, dashed past me at a hammering trot from the canton where they had been to church and market. I asked one of the children where I was. At Bouchet St. Nicholas, he told me. Thither, about a mile south of my destination, and on the other side of a respectable summit, had these confused roads and treacherous peasantry conducted me. My shoulder was cut, so that it hurt sharply; my arm ached like toothache from perpetual beating; I gave up the lake and my design to camp, and asked for the *auberge*.

A Night among the Pines

FROM

Travels with a Donkey in the Cévennes

FROM BLEYMARD after dinner, although it was already late, I set out to scale a portion of the Lozère. An ill-marked stony drove-road guided me forward; and I met nearly half-a-dozen bullock-carts descending from the woods, each laden with a whole pine-tree for the winter's firing. At the top of the woods, which do not climb very high upon this cold ridge, I struck leftward by a path among the pines, until I hit on a dell of green turf, where a streamlet made a little spout over some stones to serve me for a water-tap. "In a more sacred or sequestered bower . . . nor nymph nor faunus haunted." The trees were not old, but they grew thickly round the glade: there was no outlook, except north-eastward upon distant hill-tops, or straight upward to the sky; and the encampment felt secure and private like a room. By the time I had made my arrangements and fed Modestine, the day was already beginning to decline. I buckled myself to the knees into my sack and made a hearty meal; and as soon as the sun went down, I pulled my cap over my eyes and fell asleep.

Night is a dead monotonous period under a roof; but in the open world it passes lightly, with its stars and dews and perfumes, and the hours are marked by changes in the face of Nature. What seems a kind of temporal death to people choked between walls and curtains, is only a light and living slumber to the man who sleeps afield. All night long he can hear Nature breathing deeply and freely; even as she takes her rest, she turns and smiles; and there is one stirring hour unknown to those who dwell in houses, when a wakeful influence goes abroad over the sleeping hemisphere, and all the outdoor world are on their feet. It is then that the cock first crows, not this time to announce the dawn, but like a cheerful watchman speeding the course of night. Cattle awake on the meadows; sheep break their fast on dewy hillsides, and change to a new lair among the ferns; and houseless men, who have lain down with the fowls, open their dim eyes and behold the beauty of the night.

At what inaudible summons, at what gentle touch of Nature, are all these sleepers thus recalled in the same hour to life? Do the stars rain down an influence, or do we share some thrill of mother earth below our resting bodies? Even shepherds and old country-folk, who are the deepest read in these arcana, have not a guess as to the means or purpose of this nightly resurrection. Towards two in the morning they declare the thing takes place; and neither know nor inquire further. And at least it is a pleasant incident. We are disturbed in our slumber only, like the luxurious Montaigne, "that we may the better and more sensibly relish it". We have a moment to look upon the stars. And there is a special pleasure for some minds in the reflection that we share the impulse with all outdoor creatures in our neighbourhood, that we have escaped out of the Bastille of civilization, and are become, for the time being, a mere kindly animal and a sheep of Nature's flock.

When that hour came to me among the pines, I wakened thirsty. My tin was standing by me half full of water. I emptied it at a draught; and feeling broad awake after this internal cold aspersion, sat upright to make a cigarette. The stars were clear, coloured, and jewel-like, but not frosty. A faint silvery vapour stood for the Milky Way. All around me the black fir-points stood upright and stock-still. By the whiteness of the pack-saddle, I could see Modestine walking round and round at the length of her tether; I could hear her steadily munching at the sward; but there was not another sound, save the indescribable quiet talk of the runnel over the stones. I lay lazily smoking and studying the colour of the sky, as we call the void of space, from where it showed a reddish grey behind the pines to where it showed a glossy blue-black between the stars. As if to be more like a pedlar, I wear a silver ring. This I could see faintly shining as I raised or lowered the cigarette; and at each whiff the inside of my hand was illuminated, and became for a second the highest light in the landscape.

A faint wind, more like a moving coolness than a stream of air, passed down the glade from time to time; so that even in my great chamber the air was being renewed all night long. I thought with horror of the inn at Chasseradès and the congregated nightcaps; with horror of the nocturnal prowesses of clerks and students, of hot theatres and pass-keys and close rooms. I have not often enjoyed a more serene possession of myself, nor felt more independent of material aids. The outer world, from which we cower into our houses, seemed after all a gentle habitable place; and night after night a man's bed, it seemed, was laid and waiting for him in the fields, where God keeps an open house. I thought I had rediscovered one of those truths which are revealed to savages and hid from political economists: at the least, I had discovered a new pleasure for myself. And yet even while I was exulting in my solitude I became aware of a strange lack. I wished a companion to lie near me in the starlight, silent and not moving, but ever within touch. For there is a fellowship more quiet even than solitude, and which, rightly understood, is solitude made perfect. And to live out of doors with the woman a man loves is of all lives the most complete and free.

As I thus lay, between content and longing, a faint noise stole towards me through the pines. I thought, at first, it was the crowing of cocks or the barking of dogs at some very distant farm; but steadily and gradually it took articulate shape in my ears, until I became aware that a passenger was going by upon the high-road in the valley, and singing loudly as he went. There was more of good-will than grace in his performance; but he trolled with ample lungs; and the sound of his voice took hold upon the hillside and set the air shaking in the leafy glens. I have heard people passing by night in sleeping cities; some of them sang; one, I remember, played loudly on the bagpipes. I have heard the rattle of a cart or carriage spring up suddenly after hours of stillness, and pass, for some minutes, within the range of my hearing as I lay abed. There is a romance about all who are abroad in the black hours, and with something of a thrill we try to guess their business. But here the romance was double: first, this glad passenger, lit internally with wine, who sent up his voice in music through the night; and then I, on the other hand, buckled into my sack, and smoking alone in the pine-woods between four and five thousand feet towards the stars.

When I awoke again (Sunday, 29th September), many of the stars had disappeared; only the stronger companions of the night still burned visibly overhead; and away towards the east I saw a faint haze of light upon the horizon, such as had been the Milky Way when I was last awake. Day was at hand. I lit my lantern, and by its glow-worm light put on my boots and gaiters; then I broke up some bread for Modestine, filled my can at the water-tap, and lit my spirit-lamp to boil myself some chocolate. The blue darkness lay long in the glade where I had so sweetly slumbered; but soon there was a broad streak of orange melting into gold along the mountain-tops of Vivarais. A solemn glee possessed my mind at this gradual and lovely coming in of day. I heard the runnel with delight; I looked round me for something beautiful and unexpected; but the still black pine-trees, the hollow glade, the munching ass, remained unchanged in figure. Nothing had altered but the light, and that, indeed, shed over all a spirit of life and of breathing peace, and moved me to a strange exhilaration.

I drank my water-chocolate, which was hot if it was not rich, and strolled here and there, and up and down about the glade. While I was thus delaying, a gush of steady wind, as long as a heavy sigh, poured direct out of the quarter of the morning. It was cold, and set me sneezing. The trees near at hand tossed their black plumes in its passage; and I could see the thin distant spires of pine along the edge of the hill rock slightly to and fro against the golden east. Ten minutes after, the sunlight spread at a gallop along the hillside, scattering shadows and sparkles, and the day had come completely.

I hastened to prepare my pack, and tackle the steep ascent that lay before me, but I had something on my mind. It was only a fancy; yet a fancy will sometimes be importunate. I had been most hospitably received and punctually served in my green caravanserai. The room was airy, the water excellent, and the dawn had called me to a moment. I say nothing of the tapestries or the inimitable ceiling, nor yet of the view which I commanded from the windows; but I felt I was in someone's debt for all this liberal entertainment. And so it pleased me, in a half-laughing way, to leave pieces of money on the turf as I went along, until I had left enough for my night's lodging. I trust they did not fall to some rich and churlish drover.

The Oise in Flood

FROM

An Inland Voyage

BEFORE NINE next morning the two canoes were installed on a light country cart at Étreux: and we were soon following them along the side of a pleasant valley full of hop-gardens and poplars. Agreeable villages lay here and there on the slope of the hill; notably Tupigny, with the hop-poles hanging their garlands in the very street, and the houses clustered with grapes. There was a faint enthusiasm on our passage; weavers put their heads to the windows; children cried out in ecstasy at sight of the two "boaties"—*barquettes*: and bloused pedestrians, who were acquainted with our charioteer, jested with him on the nature of his freight.

We had a shower or two, but light and flying. The air was clean and sweet among all these green fields and green things growing. There was not a touch of autumn in the weather. And when, at Vadencourt, we launched from a little lawn opposite a mill, the sun broke forth and set all the leaves shining in the valley of the Oise.

The river was swollen with the long rains. From Vadencourt all the way to Origny it ran with ever-quickening speed taking fresh heart at each mile, and racing as though it already smelt the sea. The water was yellow and turbulent, swung with an angry eddy among half-submerged willows, and made an angry clatter along stony shores. The course kept turning and turning in a narrow and well-timbered valley. Now, the river would approach the side, and run gliding along the chalky base of the hill, and show us a few open colza-fields among the trees. Now, it would skirt the garden-walls of houses, where we might catch a glimpse through a doorway, and see a priest pacing in the chequered sunlight. Again, the foliage closed so thickly in front, that there seemed to be no issue; only a thicket of willows, overtopped by elms and poplars, under which the river ran flush and fleet, and where a kingfisher flew past like a piece of the blue sky. On these different manifestations the sun poured its clear and catholic looks. The shadows lay as solid on the swift surface of the stream as on the stable meadows. The light sparkled golden in the dancing poplar leaves, and brought the hills into communion with our eyes. And all the while the river never stopped running or took breath; and the reeds along the whole valley stood shivering from top to toe.

There should be some myth (but if there is, I know it not) founded on the shivering of the reeds. There are not many things in Nature more striking to man's eye. It is such an eloquent pantomime of terror; and to see such a number of terrified creatures taking sanctuary in every nook along the shore, is enough to infect a silly human with alarm. Perhaps they are only a-cold, and no wonder, standing waist deep in the stream. Or perhaps they have never got accustomed to the speed and fury of the river's flux, or the miracle of its continuous body. Pan once played upon their forefathers; and so, by the hands of his river, he still plays upon these later generations down all the valley of the Oise; and plays the same air, both sweet and shrill, to tell us of the beauty and the terror of the world.

The canoe was like a leaf in the current. It took it up and shook it, and carried it masterfully away, like a Centaur carrying off a nymph. To keep some command on our direction required hard and diligent plying of the paddle. The river was in such a hurry for the sea! Every drop of water ran in a panic, like as many people in a frightened crowd. But what crowd was ever so numerous, or so single-minded? All the objects of sight went by at a dance measure; the eyesight raced with the racing river; the exigencies of every moment kept the pegs screwed so tight, that our being quivered like a well-tuned instrument; and the blood shook off its lethargy, and trotted through all the highways and byways of the veins and arteries, and in and out of the heart, as if circulation were but a holiday journey, and not the daily moil of threescore years and ten. The reeds might nod their heads in warning, and with tremulous gestures tell how the river was as cruel as it was strong and cold, and how death lurked in the eddy underneath the willows. But the reeds had to stand where they were; and those who stand still are always timid advisers. As for us, we could have shouted aloud. If this lively and beautiful river were, indeed, a thing of death's contrivance, the old ashen rogue had famously outwitted himself with us. I was living three to the minute. I was scoring points against him every stroke of my paddle, every turn of the stream. I have rarely had better profit of my life.

For I think we may look upon our little private war with death somewhat in this light. If a man knows he will sooner or later be robbed upon a journey, he will have a bottle of the best in every inn, and look upon all his extravagances as so much gained upon the thieves. And above all, where instead of simply spending, he makes a profitable investment for some of his money, then it will be out of risk of loss. So every bit of brisk living, and above all when it is healthful, is just so much gained upon the wholesale filcher, death. We shall have the less in our pockets, the more in our stomach, when he cries stand and deliver. A swift stream is a favourite artifice of his, and one that brings him in a comfortable thing per annum; but when he and I come to settle our accounts, I shall whistle in his face for these hours upon the upper Oise.

Towards afternoon we got fairly drunken with the sunshine and the exhilaration of the pace. We could no longer contain ourselves and our content. The canoes were too small for us; we must be out and stretch ourselves on shore. And so in a green meadow we bestowed our limbs on the grass, and smoked deifying tobacco and proclaimed the world excellent. It was the last good hour of the day, and I dwell upon it with extreme complacency.

On one side of the valley, high upon the chalky summit of the hill, a ploughman with his team appeared and disappeared at regular intervals. At each revelation he stood still for a few seconds against the sky: for all the world (as the *Cigarette* declared) like a toy Burns who had just ploughed up the Mountain Daisy. He was the only living thing within view, unless we are to count the river.

On the other side of the valley a group of red roofs and a belfry showed among the foliage. Thence some inspired bell-ringer made the afternoon musical on a chime of bells. There was something very sweet and taking in the air he played; and we thought we had never heard bells speak so intelligibly, or sing so melodiously, as these. It must have been to some such measure that the spinners and the young maids sang, "Come away, Death," in the Shakespearean Illyria. There is so often a threatening note, something blatant and metallic, in the voice of bells, that I believe we have fully more pain than pleasure from hearing them; but these, as they sounded abroad, now high, now low, now with a plaintive cadence that caught the ear like the burthen of a popular song, were always moderate and tunable, and seemed to fall in with the spirit of still, rustic places, like the noise of a waterfall or the babble of a rookery in spring. I could have asked the bell-ringer for his blessing, good, sedate old man, who swung the rope so gently to the time of his meditations. I could have blessed the priest or the heritors or whoever may be concerned with such affairs in France, who had left these sweet old bells to gladden the afternoon, and not held meetings, and made collections, and had their names repeatedly printed in the local paper, to rig up a peal of brand-new, brazen, Birmingham-hearted substitutes, who should bombard their sides to the provocation of a brand-new bell-ringer, and fill the echoes of the valley with terror and riot.

At last the bells ceased, and with their note the sun withdrew. The piece was at an end; shadow and silence possessed the valley of the Oise. We took to the paddle with glad hearts, like people who have sat out a noble performance and return to work. The river was more dangerous here; it ran swifter, the eddies were more sudden and violent. All the way down we had had our fill of difficulties. Sometimes it was a weir which could be shot, sometimes one so shallow and full of stakes that we must withdraw the boats from the water and carry them round. But the chief sort of obstacle was a consequence of the late high winds. Every two or three hundred yards a tree had fallen across the river and usually involved more than another in its fall. Often there was free water at the end, and we could steer round the leafy promontory and hear the water sucking and bubbling among the twigs. Often, again, when the tree reached from bank to bank. there was room, by lying close, to shoot through underneath, canoe and all. Sometimes it was necessary to get out upon the trunk itself and pull the boats across; and sometimes, where the stream was too impetuous for this, there was nothing for it but to land and "carry over." This made a fine series of accidents in the day's career, and kept us aware of ourselves.

Shortly after our re-embarkation, while I was leading by a long way, and still full of a noble, exulting spirit in honour of the sun, the swift pace, and the church bells, the river made one of its leonine pounces round a corner, and I was aware of another fallen tree within a stone-cast. I had my backboard down in a trice, and aimed for a place where the trunk seemed high enough above the water, and the branches not too thick to let me slip below. When a man has just vowed eternal brotherhood with the universe, he is not in a temper to take great determinations coolly, and this, which might have been a very important determination for me, had not been taken under a happy star. The tree caught me about the chest, and while I was yet struggling to make less of myself and get through, the river took the matter out of my hands and bereaved me of my boat. The *Arethusa* swung round broadside on, leaned over, ejected so much of me as still remained on board, and thus disencumbered, whipped under the tree, righted, and went merrily away down-stream.

I do not know how long it was before I scrambled on to the tree to which I was left clinging, but it was longer than I cared about. My thoughts were of a grave and almost sombre character, but I still clung to my paddle. The stream ran away with my heels as fast as I could pull up my shoulders, and I seemed, by the weight, to have all the water of the *Oise* in my trouser pockets. You can never know, till you try it, what a dead pull a river makes against a man. Death himself had me by the heels, for this was his last ambuscade, and he must now join personally in the fray. And still I held to my paddle. At last I dragged myself on to my stomach on the trunk, and lay there a breathless sop, with a mingled sense of humour and injustice. A poor figure I must have presented to Burns upon the hilltop with his team. But there was the paddle in my hand. On my tomb, if ever I have one, I mean to get these words inscribed: "He clung to his paddle."

The *Cigarette* had gone past a while before; for, as I might have observed, if I had been a little less pleased with the universe at the moment, there was a clear way round the treetop at the farther side. He had offered his services to haul me out, but as I was then already on my elbows, I had declined, and sent him down-stream after the truant *Arethusa*. The stream was too rapid for a man to mount with one canoe, let alone two, upon his hands. So I crawled along the trunk to shore, and proceeded down the meadows by the river-side. I was so cold that my heart was sore. I had now an idea of my own, why the reeds so bitterly shivered. I could have given any of them a lesson. The *Cigarette* remarked facetiously, that he thought I was "taking exercise" as I drew near, until he made out for certain that I was only twittering with cold. I had a rub down with a towel, and donned a dry suit from the india-rubber bag. But I was not my own man again for the rest of the voyage. I had a queasy sense that I wore my last dry clothes upon my body. The struggle had tired me; and perhaps, whether I knew it or not, I was a little dashed in spirit. The devouring element in the universe had leaped out against me, in this green valley quickened by a running stream. The bells were all very pretty in their way, but I had heard some of the hollow notes of Pan's music. Would the wicked river drag me down by the heels, indeed? And look so beautiful all the time? Nature's good-humour was only skin-deep after all.

There was still a long way to go by the winding course of the stream, and darkness had fallen, and a late bell was ringing in Origny Sainte-Benoîte, when we arrived.

33. John Barrymore as Mr. Hyde in the splendidly effective 1920 silent film version of *Dr. Jekyll and Mr. Hyde*, directed by John S. Robertson.

34. Blind Pew arrives at the Admiral Benbow inn and meets Jim Hawkins (played by a woman, Shirley Mason) and his mother in Maurice Tourneur's *Treasure Island* (1920).

35. A scene from *Ebb Tide* (1920), directed by George Melford.

38. Robert Montgomery as the prince and Frank Morgan as the faithful colonel in *Trouble for Two*, a 1936 film version of "The Suicide Club," directed by J. Walter Ruben.

39. Ray Milland (in the back seat) in a 1937 Paramount remake of *Ebb Tide,* directed by James Hogan.

40. Freddie Bartholomew and Warner Baxter in Twentieth Century-Fox's insipid *Kidnapped* (1938), directed by Alfred Werker.

41. Spencer Tracy as Dr. Jekyll in Metro-Goldwyn-Mayer's 1941 remake of *Dr. Jekyll and Mr. Hyde*, directed by Victor Fleming.

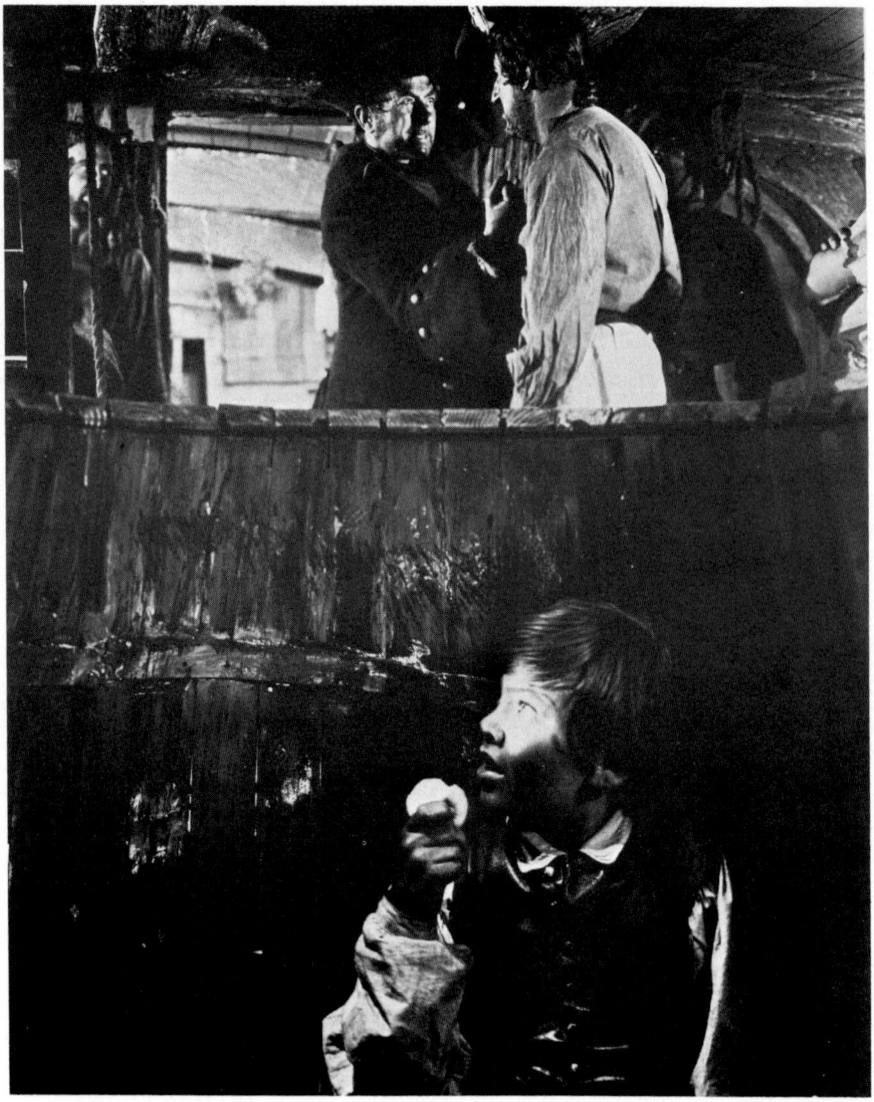

42. The apple-barrel scene from *Treasure Island* (1950), with Robert Newton as Long John Silver and Bobby Driscoll as Jim Hawkins. This gloriously rumbustious film, directed by Byron Haskin, was Walt Disney's first completely live-action production.

43. Charles Laughton, Richard Stapley, and Sally Forrest in Joseph Pevney's *The Strange Door* (1951), the only film version so far of Stevenson's story "The Sire of Maletroit's Door."

44. The duel between the "bad" and the "good" brothers, played respectively by Errol Flynn and Anthony Steel, in *The Master of Ballantrae* (1953), directed by William Keighley.

45. Peter Finch as David Balfour in Robert Stevenson's *Kidnapped* (1960).

46. Paul Massie and Dawn Addams in yet another "version" of the Jekyll-Hyde story, Terence Fisher's *The Two Faces of Dr. Jekyll* (1960). The film's only claim to remembrance is that in it Mr. Hyde was made to look more handsome and behave more charmingly than Dr. Jekyll.

47. A scene from the messy, over-indulgent (and over-starred) British film *The Wrong Box* (1966), directed by Bryan Forbes.

48. Michael Caine as David Balfour in Delbert Mann's *Kidnapped* (1972).

Noyon Cathedral

FROM

An Inland Voyage

NOYON STANDS about a mile from the river, in a little plain surrounded by wooded hills, and entirely covers an eminence with its tile roofs, surmounted by a long, straight-backed cathedral with two stiff towers. As we got into the town, the tile roofs seemed to tumble uphill one upon another, in the oddest disorder; but for all their scrambling, they did not attain above the knees of the cathedral, which stood, upright and solemn, over all. As the streets drew near to this presiding genius, through the market-place under the *Hôtel de Ville*, they grew emptier and more composed. Blank walls and shuttered windows were turned to the great edifice, and grass grew on the white causeway. "Put off thy shoes from off thy feet, for the place whereon thou standest is holy ground." The *Hôtel du Nord*, nevertheless, lights its secular tapers within a stone-cast of the church; and we had the superb east end before our eyes all morning from the window of our bedroom. I have seldom looked on the east end of a church with more complete sympathy. As it flanges out in three wide terraces, and settles down broadly on the earth, it looks like the poop of some great old battleship. Hollow-backed buttresses carry vases, which figure for the stern lanterns. There is a roll in the ground, and towers just appear above the pitch of the roof, as though the good ship were bowling lazily over an Atlantic swell. At any moment it might be a hundred feet away from you, climbing the next billow. At any moment a window might open, and some old admiral thrust forth a cocked hat, and proceed to take an observation. The old admirals sail the sea no longer; the old ships of battle are all broken up, and live only in pictures; but this, that was a church before ever they were thought upon, is still a church, and makes as brave an appearance by the Oise. The cathedral and the river are probably the two oldest things for miles around; and certainly they have both a grand old age.

The Sacristan took us to the top of one of the towers, and showed us the five bells hanging in their loft. From above, the town was a tessellated pavement of roofs and gardens; the old line of rampart was plainly traceable; and the Sacristan pointed out to us, far across the plain, in a bit of gleaming sky between two clouds, the towers of *Château Coucy*.

I find I never weary of great churches. It is my favourite kind of mountain scenery. Mankind was never so happily inspired as when it made a cathedral: a thing as single and specious as a statue to the first glance, and yet, on examination, as lively and interesting as a forest in detail. The height of spires cannot be taken by trigonometry; they measure absurdly short, but how tall they are to the admiring eye! And where we have so many elegant proportions, growing one out of the other, and all together into one, it seems as if proportion transcended itself and became something different and more imposing. I could never fathom how a man dares to lift up his voice to preach in a cathedral. What is he to say that will not be an anti-climax? For though I have heard a considerable variety of sermons, I never yet heard one that was so expressive as a cathedral. 'Tis the best preacher itself, and preaches day and night; not only telling you of man's art and aspirations in the past, but convicting your own soul of ardent sympathies; or rather, like all good preachers, it sets you preaching to yourself;—and every man is his own doctor of divinity in the last resort.

As I sat outside of the hotel in the course of the afternoon, the sweet groaning thunder of the organ floated out of the church like a summons. I was not averse, liking the theatre so well, to sit out an act or two of the play, but I could never rightly make out the nature of the service I beheld. Four or five priests and as many choristers were singing *Miserere* before the high altar when I went in. There was no congregation but a few old women on chairs and old men kneeling on the pavement. After a while a long train of young girls, walking two and two, each with a lighted taper in her hand, and all dressed in black with a white veil, came from behind the altar and began to descend the nave; the four first carrying a Virgin and Child upon a table. The priests and choristers arose from their knees and followed after, singing "Ave Mary" as they went. In this order, they made the circuit of the cathedral, passing twice before me where I leaned against a pillar. The priest who seemed of most consequence was a strange, down-looking old man. He kept mumbling prayers with his lips; but as he looked upon me darkling, it did not seem as if prayer were uppermost in his heart. Two others, who bore the burthen of the chaunt, were stout, brutal, military-looking men of forty, with bold, overfed eyes; they sang with some lustiness, and trolled forth "Ave Mary" like a garrison catch. The little girls were timid and grave. As they footed slowly up the aisle, each one took a moment's glance at the *Englishman*; and the big nun who played marshal fairly stared him out of countenance. As for the choristers, from first to last they misbehaved as only boys can misbehave; and cruelly marred the performance with their antics.

I understood a great deal of the spirit of what went on. Indeed it would be difficult not to understand the *Miserere,* which I take to be the composition of an atheist. If it ever be a good thing to take such despondency to heart, the *Miserere* is the right music and a cathedral a fit scene. So far I am at one with the Catholics:—an odd name for them, after all! But why, in *God's* name, these holiday choristers? why these priests who steal wandering looks about the congregation while they feign to be at prayer? why this fat nun, who rudely arranges her procession and shakes delinquent virgins by the elbow? why this spitting, and snuffing, and forgetting of keys, and the thousand and one little misadventures that disturb a frame of mind, laboriously edified with chaunts and organings? In any playhouse reverend fathers may see what can be done with a little art, and how, to move high sentiments, it is necessary to drill the supernumeraries and have every stool in its proper place.

One other circumstance distressed me. I could bear a *Miserere* myself, having had a good deal of open-air exercise of late; but I wished the old people somewhere else. It was neither the right sort of music nor the right sort of divinity for men and women who have come through most accidents by this time, and probably have an opinion of their own upon the tragic element in life. A person up in years can generally do his own *Miserere* for himself; although I notice that such an one often prefers *Jubilate Deo* for his ordinary singing. On the whole, the most religious exercise for the aged is probably to recall their own experience; so many friends dead, so many hopes disappointed, so many slips and stumbles, and withal so many bright days and smiling providences; there is surely the matter of a very eloquent sermon in all this.

On the whole, I was greatly solemnized. In the little pictorial map of our whole *Inland Voyage*, which my fancy still preserves, and sometimes unrolls for the amusement of odd moments, Noyon cathedral figures on a most preposterous scale, and must be nearly as large as a department. I can still see the faces of the priests as if they were at my elbow, and hear *Ave Maria, ora pro nobis* sounding through the church. All Noyon is blotted out for me by these superior memories; and I do not care to say more about the place. It was but a stack of brown roofs at the best, where I believe people live very reputably in a quiet way; but the shadow of the church falls upon it when the sun is low, and the five bells are heard in all quarters, telling that the organ has begun. If ever I join the church of Rome, I shall stipulate to be a Bishop of Noyon on the Oise.

Changed Times

FROM

An Inland Voyage

THERE IS A SENSE in which those mists never rose from off our journey; and from that time forth they lie very densely in my notebook. As long as the Oise was a small, rural river, it took us near by people's doors, and we could hold a conversation with natives in the riparian fields. But now that it had grown so wide, the life along shore passed us by at a distance. It was the same difference as between a great public highway and a country bypath that wanders in and out of cottage gardens. We now lay in towns, where nobody troubled us with questions; we had floated into civilized life, where people pass without salutation. In sparsely inhabited places, we make all we can of each encounter; but when it comes to a city, we keep to ourselves, and never speak unless we have trodden on a man's toes. In these waters we were no longer strange birds, and nobody supposed we had travelled farther than from the last town. I remember, when we came into L'Isle Adam, for instance, how we met dozens of pleasure-boats outing it for the afternoon, and there was nothing to distinguish the true voyager from the amateur, except, perhaps, the filthy condition of my sail. The company in one boat actually thought they recognized me for a neighbour. Was there ever anything more wounding? All the romance had come down to that. Now, on the upper Oise, where nothing sailed as a general thing but fish, a pair of canoeists could not be thus vulgarly explained away; we were strange and picturesque intruders; and out of people's wonder sprang a sort of light and passing intimacy all along our route. There is nothing but tit for tat in this world, though sometimes it be a little difficult to trace: for the scores are older than we ourselves, and there has never yet been a settling-day since things were. You get entertainment pretty much in proportion as you give. As long as we were a sort of odd wanderers, to be stared at and followed like a quack doctor or a caravan, we had no want of amusement in return; but as soon as we sank into commonplace ourselves, all whom we met were similarly disenchanted. And here is one reason of a dozen why the world is dull to dull persons.

In our earlier adventures there was generally something to do, and that quickened us. Even the showers of rain had a revivifying effect, and shook up the brain from torpor. But now, when the river no longer ran in a proper sense, only glided seaward with an even, outright, but imperceptible speed, and when the sky smiled upon us day after day without variety, we began to slip into that golden doze of the mind which follows upon much exercise in the open air. I have stupefied myself in this way more than once; indeed, I dearly love the feeling; but I never had it to the same degree as when paddling down the Oise. It was the apotheosis of stupidity.

We ceased reading entirely. Sometimes when I found a new paper, I took a particular pleasure in reading a single number of the current novel; but I never could bear more than three instalments; and even the second was a disappointment. As soon as the tale became in any way perspicuous, it lost all merit in my eyes; only a single scene, or, as is the way with these *feuilletons*, half a scene, without antecedent or consequence, like a piece of a dream, had the knack of fixing my interest. The less I saw of the novel, the better I liked it: a pregnant reflection. But for the most part, as I said, we neither of us read anything in the world, and employed the very little while we were awake between bed and dinner in poring upon maps. I have always been fond of maps, and can voyage in an atlas with the greatest enjoyment. The names of places are singularly inviting; the contour of coasts and rivers is enthralling to the eye, and to hit, in a map, upon some place you have heard of before, makes history a new possession. But we thumbed our charts, on these evenings, with the blankest unconcern. We cared not a fraction for this place or that. We stared at the sheet as children listen to their rattle; and read the names of towns or villages to forget them again at once. We had no romance in the matter; there was nobody so fancy-free. If you had taken the maps away while we were studying them most intently, it is a fair bet whether we might not have continued to study the table with the same delight.

About one thing we were mightily taken up, and that was eating. I think I made a god of my belly. I remember dwelling in imagination upon this or that dish till my mouth watered, and long before we got in for the night my appetite was a clamant, instant annoyance. Sometimes we paddled alongside for a while and whetted each other with gastronomical fancies as we went. Cake and sherry, a homely reflection, but not within reach upon the Oise, trotted through my head for many a mile; and once, as we were approaching Verberie, the *Cigarette* brought my heart into my mouth by the suggestion of oyster patties and *Sauterne*.

I suppose none of us recognize the great part that is played in life by eating and drinking. The appetite is so imperious, that we can stomach the least interesting viands, and pass off a dinner hour thankfully enough on bread and water; just as there are men who must read something, if it were only *Bradshaw's Guide*. But there is a romance about the matter after all. Probably the table has more devotees than love; and I am sure that food is much more generally entertaining than scenery. Do you give in, as Walt Whitman would say, that you are any the less immortal for that? The true materialism is to be ashamed of what we are. To detect the flavour of an olive is no less a piece of human perfection than to find beauty in the colours of the sunset.

Canoeing was easy work. To dip the paddle at the proper inclination, now right, now left; to keep the head down-stream; to empty the little pool that gathered in the lap of the apron; to screw up the eyes against the glittering sparkles of sun upon the water; or now and again to pass below the whistling tow-rope of the *Deo Gratias* of Condé, or the *Four Sons of Aymon*—there was not much art in that; certain silly muscles managed it between sleep and waking; and meanwhile the brain had a whole holiday, and went to sleep. We took in, at a glance, the larger features of the scene, and beheld, with half an eye, bloused fishers and dabbling washerwomen on the bank. Now and again we might be half wakened by some church spire, by a leaping fish, or by a trail of river grass that clung about the paddle and had to be plucked off and thrown away. But these luminous intervals were only partially luminous. A little more of us was called into action, but never the whole. The central bureau of nerves, what in some moods we call *Ourselves*, enjoyed its holiday without disturbance like a Government Office. The great wheels of intelligence turned idly in the head, like fly-wheels, grinding no grist. I have gone on for half an hour at a time, counting my strokes and forgetting the hundreds. I flatter myself the beasts that perish could not underbid that, as a low form of consciousness. And what a pleasure it was! What a hearty, tolerant temper did it bring about! There is nothing captious about a man who has attained to this, the one possible apotheosis in life, the Apotheosis of Stupidity; and he begins to feel dignified and longœvous like a tree.

There was one odd piece of practical metaphysics which accompanied what I may call the depth, if I must not call it the intensity, of my abstraction. What philosophers call *me* and *not me, ego* and *non ego*, preoccupied me whether I would or no. There was less *me* and more *not me* than I was accustomed to expect. I looked on upon somebody else, who managed the paddling; I was aware of somebody else's feet against the stretcher; my own body seemed to have no more intimate relation to me than the canoe, or the river, or the river banks. Nor this above: something inside my mind, a part of my brain, a province of my proper being, had thrown off allegiance and set up for itself, or perhaps for the somebody else who did the paddling. I had dwindled into quite a little thing in a corner of myself. I was isolated in my own skull. Thoughts presented themselves unbidden; they were not my thoughts, they were plainly someone else's; and I considered them like a part of the landscape. I take it, in short, that I was about as near Nirvana as would be convenient in practical life; and if this be so, I make the Buddhists my sincere compliments; 'tis an agreeable state, not very consistent with mental brilliancy, not exactly profitable in a money point of view, but very calm, golden and incurious, and one that sets a man superior to alarms. It may be best figured by supposing yourself to get dead drunk, and yet keep sober to enjoy it. I have a notion that open-air labourers must spend a large portion of their days in this ecstatic stupor, which explains their high composure and endurance. A pity to go to the expense of laudanum, when here is a better paradise for nothing!

This frame of mind was the great exploit of our voyage, take it all in all. It was the farthest piece of travel accomplished. Indeed, it lies so far from the beaten paths of language, that I despair of getting the reader into sympathy with the smiling, complacent idiocy of my condition; when ideas came and went like motes in a sunbeam; when trees and church spires along the bank surged up from time to time into my notice, like solid objects through a rolling cloudland; when the rhythmical swish of boat and paddle in the water became a cradle-song to lull my thoughts asleep; when a piece of mud on the deck was sometimes an intolerable eyesore, and sometimes quite a companion for me, and the object of pleased consideration;—and all the time, with the river running and the shores changing upon either hand, I kept counting my strokes and forgetting the hundreds, the happiest animal in France.

Walking Tours

IT MUST NOT be imagined that a walking tour, as some would have us fancy, is merely a better or worse way of seeing the country. There are many ways of seeing landscape quite as good; and none more vivid, in spite of canting dilettantes, than from a railway train. But landscape on a walking tour is quite accessory. He who is indeed of the brotherhood does not voyage in quest of the picturesque but of certain jolly humours—of the hope and spirit with which the march begins at morning, and the peace and spiritual repletion of the evening's rest. He cannot tell whether he puts his knapsack on, or takes it off, with more delight. The excitement of the departure puts him in key for that of the arrival. Whatever he does is not only a reward in itself, but will be further rewarded in the sequel; and so pleasure leads on to pleasure in an endless chain. It is this that so few can understand; they will either be always lounging or always at five miles an hour; they do not play off the one against the other, prepare all day for the evening, and all evening for the next day. And, above all, it is here that your overwalker fails of comprehension. His heart rises against those who drink their curaçao in liqueur glasses, when he himself can swill it in a brown John. He will not believe that the flavour is more delicate in the smaller dose. He will not believe that to walk this unconscionable distance is merely to stupefy and brutalize himself, and come to his inn, at night, with a sort of frost on his five wits, and a starless night of darkness in his spirit. Not for him the mild luminous evening of the temperate walker! He has nothing left of man but a physical need for bedtime and a double nightcap; and even his pipe, if he be a smoker, will be savourless and disenchanted. It is the fate of such an one to take twice as much trouble as is needed to obtain happiness, and miss the happiness in the end; he is the man of the proverb, in short, who goes farther and fares worse.

Now, to be properly enjoyed, a walking tour should be gone upon alone. If you go in a company, or even in pairs, it is no longer a walking tour in anything but name; it is something else and more in the nature of a picnic. A walking tour should be gone upon alone, because freedom is of the essence; because you should be able to stop and go on, and follow this way or that, as the freak takes you; and because you must have your own pace, and neither trot alongside a champion walker, nor mince in time with a girl. And then you must be open to all impressions and let your thoughts take colour from what you see. You should be as a pipe for any wind to play upon. "I cannot see the wit," says Hazlitt, "of walking and talking at the same time. When I am in the country, I wish to vegetate like the country,"—which is the gist of all that can be said upon the matter. There should be no cackle of voices at your elbow, to jar on the meditative silence of the morning. And so long as a man is reasoning he cannot surrender himself to that fine intoxication that comes of much motion in the open air, that begins in a sort of dazzle and sluggishness of the brain, and ends in a peace that passes comprehension.

During the first day or so of any tour there are moments of bitterness, when the traveller feels more than coldly towards his knapsack, when he is half in a mind to throw it bodily over the hedge, and like Christian on a similar occasion, "give three leaps and go on singing." And yet it soon acquires a property of easiness. It becomes magnetic; the spirit of the journey enters into it. And no sooner have you passed the straps over your shoulder than the lees of sleep are cleared from you, you pull yourself together with a shake, and fall at once into your stride. And surely, of all possible moods, this, in which a man takes the road, is the best. Of course, if he *will* keep thinking of his anxieties, if he *will* open the merchant Abudah's chest and walk arm-in-arm with the hag—why, wherever he is, and whether he walk fast or slow, the chances are that he will not be happy. And so much the more shame to himself! There are perhaps thirty men setting forth at that same hour, and I would lay a large wager there is not another dull face among the thirty. It would be a fine thing to follow, in a coat of darkness, one after another of these wayfarers, some summer morning, for the first few miles upon the road. This one, who walks fast, with a keen look in his eyes, is all concentrated in his own mind; he is up at his loom, weaving and weaving, to set the landscape to words. This one peers about, as he goes, among the grasses; he waits by the canal to watch the dragon-flies; he leans on the gate of the pasture, and cannot look enough upon the complacent kine. And here comes another, talking, laughing, and gesticulating to himself. His face changes from time to time, as indignation flashes from his eyes or anger clouds his forehead. He is composing articles, delivering orations, and conducting the most impassioned interviews by the way. A little farther on, and it is as like as not he will begin to sing. And well for him, supposing him to be no great master in that art, if he stumble across no stolid peasant at a corner; for on such an occasion, I scarcely know which is the more troubled, or whether it is worse to suffer the confusion of your troubador, or the unfeigned alarm of your clown. A sedentary population, accustomed, besides, to the strange mechanical bearing of the common tramp, can in no wise explain to itself the gaiety of these passers-by. I knew one man who was arrested as a runaway lunatic, because, although a full-grown person with a red beard, he skipped as he went like a child. And you would be astonished if I were to tell you all the grave and learned heads who have confessed to me that, when on walking tours, they sang—and sang very ill—and had a pair of red ears when, as described above, the inauspicious peasant plumped into their arms from round a corner. And here, lest you should think I am exaggerating, is Hazlitt's own confession, from his essay *On going on a Journey,* which is so good that there should be a tax levied on all who have not read it:—

"Give me the clear blue sky over my head," says he, "and the green turf beneath my feet, a winding road before me, and a three hours' march to dinner—and then to thinking! It is hard if I cannot start some game on these lone heaths. I laugh, I run, I leap, I sing for joy."

Bravo! After that adventure of my friend with the policeman, you would not have cared, would you, to publish that in the first person? But we have no bravery nowadays, and, even in books, must all pretend to be as dull and foolish as our neighbours. It was not so with Hazlitt. And notice how learned he is (as, indeed, throughout the essay) in the theory of walking tours. He is none of your athletic men in purple stockings, who walk their fifty miles a day: three hours' march is his ideal. And then he must have a winding road, the epicure!

Yet there is one thing I object to in these words of his, one thing in the great master's practice that seems to me not wholly wise. I do not approve of that leaping and running. Both of these hurry the respiration; they both shake up the brain out of its glorious open-air confusion; and they both break the pace. Uneven walking is not so agreeable to the body, and it distracts and irritates the mind. Whereas, when once you have fallen into an equable stride, it requires no conscious thought from you to keep it up, and yet it prevents you from thinking earnestly of anything else. Like knitting, like the work of a copying clerk, it gradually neutralizes and sets to sleep the serious activity of the mind. We can think of this or that, lightly and laughingly, as a child thinks, or as we think in a morning doze; we can make puns or puzzle out acrostics, and trifle in a thousand ways with words and rhymes; but when it comes to honest work, when we come to gather ourselves together for an effort, we may sound the trumpet as loud and long as we please; the great barons of the mind will not rally to the standard, but sit, each one, at home, warming his hands over his own fire and brooding on his own private thought!

In the course of a day's walk, you see, there is much variance in the mood. From the exhilaration of the start, to the happy phlegm of the arrival, the change is certainly great. As the day goes on, the traveller moves from the one extreme towards the other. He becomes more and more incorporated with the material landscape, and the open air drunkenness grows upon him with great strides, until he posts along the road, and sees everything about him, as in a cheerful dream. The first is certainly brighter, but the second stage is the more peaceful. A man does not make so many articles towards the end, nor does he laugh aloud; but the purely animal pleasures, the sense of physical well-being, the delight of every inhalation, of every time the muscles tighten down the thigh, console him for the absence of the others, and bring him to his destination still content.

Nor must I forget to say a word on bivouacs. You come to a milestone on a hill, or some place where deep ways meet under trees; and off goes the knapsack, and down you sit to smoke a pipe in the shade. You sink into yourself, and the birds come round and look at you; and your smoke dissipates upon the afternoon under the blue dome of heaven; and the sun lies warm upon your feet, and the cool air visits your neck and turns aside your open shirt. If you are not happy, you must have an evil conscience. You may dally as long as you like by the roadside. It is almost as if the millennium were arrived, when we shall throw our clocks and watches over the housetop, and remember time and seasons no more. Not to keep hours for a lifetime is, I was going to say, to live for ever. You have no idea, unless you have tried it, how endlessly long is a summer's day, that you measure out only by hunger, and bring to an end only when you are drowsy. I know a village where there are hardly any clocks, where no one knows more of the days of the week than by a sort of instinct for the fete on Sundays, and where only one person can tell you the day of the month, and she is generally wrong; and if people were aware how slow Time journeyed in that village, and what armfuls of spare hours he gives, over and above the bargain, to its wise inhabitants, I believe there would be a stampede out of London, Liverpool, Paris, and a variety of large towns, where the clocks lose their heads, and shake the hours out each one faster than the other, as though they were all in a wager. And all these foolish pilgrims would each bring his own misery along with him, in a watch-pocket! It is to be noticed, there were no clocks and watches in the much vaunted days before the Flood. It follows, of course, there were no appointments, and punctuality was not yet thought upon. "Though ye take from a covetous man all his treasure," says Milton, "he has yet one jewel left; ye cannot deprive him of his covetousness." And so I would say of a modern man of business, you may do what you will for him, put him in Eden, give him the elixir of life—he has still a flaw at heart, he still has his business habits. Now, there is no time when business habits are more mitigated than on a walking tour. And so during these halts, as I say, you will feel almost free.

But it is at night, and after dinner, that the best hour comes. There are no such pipes to be smoked as those that follow a good day's march; the flavour of the tobacco is a thing to be remembered, it is so dry and aromatic, so full and so fine. If you wind up the evening with grog, you will own there was never such grog; at every sip a jocund tranquillity spreads about your limbs, and sits easily in your heart. If you read a book—and you will never do so save by fits and starts—you find the language strangely racy and harmonious; words take a new meaning; single sentences possess the ear for half an hour together; and the writer endears himself to you, at every page, by the nicest coincidence of sentiment. It seems as if it were a book you had written yourself in a dream. To all we have read on such occasions we look back with special favour. "It was on the 10th of April, 1798," says Hazlitt, with amorous precision, "that I sat down to a volume of the new *Héloïse*, at the Inn at Llangollen, over a bottle of sherry and a cold chicken." I should wish to quote more, for though we are mighty fine fellows nowadays, we cannot write like Hazlitt. And, talking of that, a volume of Hazlitt's essays would be a capital pocket-book on such a journey; so would a volume of Heine's songs; and for *Tristram Shandy* I can pledge a fair experience.

If the evening be fine and warm, there is nothing better in life than to lounge before the inn door in the sunset, or lean over the parapet of the bridge, to watch the weeds and the quick fishes. It is then, if ever, that you taste Joviality to the full significance of that audacious word. Your muscles are so agreeably slack, you feel so clean and so strong and so idle, that whether you move or sit still, whatever you do is done with pride and a kingly sort of pleasure. You fall in talk with any one, wise or foolish, drunk or sober. And it seems as if a hot walk purged you, more than of anything else, of all narrowness and pride, and left curiosity to play its part freely, as in a child or a man of science. You lay aside all your own hobbies, to watch provincial humours develop themselves before you, now as a laughable farce, and now grave and beautiful like an old tale.

Or perhaps you are left to your own company for the night, and surly weather imprisons you by the fire. You may remember how Burns, numbering past pleasures, dwells upon the hours when he has been "happy thinking." It is a phrase that may well perplex a poor modern, girt about on every side by clocks and chimes, and haunted, even at night, by flaming dial-plates. For we were all so busy, and have so many far-off projects to realize, and castles in the fire to turn into solid habitable mansions on a gravel soil, that we can find no time for pleasure trips into the Land of Thought and among the Hills of Vanity. Changed times, indeed, when we must sit all night, beside the fire with folded hands; and a changed world for most of us, when we find we can pass the hours without discontent, and be happy thinking. We are in such haste to be doing, to be writing, to be gathering gear, to make our voice audible a moment in the derisive silence of eternity, that we forget that one thing, of which these are but the parts—namely, to live. We fall in love, we drink hard, we run to and fro upon the earth like frightened sheep. And now you are to ask yourself if, when all is done, you would not have been better to sit by the fire at home and be happy thinking. To sit still and contemplate—to remember the faces of women without desire, to be pleased by the great deeds of men without envy, to be everything and everywhere in sympathy, and yet content to remain where and what you are—is not this to know both wisdom and virtue, and to dwell with happiness? After all, it is not they who carry flags, but they who look upon it from a private chamber, who have the fun of the procession. And once you are at that, you are in the very humour of all social heresy. It is no time for shuffling, or for big, empty words. If you ask yourself what you mean by fame, riches, or learning, the answer is far to seek; and you go back into that kingdom of light imaginations, which seem so vain in the eyes of Philistines perspiring after wealth, and so momentous to those who are stricken with the disproportions of the world, and, in the face of the gigantic stars, cannot stop to split differences between two degrees of the infinitesimally small, such as a tobacco-pipe or the Roman Empire, a million of money or a fiddlestick's end.

You lean from the window, your last pipe reeking whitely into the darkness, your body full of delicious pains, your mind enthroned in the seventh circle of content; when suddenly the moon changes, the weathercock goes about, and you ask yourself one question more: whether, for the interval, you have been the wisest philosopher or the most egregious of donkeys? Human experience is not yet able to reply; but at least you have had a fine moment, and looked down upon all the kingdoms of the earth. And whether it was wise or foolish, to-morrow's travel will carry you, body and mind, into some different parish of the infinite.

Poems

Consolation

THOUGH he, that ever kind and true,
Kept stoutly step by step with you
Your whole long gusty lifetime through,
    Be gone a while before,
Be now a moment gone before,
Yet, doubt not, soon the seasons shall restore
    Your friend to you.

He has but turned a corner – still
He pushes on with right good will,
Through mire and marsh, by heugh and hill,
    That self-same arduous way –
That self-same upland, hopeful way,
That you and he through many a doubtful day
    Attempted still.

He is not dead, this friend – not dead,
But in the path we mortals tread
Got some few, trifling steps ahead
    And nearer to the end;
So that you too, once past the bend,
Shall meet again, as face to face, this friend
    You fancy dead.

Push gaily on, strong heart! The while
You travel forward mile by mile,
He loiters with a backward smile
    Till you can overtake,
And strains his eyes to search his wake,
Or whistling, as he sees you through the brake,
    Waits on a stile.

Nous n'irons plus aux bois

WE'LL walk the woods no more
But stay beside the fire,
To weep for old desire
And things that are no more.
    The woods are spoiled and hoar,
The ways are full of mire;
We'll walk the woods no more
But stay beside the fire.
    We loved, in days of yore
Love, laughter, and the lyre.
Ah God, but death is dire
And death is at the door –
We'll walk the woods no more.

Untitled

I WILL make you brooches and toys for your delight
Of bird-song at morning and star-shine at night.
I will make a palace fit for you and me
Of green days in forests and blue days at sea.

I will make my kitchen, and you shall keep your room,
Where white flows the river and bright blows the broom,
And you shall wash your linen and keep your body white
In rainfall at morning and dewfall at night.

And this shall be for music when no one else is near,
The fine song for singing, the rare song to hear!
That only I remember, that only you admire,
Of the broad road that stretches and the roadside fire.

Untitled

BRIGHT is the ring of words
    When the right man rings them,
Fair the fall of songs
    When the singer sings them.
Still they are carolled and said –
    On wings they are carried –
After the singer is dead
    And the maker buried.

Low as the singer lies
    In the field of heather,
Songs of his fashion bring
    The swains together.
And when the west is red
    With the sunset embers,
The lover lingers and sings
    And the maid remembers.

Untitled

IN THE highlands, in the country places,
Where the old plain men have rosy faces,
And the young fair maidens
Quiet eyes;
Where essential silence cheers and blesses,
And for ever in the hill-recesses
Her more lovely music
Broods and dies.

O to mount again where erst I haunted;
Where the old red hills are bird-enchanted,
And the low green meadows
Bright with sward;
And when even dies, the million-tinted,
And the night has come, and planets glinted,
Lo, the valley hollow
Lamp-bestarred!

O to dream, O to awake and wander
There, and with delight to take and render,
Through the trance of silence,
Quiet breath;
Lo! for there, among the flowers and grasses,
Only the mightier movement sounds and passes;
Only winds and rivers,
Life and death.

Requiem

UNDER the wide and starry sky,
Dig the grave and let me lie.
Glad did I live and gladly die,
    And I laid me down with a will.

This be the verse you grave for me:
Here he lies where he longed to be;
Home is the sailor, home from sea,
    And the hunter home from the hill.

Bibliography

THE LIST OF Stevenson's works that follows is not intended to be all-embracing, but it includes all his important works.

FICTION

New Arabian Nights, 1882. *Treasure Island*, 1883. *More New Arabian Nights*, 1885. *The Merry Men and Other Tales and Fables*, 1885. *Prince Otto*, 1885. *The Strange Case of Dr. Jekyll and Mr. Hyde*, 1886. *Kidnapped*, 1886. *The Black Arrow*, 1888. *The Master of Ballantrae*, 1889. *The Wrong Box* (with Lloyd Osbourne), 1889. *The Wrecker* (with Lloyd Osbourne), 1892. *Catriona* (US title *David Balfour*), 1893. *Island Nights' Entertainments*, 1893. *The Ebb Tide* (with Lloyd Osbourne), 1894. *Weir of Hermiston* (unfinished), 1896. *St. Ives* (also unfinished, completed by Sir Arthur Quiller-Couch), 1898.

ESSAYS AND TRAVEL

An Inland Voyage, 1878. *Picturesque Notes on Edinburgh*, 1878. *Travels with a Donkey in the Cévennes*, 1879. *Virginibus Puerisque*, 1881. *Familiar Studies of Men and Books*, 1882. *The Silverado Squatters*, 1883. *Memories and Portraits*, 1887. *Across the Plains*, 1892. *A Footnote to History*, 1892. *Fables*, 1896. *Essays of Travel*, 1900. *Essays in the Art of Writing*, 1905. *Lay Morals and Other Papers*, 1911. *The Amateur Emigrant*, 1916.

POETRY

A Child's Garden of Verses, 1885. *Underwoods*, 1887. *Ballads*, 1890. *Songs of Travel*, 1896.

There have been several collected editions of Stevenson's works, the best-known of which are:

Works of Robert Louis Stevenson edited by Lloyd Osbourne and F. Van de G. Stevenson (the "Vailima" edition). 26 volumes. New York and London, 1922-23. (This was published only in a limited edition of 1,000 copies each in the United States and Great Britain.)

The Works of Robert Louis Stevenson (the "Tusitala" edition). 35 volumes. London, 1923-24.

The standard edition of the poems is:

Robert Louis Stevenson: *Collected Poems*. Edited, with an Introduction and Notes, by Janet Adam Smith. 2nd edition. London, 1971. (A model of scholarship and editing.)

There have been many studies of Stevenson's work, by far the best of which are:

David Daiches. *Stevenson and the Art of Fiction*. New York, 1951.

R. Kiely. *Robert Louis Stevenson and the Fiction of Adventure*. London, 1965.

The first of these was written by a Scot, the second by an American.

Biographies of Stevenson have fallen into three phases. Devotional biographies began to appear soon after his death. Then, after World War I, a period of debunking set in. Stevenson seemed to be too good to be true, and he was accused of smugness and hypocrisy. The first exaggerated stories of his dissolute youth were unveiled during this period. Finally, and not until after World War II, responsible commentators and biographers put the record straight. They have relegated earlier biographers to the waste-paper basket; the only "early" biography that remains of interest is:

Lloyd Osbourne. *An Intimate Portrait of R.L.S.* New York, 1924.

The most stimulating biography remains:

Richard Aldington. *Portrait of a Rebel: the Life and Work of Robert Louis Stevenson*. London, 1957.

The fullest and most detailed is:

James Pope Hennessy. *Robert Louis Stevenson*. London, 1974.

Though Hennessy is sometimes unenthusiastic about Stevenson's work, it has been suggested that, had he lived, he would have expanded and revised his critical assessments.

A handy short biography is:

Compton Mackenzie. *Robert Louis Stevenson*. London, 1968.

It is heavy on opinion and light on fact and tells us as much about Compton Mackenzie as it does about Stevenson.

Far the most useful of modern biographies is that written by Stevenson's most acute and sympathetic modern critic, David Daiches:

Robert Louis Stevenson and his World. London, 1973.

It is essential reading. The potential reader should not be deterred by its coffee-table format and unattractive typography. It is an authoritative, balanced, and perceptive introduction to Stevenson and his work.

Filmography

STEVENSON'S WORKS have been ruthlessly quarried to provide material for the cinema, as the sheer length of the film list that follows is enough to demonstrate. If my counting is correct, and if some of the more frivolous and outlandish film treatments are ignored, I make it that *The Strange Case of Dr. Jekyll and Mr. Hyde* has been filmed no less than eleven times, *The Suicide Club* six times, *Treasure Island* five times, *Kidnapped* four times, *The Ebb Tide* three times, and *The Wrong Box* twice. *The Black Arrow, The Master of Ballantrae, St. Ives,* "The Sire of Maletroit's Door," and "The Pavilion on the Links" have also, at various times, been adapted for the screen. This must be a score sheet that few other writers can equal. It is also a score sheet that reflects with remarkable accuracy the order of precedence, or, at least, of popularity, in which most present-day readers and critics would arrange Stevenson's fiction. Compare, for example, James Pope Hennessy's shorthand—and misleadingly unenthusiastic—summing-up in his *Robert Louis Stevenson* (London, 1974. p. 264): "*Treasure Island* and *Kidnapped* have survived. . . . *The Master of Ballantrae,* so admirable for the first two-thirds of the book, then proves a bitter disappointment. . . . *The Strange Case of Dr. Jekyll and Mr. Hyde* is known throughout the civilized world. *The Ebb Tide* is excellent and thrilling. *The Wrong Box* can never fail to amuse." Only *The Suicide Club,* in fact, seems to have been more highly rated by film-makers than by readers.

Stevenson-inspired films are remarkable in their quality as well as in their quantity. There are few total disasters in this long list, and some memorable successes – in particular, perhaps, Rouben Mamoulian's masterly *Dr. Jekyll and Mr. Hyde* (1931), with Fredric March in the title role, and Byron Haskin's *Treasure Island* (1950), with Robert

Newton as Long John Silver. Both films, however, have some strong competition.

Three other versions of the Jekyll-and-Hyde story are worthy of note along with Mamoulian's. In a 1920 silent version John Barrymore's performance in the dual role still seems, half a century later, totally compelling. The film is also a rarity in the Jekyll-and-Hyde corpus in that the transformation scenes are achieved without the help of special-effects cinematography and with the minimal use of make-up. A 1941 remake, with Spencer Tracy, has, it seems to me, been consistently over-rated. It is virtually a frame-by-frame re-creation of the 1931 version (even the sets look identical) and whatever Tracy's strengths as an actor were, and they were many, his performance lacks the psychological depth, credibility, and conviction of Fredric March's which, rightly, had earned the latter an Oscar. But Tracy's acting aside, the make-up for Mr. Hyde was exaggerated – Tracy stumbles around in the film looking like a gorilla for much of the time and to assume that just his *appearance* in public would fail to excite on-lookers into a panic of fright forces a suspension of belief on the part of the movie-goer for most of the Mr. Hyde sequences. The "definitive" Jekyll-Hyde portrayal, then as now, must remain with one of the finest actors ever to come out of Hollywood, Fredric March. Finally, quite different from any other version, but chillingly effective, is Jean Renoir's updating of Stevenson's theme in *Le Testament du Docteur Cordelier* (1961).

Robert Newton's chief competitor in the role of Long John Silver is Wallace Beery, in Metro-Goldwyn-Mayer's *Treasure Island* (1934), directed by Victor Fleming. This is good, rumbustious stuff. But Robert Newton's controlled hamming must make him the winner; he became everyman's image of Long John Silver. He and the film became so popular that a sequel was made. This was *Long John Silver* (1954), directed by Byron Haskin; it was as unsatisfactory as most such sequels are.

This filmography is as complete as I can make it, although I have no doubt that ignorance has led me into sins of omission. Some omissions are, however, deliberate. I have not, for example, listed *Long John Silver,* considering it, perhaps over-fussily, to be too far removed from the "pure" Stevenson. On the same grounds I have excluded the 1971 Hammer film *Dr. Jekyll and Sister Hyde*, which exists only on the outer fringes of Stevensoniana. I am aware that this may seem an arbitrary decision; almost every film listed takes at least some liberties with its original. But Sister Hyde, I feel, goes too far. I have similarly refused to take seriously Louis Hayward as *Son of Dr. Jekyll* (1951) and Gloria Talbott as *Daughter of Dr. Jekyll* (1957). I have rejected too, with less heart-searching but more regret, two burlesques – *Abbott and Costello meet Dr. Jekyll and Mr. Hyde* (1956) and Jerry Lewis's *The Nutty Professor* (1963).

The list does include, in common with the filmographies of other volumes in this series, major television films – but not television serials. The arrangement is chronological. In an ideal entry the information given is: date, film title (with variant titles where they exist), production company, director, and chief players (not necessarily in order of importance). Regrettably, however, some entries fall short of this ideal. Where the production company is unknown to me, I have noted the film's country of origin.

1908 *Dr. Jekyll and Mr. Hyde*. Selig.

1909 *The Suicide Club*. American Mutoscope Biograph Company.

1910 *Dr. Jekyll and Mr. Hyde*. Nordisk.

1913 *Dr. Jekyll and Mr. Hyde*. Universal Pictures. Directed by James Cruze. With King Baggott, Jane Gail, Matt Snyder, and William Sorrell.
The Wrong Box. Solax.

1914 *The Suicide Club*. British and Colonial Kinematograph Company. Directed by Maurice Elvey. With Montagu Love, Fred Groves, and Elizabeth Risdon.

1919 *Unheimliche Geschichten*. Richard Oswald. Directed by Richard Oswald. With Anita Berber, Reinhold Schünzel, and Conrad Veidt.

1920 *Dr. Jekyll and Mr. Hyde*. Famous Players-Lasky Corporation. Directed by John S. Robertson. With John Barrymore, Brandon Hurst, Martha Mansfield, and Nita Naldi.
Dr. Jekyll and Mr. Hyde. (U.S.A.). With Sheldon Lewis.

1920 *Der Januskopf*. (Germany). Directed by F. W. Murnau. With Conrad Veidt.

Treasure Island. Paramount-Artcraft. Directed by Maurice Tourneur. With Charles Ogle, Shirley Mason, and Josie Melville.

The White Circle [The Pavilion on the Links]. Paramount. Directed by Maurice Tourneur. With Spottiswoode Aiken, Harry S. Northrup, Jack Gilbert, and Jack McDonald.

1922 *Ebb Tide*. Famous Players-Lasky Corporation. Directed by George Melford. With Lila Lee, James Kirkwood, George Fawcett, and Jacqueline Logan.

1931 *Dr. Jekyll and Mr. Hyde*. Paramount Pictures Corporation. Directed by Rouben Mamoulian. With Fredric March, Miriam Hopkins, Edgar Norton, Rose Hobart, and Holmes Herbert.

1933 *The Living Dead* [The Suicide Club]. (Germany). Directed by Richard Oswald. With Paul Wegener.

1934 *Treasure Island*. Metro-Goldwyn-Mayer. Directed by Victor Fleming. With Wallace Beery, Jackie Cooper, and Lionel Barrymore.

1936 *Trouble for Two* (British title *The Suicide Club*). Metro Goldwyn-Mayer. Directed by J. Walter Ruben. With Robert Montgomery, Rosalind Russell, and Frank Morgan.

1937 *Ebb Tide*. Paramount Pictures Corporation. Directed by James Hogan. With Oscar Homolka, Frances Farmer, Ray Milland, Lloyd Nolan, and Barry Fitzgerald.

1938 *Kidnapped*. Twentieth Century-Fox Film Corporation. Directed by Alfred Werker. With Warner Baxter, Freddie Bartholomew, and Aileen Wheelan.

1941 *Dr. Jekyll and Mr. Hyde*. Metro-Goldwyn-Mayer. Directed by Victor Fleming. With Spencer Tracy, Ingrid Bergman, and Lana Turner.

1947 *Adventure Island* [The Ebb Tide]. Paramount Pictures Corporation. With Rory Calhoun, Rhonda Fleming, and Paul Kelly.

End of the River [Blue Days and Green Days]. The Archers. Directed by Derek Twist. With Milton Rosmer.

1948 *The Black Arrow* (British title *The Black Arrow Strikes*). Columbia Pictures. Directed by Gordon Douglas. With Louis Hayward, Janet Blair, and George Macready.

Kidnapped. Monogram Picture Corporation. Directed by William Beaudine. With Roddy McDowall, Sue England, and Dan O'Herlihy.

1949 *The Secret of St. Ives*. Columbia Pictures. Directed by Philip Rosen. With Richard Ney, Vanessa Brown, Henry Daniell, and Aubrey Mather.

1950 *Treasure Island*. RKO-Walt Disney. Directed by Byron Haskin. With Robert Newton, Bobby Driscoll, and Basil Sydney.

1951 *The Strange Door* [The Sire of Maletroit's Door]. Universal-International. Directed by Joseph Pevney. With Charles Laughton, Boris Karloff, Sally Forrest, and Richard Stapley.

1953 *The Master of Ballantrae*. Warner-First National Productions. Directed by William Keighley. With Errol Flynn, Beatrice Campbell, Roger Livesey, Anthony Steel, and Yvonne Furneaux. Narrated by Robert Beatty.

1960 *Kidnapped*. Walt Disney Productions. Directed by Robert Stevenson [*sic*]. With Peter Finch, James MacArthur, Bernard Lee, Peter O'Toole, and John Laurie.

The Two Faces of Dr. Jekyll (US title *House of Fright*). Hammer Film Productions. Directed by Terence Fisher. With Paul Massie, Dawn Addams, Christopher Lee, David Kossoff, and Norma Marla.

1961 *Le Testament du Docteur Cordelier* [Dr. Jekyll and Mr. Hyde] (US title *Experiment in Evil*). Jean Renoir. Directed by Jean Renoir. With Jean-Louis Barrault.

1966 *The Wrong Box*. Salamander. Directed by Bryan Forbes. With John Mills, Sir Ralph Richardson, Michael Caine, Nanette Newman, Peter Cook, Dudley Moore, Tony Hancock, and Peter Sellers.

1971 *Dobotsu Takarajima* [Treasure Island]. (Cartoon). Toei Company. Directed by Hiroshi Ikeda.

Treasure Island. Towers Production. Directed by John Hough. With Orson Welles, Kim Burfield, Walter Slezak, Lionel Standen, and Paul Muller.

1972 *Kidnapped*. Omnibus Productions. Directed by Delbert Mann. With Michael Caine, Trevor Howard, Jack Hawkins, Donald Pleasance, James Stewart, and Vivien Heilbron.

1973 *Dr. Jekyll and Mr. Hyde*. (TV film musical). Timex-NBC-TV. Directed by David Winters. With Kirk Douglas, Susan George, Susan Hampshire, Stanley Holloway, and Donald Pleasance.

The Suicide Club. Universal Productions. With Joseph Haskell, Margot Kidder, and Joseph Wiseman.

L'ENVOI

I have trod the upward and the downward slope;
I have endured and done in days before;
I have longed for all, and bid farewell to hope;
And I have lived and loved, and closed the door.

Untitled poem first published in
THE WORKS OF ROBERT LOUIS STEVENSON,
Vol. XIV, Edinburgh, 1895.

A NOTE ON THE TYPEFACE

This book was composed on the Monotype in Garamond, Series 156, a face cut in 1922 by the Monotype Corporation and based upon punches from the Imprimerie Royale which had acquired an ascription to Claude Garamond. Four years later, when it was too late to rename the series, the researches of Beatrice Warde identified the designer as Jean Jannon, printer to the Calvinist Academy at Sedan. Owing to political disturbances in 1615, Jannon was deprived of his type supplies from Frankfurt and in the space of six years he cut and struck a magnificent range of sizes. Based on Garamond's models, his design is much lighter and more open and characterized by the sharply-cupped top serifs. The italic is taken from a fount of Robert Granjon in the repertory of the Imprimerie Royale and was probably cut about the middle of the sixteenth century. A further series of italic was cut by the Corporation some years later, Series 174, which displays none of the eccentricities of letterform of the initial issue.